THE BOYS OF ST. MARY'S

KEEP ON KEEPING ON

CAROLINE WHITEHEAD

By the same author:

Shadows In Every Corner

Surviving The Shadows

Rowland: A Heart of Sunshine

Under The Railway Clock

DEDICATION

This book is dedicated to the boys of St. Mary's, Gravesend, Kent, England, who gave their lives with honour and distinction when serving King and Country during the Second World War. We will remember them.

A Plaque Erected By St. Mary's Old Boys In Memory Of Their Companions Who Lost Their Lives in the War 1939–1945:

JOSEPH ANDERSON	PAT WALSH
JIMMIE FISHER	GEORGE BUCKLAND
JACKIE READE	DENIS BROOK
JOSEPH IZZIO	JACKIE COOGAN
RONNIE SULLIVAN	JACKIE BODINGTON
LOUIS IZZIO	WALTER GRAHAM
LEWIS BUCKTHORPE	DENIS EDMEADS
JACK McSWEENEY	JAMES O'KEEFE
JOHN BARZEE	GORDON KANE
BILLE GIBBONS	GEORGE BLOXHAM
JAMES WARREN	

R. I. P.

ACKNOWLEDGEMENTS

First and foremost, to the members of the KOKO writers group worldwide who approved publication of their memoirs from the 1920s era of St. Mary's, Gravesend, Kent, England, by Agio Publishing House, Victoria, British Columbia, Canada.

Special thanks to (Delvin) John Flynn for setting in motion a "network" of old boys in 1988 and encouraging them to write their stories so they can now be told. His invaluable time and energy in compiling their emails is much appreciated.

Terry McKenna for his contribution and invaluable time in collating the emails sent to the writers group, worldwide. His ongoing communication between England, Canada and Australia was instrumental in achieving this goal through his contact with John Flynn.

Antony Hayman for providing the article by *Reporter Ltd*, Gravesend of Schoolboy Football – St. Mary's v St. Joseph's, Rotherhithe, Stonebridge Road Ground, and many photographs of the school.

To those group members around the world who generously contributed towards the cost of this publication, and who set me on this journey in the first place.

Tony Larkin, an historian of Gravesend, Kent who diligently takes care of the St. Mary's Boys' Remembrance Plaque, of those who gave their lives during the Second World War.

Social Workers past and present: Cabrini/Irene Coppock, Irena Lyczkowska, Teresa Downy. Mr. J. Lyons, Archivist. Their excellent services over the years enabled many of our members to search their personal records at the Purley archives, which enabled them to understand their family history. Their support and respect, greatly appreciated.

My son-in-law Don Boston for his expertise and time to ensure all systems functioned on my computer to allow this manuscript to unfold. Special thanks and appreciation to Bruce and Marsha Batchelor of Agio Publishing House for their advice and support to make this publication possible. To Marsha Batchelor, an award-winning graphic designer, for the cover design.

— *Caroline Whitehead*

CONTENTS

INTRODUCTION

This is not the first time Caroline Whitehead has published about life in an institution, but this time she has lent her efforts to the St. Mary's Boys Orphanage, Gravesend, Kent.

This book is compiled and inspired by emails written by the members of a London group recalling life lived in an institution in a past era, times hopefully never to return.

Caroline writes with fluidity marrying up the thoughts of the members of the St. Mary's old boys. Each member has recorded his own unique experiences but the one question rarely answered is, WHY?

Did their mothers not want them? They felt they were to all intents and purposes like left luggage at a railway station and their mother failed to collect.

This is a book that explores the innate ties that binds a boy to a mother who did not necessarily reciprocate the longing to know and the bonds of blood that tie us all.

— *Delvin John Flynn*

ABOUT THIS BOOK, THE WRITERS AND THE SETTING

ABOUT THIS BOOK

This is the story of young children who, due to unusual circumstances, found themselves in the care of St. Mary's Home for Boys at Gravesend, Kent.

Their stories are characterized from the sublime to the ridiculous, relating to family history when parents in the twentieth century were either unable to care for their sons or so poverty-stricken, incapable of bringing them up.

It is when they reached manhood that the St. Mary's boys found they were travelling incredible journeys that would take them to unheard destinations to different parts of the globe, in search of their birthright. Many were to leave the shores of England and settle in countries abroad, leaving memories of the old regime behind.

The question was 'why me?' by some of the old boys after they discovered other siblings were allowed to remain at home, when they were the chosen ones to be taken away and put in St. Mary's, Gravesend.

ABOUT THE WRITERS

A "network" of old boys was inspired and founded in 1988 in North London, England by master-mind (Delvin) John Flynn, to give each a voice and provide them with the initiative to speak up and free ghosts of past, long held in many closets. The group's motto was KOKO (Keep on keeping on).

Memories, good and bad, were channelled across all continents. Some writers tell of happy times where they spent summer holidays at Dymchurch, Kent. Others remember their contribution and duty to the church as choir boys. Sports Day gave each boy the opportunity to extend his skill and energy on the football ground, to succeed to unheard of heights.

Mentioning Father Baker and his tuck shop brings back memories of sweet treats; albeit, not without payment.

Each writer tells his story in his own style, often with pathos, in the understanding we are who we are today. Throughout their many trials and tribulations from childhood to manhood, and through sheer perseverance, they are determined to keep on keeping on their motto, KOKO, alive.

HISTORY OF GRAVESEND, KENT, ENGLAND

Gravesend is a town in northwest Kent, England on the south bank of the Thames, opposite Tilbury in Essex. It is the administrative town of the Borough of Gravesham and because of its geographical position, has always had an important role in the history and communications of this part of England. It still retains a strong link with the river. The opening of the international railway station immediately west of the town at Ebbsfleet Valley, the arrival of high speed train services to and from Gravesend railway station itself, and the town's position in the Thames Gateway, have all added to the town's importance.

Notable personalities:
- Charles Dickens (1812-1870) is associated with Gravesend and the villages around the borough. Though he died over 140 years ago, many of the links between him and Gravesend are still in evidence – Gravesend he visited, at Chalk he spent his honeymoon, at Higham he lived and died, and at Cobham he found inspiration for *The Pickwick Papers*.
- General Charles George Gordon (1833-1885) lived in the town

during the construction of the Thames forts. For six years he devoted himself to the welfare of the town's "poor boys", setting up a Sunday school and providing food and clothes for them from his Army wage.

• Composer Nikolai Rimsky-Korsakov (1844-1908), officer in the Russian Navy, was posted to Gravesend in 1862, where he wrote part of his first symphony.

Rowing Matches have been taking place on the River Thames at Gravesend since the year of 1689, and the first organized Regatta was in 1715. The Annual Borough Regatta goes back to 1882.

HISTORY OF ST. MARY'S, PARROCK ROAD, GRAVESEND, KENT

St. Mary's was originally known as The Manor of Parrock, Gravesham. Abott and Convent of St. Mary Graces rented The Manor of Parrock to Sir Simon Burely (Lord Warden of Cinqueports).

The building which was later to become St. Mary's was built in 1873 and was originally a girls' college – Milton Mount College. The college moved away from Gravesend in 1915 because of the bombing raids in the area.

The College was bought by the Southwark Catholic Rescue Society in 1925, and in 1926 it was opened as St. Mary's orphanage and school, accommodating between 250 and 300 boys. St. Mary's was run by the Sisters of Charity, a priest and staff. During the Second World War the boys were evacuated to East Anglia and to Devon but returned to Gravesend after the war.

In 1951 St. Mary's ceased to be a school and the boys started to attend a newly opened Catholic School at Denton. During the 1950s there was a move away from the usage of large orphanages. A Family Group Home was established in Glen View in 1956 and further small homes were subsequently built in Glen View, Leith Park and Parrock Road. The original St. Mary's became more and more empty.

During the 1960s many babies were placed for adoption and there was a shortage of foster families to care for them before they went to their new families. Consequently in April 1965, a residential nursery was opened in a wing of the old main building. The nursery could accommodate 33 babies awaiting adoption. It was run by the Daughters of Charity (the new name of the Sisters of Charity) and the Matron was Rev. Sister Elizabeth.

During the second half of the 1960s a decision was made to sell the old building for demolition and a new St. Mary's Nursery was opened in 1971. This was designed to accommodate 24 pre-adoption babies. After 1970, however, fewer babies were being placed for adoption and the new nursery was never fully used. St. Mary's Nursery closed in October 1973.

St. Mary's, Parrock Road, Gravesend, Kent was demolished in 1971, and the land used for a new housing estate. St. John's Roman Catholic Primary School moved to a temporary building on the Denton site in 1950. Boys were admitted to Denton School in 1951. Permanent buildings at Denton, Gravesend commenced in 1960.

MEMORIES OF ST. MARY'S BEFORE AND AFTER

BY ANTONY HAYMAN

IT BEGAN IN ITALY

To understand this story I need to start at the beginning in Italy with something of my mother's life before she came to England with my father. My mother had fallen pregnant following a liaison with an Italian army officer who was billeted in her parent's farmhouse. This was, of course, considered a scandal in those days, unlike today when it is used to get a council flat and an easy life on benefits. My mother was hastily married off to my father and gratefully dispatched to England before my half-brother Giovanni (John) was born. Small wonder then that she later refused to go back to Italy!

I have no doubt that my father loved my mother who he named Giga (short for Luiga) but I think for my mother it was a matter of expediency and flight from her family whom she had disgraced. Then Thomas and Tina (Margerita Lambertina) were born before my parents moved to Ashford, Kent. Then followed Bernard. I came into this breathing world on April 24, 1926. (Followed by the General Strike!) I was named Antonio Domenico after some distant Italian uncle. Finally, Freda Raimonda my second sister arrived. There has always been a doubt about Freda's father. Rumour had it be a Mr. Laker, my father's friend, could have been her father. My father was desperately ill and in Lenham Sanatorium about this time.

My father died in 1928 when I was two and, with six children to look after, there is no doubt that my mother was in desperate straits. So, although she was not a practicing Catholic, my mother turned to the church for help. John had already gone to St. John's in Dartford, and Thomas and Bernard went to St. Mary's in 1930. Bernard in particular was bitterly resentful of this and, apart from one visit with his wife in 1946, never communicated with his mother again. My sister Freda was adored by a childless couple who lived next door and spent most of her time with them. So that just left Antonio (me) to look after which should not have been beyond her means. I certainly never went hungry.

My mother had male friends during the thirties, several of whom I remember. We were the first in our street to change from gas to electricity and had a mains radio thanks to John Masters. We also took in lodgers. This became complicated when Tina arrived home because we only had three bedrooms and so I had to be got rid of somehow. I could go into detail here about my so-called naughtiness but I was just a normal happy boy if a little mischievous from time to time.

SO TO ST. MARY'S

I arrived with my mother on a bleak December day. My first memory was of the strong smell of furniture polish and the austere figure of Sister Augustine. I had never seen a Sister of Charity before. My mother departed and I was hustled up to the sewing room and Sister Josephine where I was stripped and given the regulation St. Mary's clothes. This being Winter I was given shorts and shirt plus a blue jumper and long socks and boots. In Spring we changed to sandals (no socks), shirt and the same shorts. I did not know what underwear was until I was sixteen.

I was then given a long blue striped nightgown and so to bed. I missed my mother and cried myself to sleep. I wet the bed that night and was rewarded by being sent to St. Rocs dormitory where the boys who were regular bed-wetters slept. I was also rewarded with three whacks on each hand by the cruel Sister Augustine who obviously had had no training in child psychology. From St. Rocs to the toilets was through two other dormitories in the dark and, with no lights, it was quite frightening for a nine-year-old.

The worst thing about the school in those days was that it was, to all intents and purposes, a closed community. I do realise that it could not have been a free for all but I think that as we got older, we could have been gradually introduced to the outside world.

I was in Sister Patricia's class to start with and I wrote tearful letters to my mother to take me back home. I doubt that they were ever sent. I remember Sister Patricia well. She was a very large Irish lady and very kind.

She was also in charge of housekeeping and gave me my first job of dusting the ledges in the long corridor that ran the whole length of the school. From that I progressed to my own length of the corridor floor which I had to wash and scrub every day.

I was not long in Sister Patricia's class because I had already learnt to read, write and do simple arithmetic, so I progressed to Miss O'Neils and then to Miss Rumes. I think she was the best teacher in the school. I was always, with Michael Halliday, at the top of her class. Miss Rumes also left me with a lifelong friend in the Kenneth Graham's book *"The*

Wind in the Willows". Once a week Miss Rumes read us a chapter from the book and the magic has stayed with me to this day. I have a copy of this wonderful story which I read to my son when he was growing up. I have to say that the education standard was not high, and it would have been advantageous if some of the more intelligent boys had attended a better school in Gravesend.

The food which we were given was best described as adequate. Meat was never served except on Sundays where it consisted of one sausage! Followed by an apple. Breakfast was always unsweetened porridge and tea, laced once a month with Epsom salts. Tea was a doorstep (bread) with margarine and jam. Speed was essential in getting your share of the jam! Easter brought the one egg of the year.

The boys did all the housework organised by Sister Patricia. I went from corridor duty to the Chapel, polishing the brass, etc., and then, because of some minor transgression, to the laundry, where I learnt to iron shirts My wife maintains that I iron and do housework better than her! The laundry was run by two Irish ladies and the boiler room by Mr. O'Connor. Sister Patricia rescued me from this and gave me the plum job of serving the teacher's meals. This improved my diet considerably because there were always leftovers of dessert which I consumed with alacrity and gratitude. My final task at the school was to do the housework at the teacher's house.

BATH TIME – FRIDAY NIGHTS

No tin bath in front of the copper as at home. Sister stood at the entrance of the washroom and deposited a dollop of soft soap on your head. Then into a footbath with everybody else, followed by the showers. All this wearing red shorts so as not to embarrass the Sister. We then struggled to dry ourselves with a towel while divesting ourselves of the red shorts. Then a further examination by Sister, of ears and nails. And so to bed.

The Sisters I remember most were: Sister Patricia, Sister Ann (Kitchen), Sister Josephine (Sewing Room), and Sister Clare (too lovely to be a nun). The infamous Sister Augustine, who actually cried when she had to leave, when we were in Wells-next-the-Sea. I felt like cheering!

Sister Vincent known to the boys as Vinnie who was the Superior for most of my time there.

Perhaps I should recount here the one escapade I had for which I would have been severely punished had I been caught. It was on Christmas Day and we were all in the Shed. Boys were all opening parcels sent in by their parents. But not me!

I had heard on the school grapevine that some good folk in Gravesend had sent in toys which were stored in the teacher's old dining room. Envy got the better of me. I slipped out of the Shed, climbed over the seven-foot gate quickly, and on to the front of the school. Pushing up the sash window, which was unlocked, I climbed inside and looked around. Then I heard footsteps coming along the passage – footsteps I knew only too well. It was the dreaded Sister Augustine! I hid behind a corner unit in the nick of time.

Key turned in the lock and Sister Augustine came into the room. I held my breath for what seemed an eternity. But after a few minutes she turned and left. All I had for my trouble was a toy cannon that fired matchsticks. Where do you find matchsticks in a Convent? Anyway the episode cured me of envy!

Bullying was not something that I experienced except for two incidents. Firstly I had only been at the school a few months when I was approached by a boy two or three years older than myself who teased me and began to slap me around. The boy's name was Valentine Dorenbecher and he would have been in probably the same Class as my brother Bernard. I can only assume that he must have fallen out with my brother and decided to take it out on a small opponent. My brother intervened and that was that!

Or so I thought. When my brother left the school, he gave me his most precious possession, a cricket bat. Playing with the bat while on holiday in Dymchurch, V.D. asked if he could borrow it and when I refused he snatched the bat away and proceeded to smash it to pieces on a rock. A Nazi in the making! I never forgot this incident, and years later I received a letter from V.D. asking for money to pay for a Mass for Sister Patricia. Normally I would have been happy to oblige but not from him. I regretted this decision in later years.

RELIGION

We had plenty of that! Firstly, I was given a medal to wear around my neck on a blue cord. This was "Our Lady of the Immaculate Conception". I should mention here that when I was taken into hospital in 1940 it was removed and I never saw it again. Many years later I was in the Cathedral in Kerry (Ireland) and I found one that someone had dropped. I still have it.

Mass and Benediction on Sundays and Mass on many other feast days as well. Not to mention numerous Rosaries which I disliked. All that gabbling of Hail Marys and all I had to show for it was sore knees. I loved the Mass in Latin and regretted the change to English. I felt that the Mass lost all of its mystery and magic. Benediction too was great. I will always remember "O Salutaris, Tantum Ergo and Adoremus". And the great moment of raising the Monstrance and the Incense. Pure theatre.

There was so much talk of the SOUL that, in my childish imagination, I thought of it as fleshy and shaped like a rugby ball!

EASTER 1937

The choir spent hours learning a sung Mass only for our efforts to be in vain when the Sister who had organised it and also played the organ, fell ill so it was all cancelled. Towards the end of 1939 the school was sent a young Irish Priest who flew through the Mass so fast that the Altar boys could scarcely keep up. He also had a vile temper. He struck me round the ear for supposedly talking at the wrong time (he got the wrong boy) and I have been deaf in that ear ever since.

I particularly liked our three day Retreats despite the enforced silence. We had a visiting Priest for the Retreats who gave brilliant and humorous talks which were very enjoyable. Strange that after all that religious instruction I should lose my faith.

Another memory, which has always stayed with me, was singing "Bless This House" in the school hall. It was a dark and dismal day and there were no lights on. When it came to the line "Bless these windows shining bright – letting in God's heavenly light" a burst of sunlight came through the windows, illuminating the whole room. The look on the Sister's face and the smile was something I shall never forget!

SPORTS

Apart from drill in the bleak and inhospitable Shed which in winter was so cold most of us wound up with chilblains, we were marched down to the field. We were divided into "Houses" in those days – Crusaders, Wasps, Ramblers, etc. So events were arranged with Houses playing against each other. From these Houses were picked the boys to play for "The School Team". It was every boy's ambition to play for the School and I did not make it until 1940. More of that later. St. Mary's played against teams from other Schools on different pitches in the town, with proceeds going to local Charities.

Grounds, I remember, were Imperial Paper Mills and the Barracks. I also remember that the School rallying cry was "Up St. Mary's". Some new boys tried to change this to "Two Four Six Eight, who do we appreciate" etc. Mr. Roche became very annoyed by this and made them stop and revert to the original Cry. We also had a Sports Day and I can vividly remember beating the great Billy Kiernan in the last leg of a relay. Mind you the other three boys had given me a good start!

Cricket, which I loved, was a non-starter at the School except for the games we played in the Shed. Being in the Shed or the upper playgrounds was known as being on Guard and to use Mr. Roche's words, 'woe betide you,' if you were caught – "off guard".

Football was played with a tennis ball or a "Tanner" ball obtained from the local shop in Echo Square. It was not unknown for boys, with money, to slide down the hill at the back of the Shed and buy things at the local shops.

One of Sister Augustine's favourite games was, when a box of sweets was sent to the school, to stand at the top of the playground and throw the sweets into the throng of boys. Believe me one had to be tough to get a sweet! And avoid being trampled on.

Excursions were few and far between but those I remember were: A visit to the local cinemas to see (naturally) "Boys Town" with Spencer

Tracey and Mickey Rooney, "A Tale of Two Cities" with Ronald Colman and rather surprisingly, Flanagan and Alan in "Underneath the Arches". Also a visit to Bertram Mills Circus in London. I do NOT remember much of the Circus but I do recollect being reprimanded by a man in the audience for eating my sandwiches with both hands! He remarked that only Tramps eat like that!

There were lots of things that were started but did not last long. The print room was one where we were supposed to produce a School Magazine. A gym with a vaulting horse, etc. and a hobbies room. For some reason these were all dropped. On Sundays after Mass, we assembled into a long crocodile, three abreast and marched through the town. A Sister at either end, of course.

HOLIDAYS

The two weeks holiday at St. Mary's Bay Holiday Camp was the highlight of our year. We had better food and greater freedom. We mixed freely with other schools and had great fun down on the beach, some of us learning to swim in the sea wearing of course, the ubiquitous red shorts. There were great water-pistol fights around the washrooms and we concluded the holiday with an all-school singsong in the main Hall.

In the final holiday there I was given a half-crown and put on a bus to visit my family in Ashford. I also had a half-day with my sister Tina who was working in nearby Folkestone.

EVACUATION

So to the day when we were told to leave everything, including my prize stamp collection and other "Crodge", school slang for little treasures that we had acquired. And we were marched down to Gravesend Pier. The date was September 2, 1939. On to the "Royal Daffodil" Steamer and we set sail for Lowestoft in Suffolk. We were told we were being evacuated because of the threat of War. The majority of the boys were seasick, but fortunately not me. That night we slept on straw in a dance hall only to be awoken at three in the morning by the Air Raid sirens. We had to put on our gas masks and wait for the All Clear. War was declared the next day at 11a.m.

Then we were put on coaches and taken out into the Suffolk countryside. We all had bags containing chocolate bars, a tin of condensed milk, etc. We arrived at the Village Hall where we were selected by the local people. I was with a Mr. & Mrs. Barber who had three children of their own. They were lovely people and the food was great. Too good for my constitution after the meagre diet of St. Mary's, because I developed very nasty boils on my neck. Sister Patricia, who was billeted locally, treated me with very hot poultices so they soon cleared up. Most importantly I was once again free to roam the countryside and I learned to ride a bicycle. Sister Clare, also billeted with Sister Patricia, bought me a fishing rod to fish in the village pond. As I was the only boy capable of riding a bike, I was entrusted with a message to take to some of the other Sisters. This entailed a journey of five miles there and back. We started our education again in the Village School and we also celebrated Mass there on Sundays. An idyllic life but alas it was not to last and all too soon we were gathered up and taken to Wells-next-the Sea.

There I was taken to "The Ostrich" guest house run by Mr. and Mrs. Barker, who had two young children of their own, and the event was to change my life completely. I enjoyed being by the sea. Apart from the guest house, they also had a Carriers business delivering parcels all over Norfolk and I was roped in to help at weekends and holidays. It was during one of these trips that while I was carrying a heavy package, that I slipped on a patch of ice and badly bruised my right knee. I thought nothing of it at the time. But on the day before I was due to make my first team debut I was rushed to hospital for an emergency operation on my right leg. I had developed Osteomyelitis of the femur. The treatment in those days was to cut into the leg to drain the abscess, pack it with paraffin gauze and put the leg in Plaster of Paris.

After a short stay at Drayton Hospital, outside Norwich, I was unaccountably put on an Ambulance Train and taken to a hospital in Shotley Bridge, County Durham. The train was mainly full of soldiers returning from Dunkirk, so I had no idea why I was on it. Nobody asked me if I wanted to go and as far as I know, the School was not informed. I awoke the following morning to find myself in a long Hut/Ward mainly with very elderly, and in some cases Paraplegic patients. The Hut/Ward was one of several built on the side of a very steep hill. My ward was near the top of the hill of which, more later. Patients that I remember were an eighty-year-old former boatswain of the Cromer Lifeboat, a heavyweight Boxer, and others. The Boxer had been warned about his diet of steak and chips but had ignored the advice and was very ill. He was eventually taken to another hospital. The elderly boatswain died and I was asked if I had ever seen a dead person. They were amazed when I said no and persuaded me to have a viewing. Not the best thing for a young boy still on crutches.

With no previous experience, I found myself performing the services of a hairdresser for many of the elderly, and particularly the Paraplegics. I got on very well with the Ward Sister, Mrs. Ledger, and we did Crosswords together. I also became friends with a boy in Consett, the nearest town. It always seemed peculiar to me that the hospital was situated less than a mile away from Consett, which had a major Steel Works with an open furnace, which could be seen for miles, especially at night. The Luftwaffe made several attempts to bomb it, with one of the bombs falling on the golf course next to the hospital!

Where was the school while all this was going on? I saw nobody. The SCRS knew that I was at Shotley Bridge but made no attempt to contact me or the Authorities. This resulted in my being wheeled into the operating theatre (in an attempt to cure me) only to find that they had not had permission to perform the operation. I should mention here that Penicillin which could have cured me was reserved for the Armed Forces. But I think that they were going to make an exception in my case. I think that this amounted to a failure by the SCRS in their duty of care of me. The result of all this was my being sent home to my mother who did not want me there. I also still had an open wound on my leg which had to be dressed twice a day and this I did until 1946.

My mother dispatched me to work in a hotel in Folkstone in 1943 which at that time was being heavily shelled from across the Channel. When this fell through she then sent me to work in a friend's restaurant in London, where I stayed until I received my Calling up papers. Not that the government had no trouble finding me. This proved a major turning point in my life because having failed the medical, for obvious reasons, the examining doctor asked if my own doctor had ever heard of Penicillin. That resulted in my being sent to the Middlesex Hospital in London where after a couple of operations (the problem had broken out on my clavicle) and millions of units of Penicillin I was finally cured. This was in 1946.

The rest as they say is history. Apart from a couple of near misses my health has been good. I have been happily married for over 58 years to my dear wife Gwen and we had one son Paul. My mother eventually married a Russian ex-soldier she met in London and settled in Maidstone, Kent. She died at the age of eighty. She always complained that I did not visit her often enough!

As I have said before I do not regret my time at St. Mary's. It taught me many things such as loyalty, always to tell the truth and discipline. Apart from three points on my Driving License when I was 83, I have never been in trouble with the Law. It is perhaps a sobering thought that had I not gone to St. Mary's and had the accident in Norfolk, I would have had to join the forces in 1944, and therefore maybe not survived to tell the story!

I eventually went into the Printing trade, my father's profession, retiring as a Director when I reached the age of 67.

BACKGROUND HISTORY

Here I would like to record my grateful thanks to Teresa Downey for her help and research, which gave me an insight into my early history....

Dear Antony,

I am pleased to enclose the records we hold concerning you. I would be grateful if you could sign the attached receipt of records and return one copy to me. I am also enclosing an evaluation sheet, and would be pleased if you could take the time to complete and return this in the SAE. We welcome feedback from our service users, as this helps shape the delivery of our services in the future.

You will see that there was contact between your mother and this Society (then called Southwark Catholic Rescue Society – SCRS) from 1930, when your mother made an application for assistance in connection with Walter, Bernard and yourself. John at this time was at St. Vincent's Industrial School, Dartford; Margaret was at a Convent School in France; and Freda was living at home. Your mother was a widow. Your father's name was given as Walter Leslie Hayman, age 35, and a convert to Catholicism. He was deceased. Your mother was in receipt of a widow's pension.

The SCRS committee decided to accept her application on behalf of Walter and Bernard, and they were subsequently placed at St. Mary's Gravesend on 13th September 1930. The committee decided not to accept you into Care as you were still quite young. You therefore remained at home with your mother and younger sister.

Your mother applied again in August 1931 and in May 1934 asking the SCRS to admit you to Gravesend. The SCRS wrote back to her saying they were unable to help her at present.

A further request for assistance was made by your mother in August 1935. The SCRS accepted you into their Care and you were placed at St. Mary's Gravesend on 11th December 1935.

I'm afraid no records of your time at St. Mary's were

made – it just wasn't the practice in those days. The file records therefore became very brief after your admission to St. Mary's.

The school was evacuated to Great Yarmouth in September 1939 and boys dispersed to families in Suffolk and Norfolk. You were admitted to Norwich Hospital on May 4th 1940, and then on to the Drayton Emergency Hospital on 22nd July 1940. It seems there was a breakdown in communications at this time, probably due to the enormous upheaval of the War. The SCRS clearly thought you were still attached to the school, which by February 1941 had been transferred to Ugbrooke. We do not know the date when you transferred from Drayton to the Emergency Hospital at Shotley Bridge, Co. Durham, but you were clearly there by May 1941.

You were discharged to your mother at 4 West Street, Ashford, on 11th May 1941. It seems this discharge surprised the SCRS – there is no record on file of any discussions between the SCRS and hospital about your discharge.

Once you have had time to go through the records and absorb all the information I would be pleased to hear from you if you have any further questions or would like to discuss the records further. I look forward to reading your memoirs in due course!

Sincerely,

Teresa Downy, Team Manager, Post Adoption & Care Service, Cabrini Children's Society.

Dated: 31 August 2011

POSTCARDS

Year: 1936 – 1d postage stamp.

Addressed to the   Rev. Canon Crea,

59 Westminster Bridge Road, London, S.E.1

Dear Sir, I would be very pleased if you could let me have a permit to take my brothers Tony and Bernard Hayman out on Saturday, the seventh. Yours Obliged, J.L. Hayman. 101 Highfield Road, Dartford, Kent. Dated: 4th November 1936.

(There is a notation on this card – "If he has had this before, OK)

Permit requested, sent 5/11/36

Dear Sir, I would be very pleased if you would kindly send me a permit to see my brothers on the schools Reunion Day (Bernard and Tony Hayman). Thanking you and trusting that everything will be alright. Yours obliged, John Hayman. 101 Highfield Road, Dartford, Kent.

Dated: 28/12/1936 Permission approved 30/12/36

WELCOME TO YOUR NEW HOME

BY TERRY S. MCKENNA

"Welcome to your New Home." It was most probably the first sentence I ever heard uttered and it certainly was life-defining. After four months in hospital recovering from whooping cough, my "new home" was St. Mary's Catholic Children's Home in Gravesend, Kent. A giant step for a small frightened Catholic boy.

On arrival to this "home" I remember the very wide flagstone steps to the huge, imposing building at the end of a long driveway, and being "greeted" by nuns attired in black, whose faces you could not quite make out. Where is this place? Had I died and were these apparitions actually the "Grim Reapers"?

'Come on, Terence,' a voice within the nearest black shroud boomed.

With one swoop, I was engulfed in the shroud and whisked inside. Life was never going to be the same again.

'My name is Sister Josephine and I am your new mother. Come with me and I will bathe you and give you some new clothes.'

At this point I cried out for my mum, but of course she couldn't hear me. She never heard me again.

My new clothes were flannel grey short trousers, a white shirt, a grey tank top jumper, grey socks and some ill-fitting highly polished but worn boots, with leather laces a mile long. Grey seemed an appropriate colour. The smell of carbolic was powerful and ever-present – I can smell it in my mind even today.

All the other boys were dressed the same and we looked like a swarm of shiny-faced Mini-Me's. The polished wooden floors echoed to the sound of nervous stuttering feet of little boys; yet not a sound came from these "lost souls". No laughter, no talking, just vacant expressions of despair! Where is this place?

'Right, children, follow me,' a voice in the distance commanded and we followed like sheep.

The gloomy carbolic smelling inside was left behind and we were in a hard court area bathed in brightness. The whole of this area was protected by high wire fencing. Most of the time there would be people walking round, pointing and chatting with the Grim Reapers. Little did we know this was the "reviewing" area for prospective Mums and Dads; a sort of "Pick 'n' Mix" of kids!

Often kids would "disappear" on a Friday or Saturday and return on Sunday afternoons. I was "returned" many times. Some of the kids did not come back and as I was to find out eventually, they had either been adopted or sent to Australia or Canada.

After the Second World War, Australia in particular was left bereft of fathers to "make children" and the UK became a source of supply with all the displaced children from the war, and the "unwanted" from the late

1940s and '50s. At this time it was a huge stigma for unmarried mothers to bear children and for those women left by the child's father to fend for themselves. Unless they came from a wealthy family, mothers were often forced to give up their children. Most women were traumatised by these events and never came to terms with what they were made to do. Nearly all of these children were told their parents were dead. This is a dreadful reflection of society as a whole from this time and I am pleased attitudes have changed.

Every new friend I made seemed to leave me behind and after a year or so I was still a lonely friendless little chap, lost in my strange "grey" world. On most of my returns I cried. Perhaps it was because the "magical" weekends were over too quickly or maybe it was the return to my "grey" world.

Meal times were good. There was plenty to eat and drink, though I was "special" because I had lots of orange juice. Oranges were apparently good for me and my bones! There were tables of different colours, seating eight. Mine was red. We also had lots of thick broth with barley in the winter months to keep us warm when we played in the hard court area. It was important that we looked well-fed, as we played for our very existence though, of course, none of this was known to us. Maybe this might explain my abhorrence to "caged" animals and I never felt comfortable at the circus or the zoo.

The nuns were never allowed to smack you, so if you misbehaved you were sat in a tiny room (I think it was an old style confessional box) which had very deep black velvet curtains, drawn together. You were left in total darkness and isolation for as long as the nun felt fit. I was a naughty boy a lot and as a result I am still frightened of total darkness.

Although I was very young I do remember my early education and could read and write (after a fashion) when I was just four years old, so there must have been a good seat of learning. When I went to "proper" school aged five, my teachers were pleasantly surprised at my advance skills. I have to say that the 3Rs today's children learn is way behind the levels that in my days were expected to attain, even with classes for fifty children.

At my primary school (a Catholic one) discipline was "fierce" and the teachers stood no nonsense, nor took any "prisoners". Friday afternoons were the day I enjoyed most. We used to do country dancing to the radio for about an hour and then end up with spelling. The kids used to all stand up and were given a word to spell. If we got it right we would remain standing; if not we sat down. I used to nearly always be one of the last to sit down.

THEN ONE DAY IT HAPPENED! A lady, a man, and a boy three years older than me, and a priest announced that I was leaving my "grey" world for good. The "Pick 'n' Mix" had finally worked for me too! As a four-and-a-half-year-old boy I didn't know what to do or say. The clinical carbolic smell suddenly hit me as never before, as I was given my worldly goods – a change of clothes. All I wanted to do was to take my three toys with me – a large Teddy Bear, a fire engine and a football.

The "Grim Reapers" said I couldn't take them with me, so I screamed the place down and they relented, and said I could take one of them with me and made me choose. My parents must have wondered what they had let themselves in for. Although very unhappy I chose the football and the other toys were left behind for the next wave of "Lost Souls".

I never saw the "Grim Reapers" again.

Life was never going to be the same again for me.

EMAILS FROM THE KOKO WRITING GROUP

Editor's Note: The following emails from a group of writers in England, Australia and Canada have been kept in their original form, except where this would have made them difficult to read. This gives the reader a picture of events then and now and how the old boys of St. Mary's viewed their childhood memories. Several honorary members of the London Group who were not brought up at St. Mary's include Ann Phyall (Buckinghamshire, England), Caroline Whitehead (British Columbia, Canada), Mavis Heffernan (Australia) and Christine Shrosbree (England) who are contributors to the old boys "network".

FANTASY WORLD OF FOOTBALL

Delvin. Hope you and your family and the rest of the group are in the best of form. Your member I think new member John (Michael) Murray brought back some very happy memories about Dymchurch and some of the boys who were good at football. Football was the fantasy world I lived in when I was at St. Mary's and when we went to camp at Dymchurch I was in another fantasy world. I used to love the miniature railway at Dymchurch. I think I remember the names of two of the engines: one was called Hercules and one was called Samson.

About not ever getting fried eggs, I used to dream about them. I remember there was a café just outside the Dymchurch camp. It was 1956 and you could get fried egg and chips, and the café had a jukebox. We would sit there hoping someone would put a thruppenny bit in it. It was the first time I heard Rock & Roll. That was the last time I went to Dymchurch. I left St. Mary's March 1957. What beautiful memories.

I remember Bill Kiernan the Charlton Athletic Player came to visit St. Mary's and he was looking for some boys to help him clear some waste ground at a new house he had bought; it was back-breaking work on a very hot day; taught me a lesson about hero worshiping I never forgot. I don't remember St. Mary's football team there. Myself and Alan Johnson who brilliantly got reunited with his family last year, used to be pulled out of the class one afternoon a week, when we were in the year below the rest of the team.

A Mr. Rawlings who came from up north; he should have stayed up north. (Claimed he trained Albert Quixall to play football). He used to get one of them old leather footballs, soak in a bucket of water and make us kick it against the wind all afternoon. Thank God he left and Mr. Staunton came and took over. I remember him to be a lovely man. I remember going for a trial for area school boys' team; Thames-side I think it was with Alan Johnson. We had to take our kit and walk all the way there as we had no money for bus fares. I remember we were knackered when we arrived.

Here are some of the boys I seem to remember: Colin Dobson I think he came from the town, had a very nice sister who went to St. John's. There was another boy from the town called Casey, he had ginger hair and went on to play for Gravesend & Northfleet. The boys from St. Mary's I remember were Micky Lenahan, they said he went to Arsenal. Wally Hanson, Roy Brown, Chris Kelly he played wearing glasses – wouldn't be allowed nowadays but he was very good. Jock Thomson, Gordon Gauntlet.

On a Saturday afternoon when we were allowed out I used to enjoy going to Windmill Hill from where you could look down the high street towards the ferry and go into the under cover market. All this I think I remember. I could be wrong. I say this because in some of your emails I remember different. Lots I remember the same, and some awoke memory I never knew I had. Pardon the bad grammar I have never been very good at it. Since I have been receiving the emails it's been a brilliant trip down memory lane.

Thank you very much.

Tony Ledger

MR. RAWLINGS

Tony, Thank you for your kind words about the emails. Your latest email has been so informative I haven't thought about Mr. Rawlings for years. I recall his quality hair – the colour somewhere between bronze and what we used to call ginger which was enhanced by Brylcream. Here is a memory for the younger members of the group. Mr. Hawket, another teacher, who hasn't been mentioned recently is still alive and living with his daughter in the Gravesend area. Surely he must be the oldest surviving teacher. I have received a couple of letters from him and like many of his generation his handwriting has to be admired. What a fine list of boys names you have conjured up. Our memories are dormant until someone like yourself revives them and they say it's not worth giving artificial respiration to a headless corpse.

Just as I was thinking our writings have gone as far as they can go, you Tony and our new entrant John, have totally reinvigorated our group with fresh memories. I have been very wary about how things have been going. I mean we can only continue so long as the membership show enthusiasm and there seems to be a lot of it out there. Sure, some of us do most of the writing yet the interested like an iceberg is mostly below the surface. I "cut and pasted" a section of John Murray's email on the Gravesend facebook site and was amazed at the early response. I have had a mature lady asking about how we were treated at St. Mary's. Another lady remembers, she thinks, taking John Murray into the family home and feeding him up and again there was another enquiry asking about a boy who may have gone to Australia in the early fifties. I was able to look at the passenger list of the "SS New Australia" on which some of the boys travelled to Australia but did not see the name of the boy to whom it referred. By the way the name of the boy was Clive Church and perhaps one of you out there may remember him.

Tony, I remember Windmill Hill. Some of us voyeurs used to go there in the late evenings to watch the courting couples. Because of the shady shadowy outlines we used to call them logs. Of course we didn't see anything and besides who ever heard of the word voyeurism in those days?

We had four cinemas in the town: Regal, Plaza, Super and Majestic. The week's programme would start on a Monday and change midweek and then again on Sunday. There was the main film and a supporting film. Imagine the total number of films that one could possibly see. And if that wasn't enough one could enjoy the monopoly advertising by Peal and Dean. We all loved the Cowboy and Indian films in those days. Who remembers Hopalong Cassidy?

The under cover market in the town was fascinating. I used to enjoy the spiel of the market traders and their humour. I remember one chap pleading with the ladies to come closer to his stall. 'Close up. Close up, ladies,' he would say then follow it up with a smart arse remark like. 'Put your dress down. I said close up, not clothes up.' They were so funny. 'Don't say you bought it, say you stole it at these prices.'

I could go on about their chat but I haven't the gift to convey it as it was. Does anyone recall the little monkey in the cage in the market? We were horrible children. We used to poke the monkey with a stick and watch it lose its temper. The look it gave us was a tad frightening but remember it was safely in its cage. Kids, eh! Don't ever let them be in charge. We had the potential to supersede the film "Lord of the Files".

KOKO

Delvin

KID NAMED DOBSON

Hi John and the rest of the gang.

You all seem to be talking in your emails about someone named DOBSON? I think you may be mistaking him for an OUTSIDE kid named DAVID DOBSON all-round athlete from St. John's who was brilliant at football, cricket, running, swimming and just about everything else and was a great favourite of Copper Knob, Mr. Rawlison or Rollinson.

I hope you are all keeping well out there. Keep smiling and maybe the sun will shine through. John, I can't remember if I sent you an email of the CD I made, arranged for me to make a couple of years ago by my son Stephen?

KOKO

Bernie Francis

MR. R'S HAIR

Bernie, as usual you are demonstrating your good memory. I like your refined description of Mr. R's hair. A fine head of hair by any standards. I never heard of Dobson again after I left St. M but being as you said an "outsider" kid that is understandable. We didn't need to get close to other kinds as we had plenty of "brothers" at St. M to play with.

Now about the CD. We would love to obtain a copy as you have already demonstrated that you have a fine voice even though you were booted out of the singing class when we were infants.

KOKO

J&J (Josie & John)

FRAME CANVAS BEDS

Hello again,

Can anybody remember the two weeks summer holiday in August each year to St. Mary's Bay Holiday Camp at Dymchurch?

I remember climbing aboard the blue and white coaches of AC Ltd and being ferried down to the coast.

We slept in long wooden huts which were unheated and could be quite cold at night. We slept on very low wooden frame canvas beds. If you were unlucky you had a bed where the canvas had stretched so you rested on the floor. All meals were taken in a huge shed with hundreds of other children from a variety of schools.

There used to be a souvenir/gift shop where we could spend our pocket money (those who had any). Playing on the beach was fun, particularly when the tide was really far out. We had to walk for what seemed miles to get to the water past our waist. Remember the Jellyfish? One poor boy I recall got stung and came up in a horrible rash. When the tide was in we just sat on the wall and shivered.

I used to love our annual trip to the Romney Hythe and Dymchurch Railway – the miniature trains, one was called The Green Goddess and another Dr. Syn. We went to the fair at Hythe. I loved it. Some days we were taken on long walks round the country lanes. I recall a few of us pooling our money to buy a tin of Golden Syrup and taking turns to dip our fingers in it without the nuns seeing. In the evening we used to play out in the huge field in front of huts. One year we were plagued with swarms of flying ants.

There used to be a football match arranged with other schools and if my memory serves me right we often used to win. Our senior boys were quite good. I remember two of the senior boys called Dobson and Lenahan. I think they had a trial for England Schoolboys. When they left Gravesend I heard Dobson went to Arsenal and Lenahan to Charlton Athletic. Talking of old boys who made it good there was a boy at St. Mary's with me called David Starbrook. We were always told he had to have an operation to remove his Adams apple because he used to eat ants – it may have only been boys exaggerating. He did have a scar where his Adams apple would be. A few years ago I saw a picture of him on the internet (scar and all) as having represented GB in the Olympics at Judo, he was also a world champion. The last I heard he lives in France and is still involved with Judo. I have never managed to make contact.

When it rained, and it often did, if we were lucky we had a film. An old black and white one while we sat on the cold hard floor. I loved going to Dymchurch, playing in the rock pools, gathering crabs and other creatures and being scared to death of the "quick sand" as we were told we would get stuck and vanish forever. It wasn't all bad.

More later.

John (Michael) Murray

BRASS MONKEYS

John,

This was my first introduction to the seaside. I don't want to sound like a miseryguts, but I was so disappointed I didn't anticipate how salty the sea was nor how brass monkeys it would be. From that time on, I always associated the British coast with khaki porridge until in the early 80s when we spent a few hours in Looe before getting on the ferry from Plymouth to Roscoff. I was amazed at the clarity and beautiful colour of the sea.

God was on my side as my company transferred me to Truro for two years.

A propos Dymchurch, do you remember the turkey farm with its pungency next to the camp?

Via iPad

Glen Cawdeary

Glen,

It could be cold and often was. Father Baker insisted that we duck into the freezing brine and could not retreat until there was evidence that one was soaked from head to toe. But there were more good warm days than cold ones.

St. Mary's Bay to me is filled with happy memories and it was always a sad day when we had to leave.

Like you, it was really only when other resorts were seen that it was discovered that the sea could be other than opaque grey.

My posting to Cyprus spoilt me for the chill of the south coast and my swimming was kept to the hygienic swimming pools from then on.

I have no memories of the turkey farm and it must have come along after my time.

KOKO

John F.

A RARE TREAT

John (Michael) Murray,

You refreshed my memory when talking about the miniature railway. The train named Doctor Syn was reputed to be named after a famous smuggler and clergyman. This contraband was supposed to be hidden in a local country church which we would visit on our country walks.

In those days the powers that be had an absolute aversion to giving us fried eggs for breakfast consequently we never got any, but on holiday we would travel to Hythe and call at our special café and enjoy fried egg and chips – a rare treat.

Dymchurch was about a mile along the beach from St. Mary's Bay and they had a small fun fair and a skating rink. I just loved the skating rink and we strapped on our chunky steel skates for a fun time. The bumping cars were a bit expensive but what the hell we were on holiday.

St. Mary's had over the years good football teams. Crowds would turn out to watch and sometimes Billy Kiernan an ex St. M boy and Charlton FC player would referee. I actually have a couple of old programs which if you remind me I could send.

You mentioned Dobson he was an outstanding player in a later era when we went out to school at Denton. I didn't hear of him again until you mentioned him. I recall him as having blond curly hair and he was of course an all round sportsman. I can't recall Lenahan.

KOKO

(Delvin) John Flynn

ST. MARY'S BAY

John M.

St. Mary's Bay, ah! They were great holidays or were we just simple folk? I believe we only used AC Limited coaches on one occasion but I recall Timpson's coaches. I always fancied being a coach driver and would practice in the playgrounds with the bicycle hoops and a stick or used old rubber tyres. Sometimes we would crouch inside a tyre and would be rolled along by some other lad. We kidded ourselves that riding inside the tyre was fun whereas in reality we staggered about afterwards feeling quite green. The really large tyres were great fun when we would push them along and then clamber onto them, brought to the top and over by the momentum.

I have sent you a picture of St. Mary's Bay Holiday Camp. "The largest camp for boys and girls in England" which I feel sure will bring back memories for you.

Father Baker used to carry a load of stuff in a trailer behind his vehicle and he would invite the two oldest boys to travel down with him to

Dymchurch. In 1954 Harwood and me were the oldest so had the honour of travelling down in his new Morris car. Before taking ownership of the new car he used to have a pickup truck registration CAN 161. I had mixed feelings about this as although I felt privileged I had a feeling of nausea brought on by the smell of new leather. We took a break halfway down to the camp and Fr B treated the both of us to a fish and chips lunch (it being Friday) with a glass of woodpecker cider. He then went on to tease us that this harmless drink was making us drunk.

The meals in the huge shed for us and other schools was better than what was dished up at St. Mary's. And there was plenty of it for us hungry lads exposed to the fresh sea air. Swimming was good so long as the weather was warm but Father B insisted that we get right in irrespective of whether it was warm or cold. Do you remember he held our savings for us and I never knew him to make a mistake? Had he not been a priest he would surely have been an accountant.

KOKO

(Delvin) John F.

AWFUL BEANS

Hello,

I remember the beans, they were awful. We used to say 'beans, beans good for your heart, the more you eat the more you f......t.'

We used to be given a big plate of them. I recall the change. We used to have food delivered by Kearly & Tonge and from them we got better quality beans, more reddy brown rather than grey in a thick goo.

When I first went to St. Mary's I think we were just coming to the end of having schooling there. We then went to what I think was called St. John's Infants School run by Sisters of Mercy. I can recall being in a classroom when a nun came in and told us the King was dead. We had to immediately say a prayer. That was in 1952, and I was nine/ten. The next year I took the 11+ exam. Two boys in the class passed and went to St. Mary's in Sidcup. They were Patrick Nye and David Stoddard. I was told I passed to go to a Technical School but as there was not a Catholic one I had to go to St. John's in Denton. In later life my mother showed me a letter from the Kent County Council, confirming it.

When I think back we were given a lot of freedom. After breakfast and we had washed our hands and faces again, we were sent off to school. We went off on our own accord, no supervision, just walking down the street in little groups. Can you imagine that today? A long snake of children wearing Hi-Viz vests and two or three nuns as escort. I don't recall any harm coming to any boy. We used to walk back from there at lunch time for school dinners in St. Mary's, a long chain of girls and boys. As Terry Mc says, this is where we came into contact with girls.

We had a separate playground and I remember getting the cane off one of the nuns for kissing a girl through the railings. I did it for a dare but got caught. The girl's name was Anne Hibben, a very pretty blonde girl. She had an equally pretty friend called Marilyn (not Monroe), also blonde. Anne was my first love at nine/ten. I recall buying her a box of Licorice Allsorts for her birthday which I think was in September. They cost me 7d. I knew how to give a girl a good time.

At some stage whilst at the junior school, I was selected to go and get the nuns' dinner. This entailed coming out of the class a bit early, going to the office collecting my bus fare, and the containers that the food was to be carried in. This consisted of a series of round cans with lids on which fitted into a carrying frame. Off I trotted!

I had to catch the 495 or 496 bus to Echo Square which was where St. Mary's was. I then had to walk down the road toward Denton, past a big church and the convent was up a long lane. I was given dinner there while a nun filled the container and off I would trot back to the infants' school, catching the bus at Echo Square. I used to sit at the back of the bus near the door as the smell of the food was so strong, and I felt embarrassed. On one occasion whilst waiting for the bus some boys started to pick on me, punching and pinching me and trying to get the container off me. Luckily, the bus came along just in time. They carried on, so in desperation, I swung the container at one of the boys, catching him on the side of the head. He finished up with gravy on his head.

The bus conductor saw what was happening and helped me on the bus. He would not let the other boys on. By this time the container was leaking custard and gravy, as well as the usual smell of cooked food. He told me not to worry and would not take my bus fare off me. Again "the kindness of strangers".

When I arrived back to the school, the Mother Superior was pretty upset. I do not think she believed me when I told her what happened. I think I was relieved of the job shortly afterwards.

More later.

John (Michael) Murray

THE ANGELUS

John,

Thank you for your email. I did have a brother who was not a resident at St. Mary's. He lived at home in Bromley with my mother and came to "holiday" in St. Mary's during the summer months. In my later years at St. Mary's, I did go home to Bromley on the Greenline bus for weekends.

I remember, when I was very young, a nun called Sister Alphonsus who was teaching me to play the piano and sing. It was in a downstairs playroom next to the "bootroom". She was very strict, whacking me across the knuckles if I played a wrong note. She used to make me sing the scales out loud saying, 'you must be able to hit the back of the room with your voice.' Unfortunately, she died as I recall. I never did learn the piano but I did sing in the choir in the chapel at St. John's School in Denton and in the Kent School Choir Competition. I was taken to, I think, the Festival Hall and had to sing Greensleeves, a tune I still hate to this day.

Can anyone remember the chapel? The choir was at the back and had a pump organ. Are there any former altar boys out there who were woken early in the morning to serve at Mass? I liked Benediction best, particularly if I was able to get the thurible (incense burner) and managed a good head of smoke. I was told off a few times by Father Baker for doing it. When we said Mass in those days the responses were in Latin. We said them but did not understand what we were saying.

Without wishing to be disrespectful, I really hated the Stations of the Cross where we had to keep moving round in our pew to look at the various stations. How many times did we have to say them during Lent?

Can anyone remember having to stop everything for the Angelus? I think it was rung in the afternoon, though I could be wrong. We seemed to spend a lot of time on our knees in chapel, those days. I remember being sent to the chapel with another boy and made to sit apart because we were fighting in the Shed. We seemed to be in there a long time before we were made to shake hands.

Talking of fighting, can anyone remember Mr. Smith? He was, I think, a games master and lived in a house up by the Squares. He had a nice daughter and I was invited to her birthday party one year. I digress! I think he was ex-navy, a small man with a flat nose. One day, he was taking us for PT in the Shed and we were having to do handstands, something I could not do. While I was making a bad attempt at standing on my hands he hit me on the bare legs with a plimsole. I stood up and punched him in the face; a bad mistake. He got some boxing gloves and we had a fight. Rather he hit me! I don't think I touched him. Happy days! Today, he would be in court.

When I look back at my time at St. Mary's, it was not all bad. We had some good times and lots of fun.

People often ask me if I regret being sent there. I always answer, no. I knew no different. To me, it was life. I am glad I have at last found fellow "residents" to swap memories with. I have often thought of writing a book or even a play. What a fantastic West End musical it would make! We would have the audience splitting their sides with laughter and crying in their hankies. Just a thought!

I have lots more memories. So I will be in touch very soon.

John (Michael) Murray

PUPPY LOVE

John,

Beans or peas were always served as a lump, matted together – horrible, but you had to eat something.

Kearly & Tonge. I remember that company. Do you remember Echo margarine? As we grew older we were moved up to the big refectory and Jackie Howard just that bit older, went before me. I knew that they were permitted to spread their own "butter" so I begged him to do me a slice lavished with thick butter. Oh! The disappointment! It was marge! I should have known better as in those days a little square pat of butter was only for Sunday morning with a hard boiled egg – we never had fried eggs until years later when they were available to celebrate birthdays. The boys who had their birthday in any particular month were gathered together and enjoyed a fried egg.

Not many boys passed the examination to go to Grammar or Technical School. We thought people like you were geniuses. Nobody in our year passed. Terry Russell, a couple of years younger than me, was the next boy to pass and went to Sidcup Grammar. We still meet up with Terry and his family at infrequent intervals.

I recall going out to school for the first time and chasing the girls. One of the girls passed on a message that her friend liked me. I was smitten. I hugged my pillow at bedtime and my thoughts were filled with puppy love. Patsy Hayes was the name of the girl, then another boy told her to clear off and that I was not interested. The damage was done and we parted. That was not the first time that my lack of courage lost me a girlfriend.

Talking about school, did you know that Mr. Hawkett is still alive?

I returned from my final holiday from St. Mary's Bay in 1954. It took me the whole two weeks of the holiday to summon up the courage to finally kiss the girl of my dreams. She was from St. Anne's, an orphanage at Orpington. I left St. Mary's almost immediately after the holiday and stayed with a family in Orpington. This was a great opportunity to continue with my holiday girlfriend but I thought the better of it as I believed the family I was staying with, would tease me. Even this year (2013) while attending the Orpington Orphanages' Reunion her name came up and I asked for further information. Sadly, the chap who mentioned her name, said his sister had only just lost contact with this girl. I am happily married, and all I wanted to do was to explain my actions of all those years ago.

I also experienced an occasion when I was picked on by a few boys. I was staying with a bodge-up auntie ("the kindness of strangers") when these boys started to interrogate me. You know the sort of thing. 'How old are you?' 'Where do you live?'

The impertinence! I was having none of it. I was a very slight boy for my age. This mini-mob would not have known that although we were matched physically, I was so much older than them. I tore into them with mixed results, with nobody landing a knockout blow. In my own habitat at St. M's I had found my own level and although very small for my age I was a respected, popular boy and never needed to fight.

One of the nice little earners was to be picked to go to the Sisters of Mercy convent, which you mentioned, to do an afternoon gardening. This was a double win. We were paid a silver sixpence and given afternoon tea. My grandson expects at least twenty pounds to leave a mess in my garden.

We were horrible kids on occasions. Once at the convent we were tucking in to our afternoon fare when a tramp joined us. We teased him rotten but he took it in good humour. Years later, Tommy Cooper (the comedian) came up with a laugh about similar circumstances.

A tramp knocked on the farmhouse door. 'What do you want?' said the farmer.

'I want some cake,' said the ambitious tramp.

'You're a cheeky tramp,' said the farmer. 'Most tramps settle for a piece of bread and water. Why are you asking for cake?'

'It's my birthday,' said the tramp.

The tramp wandered off mournfully down the road and the farmer felt a momentary pang of guilt at the way he had treated the unfortunate. So he called after him. 'Do you like cold rice pudding?' he said.

'Love it,' said the tramp.

'Well,' said the farmer, 'come back tomorrow because it's hot at the moment.'

(Delvin) John

THE BOYS THAT SAILED AWAY

To: Edward Butler

The boys left Southampton, England and sailed on the S.S. "New

Australia" landing at Freemantle, according to the records on 22 February 1953.

Some names: Michael Monoghan, J Murphy, L O'Connor, M Vaughan, J Sullivan, J Garrington, T O'Leary.

This is not a complete list, which would suggest the boys possibly sailed on separate dates.

Edward, we have a writing club called St. Mary's and I have taken the liberty of adding your name to the list. There is no obligation to contribute to writings. Some members write, some just read the emails and some no doubt, just delete them.

Good health and good fortunate in your undertakings.

KOKO (Keep On Keeping On)

(Delvin) John Flynn

FREEMANTLE, W. AUSTRALIA

Hi John,

The list of the SS "New Australia" to Freemantle, Western Australia stating Peter Wood and Peter Robinson are not included. Perhaps your suggestion to contact the National Archives of Australia, giving the exact address, might possibly have a few answers.

I have been reading the messages from John Michael Murray which I find interesting. If anything further comes out of the inquiry I would appreciate the details for KOKO, which is part of the ongoing social history of St. Mary's.

Information to JMM to contact St. John's Comprehensive School in Gravesend might also prove successful.

I find the memories of the group going back so many years, remarkable. It proves a point many things that happened in childhood are not easily forgotten, even in the intervening years. The yen to continue to know our history will always remain.

KOKO

Caroline

THE WAY WE WERE

To: Colin Bedford,

Tony Larkin also handed me details of those who worked at St. Mary's over the years.

Richard A Roche 1935/36 first mentioned.

Miss Kathleen Downing 1933/34 first mentioned.

Father Paul Baker first mentioned in 1945 but he was the chaplain before this date as I remember him at Lord and Lady Clifford's stately home at Ugbrook near Exeter, Devon where we were evacuated during the war.

Sydney Peacock first mentioned 1950/51

Richard Smith replaced Dicky Roche 1952

This information is not guaranteed to be correct. Sometimes there were gaps in the records.

KOKO

(Delvin) John

WE WILL REMEMBER THEM

Ann Phyall (honorary member),

The plaque (erected by St. Mary's old boys in memory of their companions who lost their lives in the war 1939-1945) is to be found at St. John's RC Church at Parrock Street, Gravesend.

Tony Larkin lovingly cares for it by polishing it on each Remembrance Day and it is his poppy and another added by someone else that can be seen in the photo.

It would be interesting to learn if any on the Graversham facebook remember the St. Mary's School football matches.

Ann, I hope all is well with you and yours.

KOKO

Delvin

ST. JOHN'S SCHOOL – SENIOR DEPARTMENT

(Headmaster: Mr S. S. C. Bray)

PROGRAMME OF ATHLETIC SPORTS

Denton Paddock, Gravesend

Thursday, 16th July, 1953, commencing at 2 p.m.

Our Sincere Thanks are due to generous friends who have presented Cups and Trophies to be competed for by the four houses of the School.

THE ST. EDMUND CUP

For Boys Games

Presented by Rev. Fr. Eamonn Mundy

THE ST. JOHN'S SILVER CHALLENGE CUP

For Scholastic Achievement

Presented by Dr. and Mrs. Charles Outred

THE ST. COLUMBA SHIELD

For Athletics and Swimming

Presented by The Knights of St. Columba.

THE CONDON BOWL

For Girls Games

Presented by Mr. and Mrs. Leo Ring

OFFICIALS

Referee: Mr. R. R.Smith   Starter: Mr. D. J. Crines

Judges: Mr. J. D. Rowlinson, Mr. L.G. Lingham and Mr. L. Ring

Recorder: Mr. V. C. Hawkett

The arrangements for Refreshments have been made by Sister M. Aidan and Mrs. A. M. Howell.

Tea for the Pupils of the School has been provided by Mother M. Aloysius and Sister M. Patrick.

PROGRAMME OF EVENTS

Events 1-28: Girls and Boys under and over 13yrs.

Skipping: 100 yds: Discus: 120 yds: Shot: 80 yds: High Jump: 220 yds: Long Jump: 440 yds. Javelin: Inter Relay Races.

BOYS WHO PARTICIPATED IN THESE EVENTS: Moore, Richie, McCarthy, Brody, Freebody, Brennan, Standen, Hughes, Cox, Chapman, Connolly, Gaffney, Finn, J. Brown, R. Dodson, Gilliam, Baker, Jordan, Hughes, R. Beadle, Cientanni, Foulger, Jordan, McFarlane, Bishop, Casey, Kavanagh, Harris, Hembrow.

**HOUSE POINTS OBTAINED IN QUALIFYING HEATS
ARE AS FOLLOWS:**

RANSOME: 954   CARMEL: 837   STELLA MARIS: 1018   LOURDES: 842

The above points include those gained for swimming, as under:

124   51   45   64

In addition to a Medal for the Winner of each Event, four Victor Medals will be awarded to the two Girls and two Boys in each age group scoring most points, in both Athletics and Swimming. Inter House Races do not score for these Medals.

An Exhibition of Needlework and Woodwork will be on show during and after the Sports. There will be no Interval but Tea and other Refreshments will be on sale.

SPORTS DAY

DENTON PADDOCK, GRAVESEND, FRIDAY 16TH JULY 1954

EVENTS: The St. Edmund Cup - For Scholastic Achievement.

The St. George's Shield - For Boxing

The St. Columba Shield - For Athletics and Swimming

The Condon Bowl - For Girls' Games

The arrangements for refreshments have been made by Sr. M Patrick, Sr. M. Aidan and Mrs. A.M. Howell.

SCHOOLBOY FOOTBALL

Terry McKenna,

I saw Tony Larkin today. What an amazing guy. He is the local amateur historian of all things Gravesend. Tony passed me on some "interesting" papers about St. Mary's Boys. I have tried sending a couple of photos but what if anything you can make of them remains to be determined. To help I will relay some of the stuff:

Schoolboy Football

Saturday, 7 January 1950

St. Mary's v St. Joseph's Rotherhithe

Our team: Goalkeeper A. Fisher; Full Backs B. Baker and G. Gillin; Half Back(s) J Duffy, J. Desmond and M. Desmond; Forward line B. Woolridge, R. Beddice, C. McGillicuddy, T. Shaw and M. Lewis.

And there was then the opposition.

And the local paper included an article which is far too long for this old banger to type in full so I will select some information which I hope you will find of some interest.

When at a quarter to seven tomorrow night, eleven young lads troop from the green painted wooden pavilion on the Imperial Paper Mills Sports Ground at Milton, Gravesend, on the football ground a roar will go up from upward to two thousand throats: 'Come on, St. Mary's.'

'Who are these lads who so capture the hearts of the local football public?' a stranger may ask. He would not be long in getting a reply. 'The best boys' team for their ages in the county.'

The reporter goes on to describe the magnificent bravery of our boys serving in the various theatres of war. There are too many for me to name here but I hope I will be excused for mentioning one little wizard on the field – Billy Kiernan who went on to play for Charlton Athletic in the 1947 or was it 1948 FA cup final, which was a good result for Charlton. As the years passed Billy would often volunteer his services to referee the St. Mary's games. How did they achieve what they did? Behind this remarkable side was a slight bespectacled sports master Mr. R. Roche (Dicky) a most unassuming man you could wish to meet. Can you imagine a manager today say 'I would much rather see them lose playing good football than win by any means fair or foul or kick and rush.'

Tomorrow there will be other boys showing their paces for the first time: C. Hayes, C. Bedford (age 11 and the youngest player), N. Hearne, P. Rose, R. Hedges, C. Stewart, D. Dutton, R. Walsh, C. McGillicuddy.

Proceeds of the match go towards financing a holiday for the boys at the largest holiday camp for boys and girls in England at St. Mary's Bay, Dymchurch, Kent.

And so the article comes to an end. Now I have had a stab of typing this but I can't vouch for my accuracy in either being faithful in every respect to the article or the typing and spelling.

KOKO

(Delvin) John

MR. ROCHE

Hi John,

In response to your email requesting the history of Mr. Roche, he was born in Eireland in 1900 and played football for a top team in the Irish football league prior to arriving at St. Mary's at Gravesend before the war. He went with the school to Ugbrooke in Devon where his main job was to teach the older boys in Standard 7 and was in the ARP as his contribution to the war effort. He was paranoid about football and produced a team that could draw a crowd of four to five thousand when he returned to Gravesend after the war; if you were no good at football, you were not on his radar. One of his prodigies was a boy named Billy Kiernan who played for Charlton Athletic when they were in the first division of the football league. When he left Gravesend he became manager of Gravesend and Northfleet (now Ebbsfleet United) after taking a timekeeper's job at a local factory. His life at the end became a little obscure but I think he must have finally returned to Eireland. He was a man with a vile temper and I think most boys respected him out of fear and he certainly knew how to use the cane, but I think to his credit he was a very good teacher. I don't think he took to Bernard very well, as

Bernard spent most of his time in the workroom and never played any games or sport. I think he made up for this when he left school.

Another story that went around was that Dennis threw the school trophy cup at Mr. Roche in a temper and this was confirmed by Malcolm. I did not witness this incident as I was too young but perhaps John you could throw some light on this, being the next in line age-wise, tell me about it!

Well, John, I hope this information prompts your memory of this rather unusual man who became one of the legends of the school in our time.

Regard to all and sundry.

Colin G. Bedford.

Senior Genealogist and Family Historian, EDIA.

GODDINGTON PARK

Hi John,

When I read the on-going emails from the group members, I am amazed at their clarity of mind to remember so far back their childhood memories.

Like St. Mary's, when the St. Jos. boys played various sport probably the most enjoyable – football, I remember the St. Anne's girls watched them two fields away play with such gusto you could hear the shouts from across the fields.

The netball, field hockey and the annual sports day at Goddington Park where we did high jump, long jump and relay racing, are truly enjoyable memories.

I often wonder if I had been brought up in the "spoils" of London, would the opportunity have availed itself of the advantage to play sport.

KOKO

Caroline (honorary member)

THE WAY WE WERE

Sadly, Caroline, much of the competitive spirit has gone out of school sport and many attribute this to politicians of the main parties selling the school's playing fields. Also teachers are told to tell the children that there is no such thing as failure – we are all winners. Sadly, that is rubbish. I was no good at sport but would give it a go, but had to come to terms that among our lot some show more prowess. I recall as a very small child racing the hundred yards and coming a poor last, but that was not fair competition. I should have competed against boys my own size irrespective of the age.

You wouldn't pit a heavy weight boxer with a featherweight. Competition is good so long as the competitors are evenly or almost evenly matched, then the result is not easy to guess.

Competition among schools can generate enormous pride in the achievements of the school. We were proud of the achievements of St. Mary's boys' football team. The spur to be good at sport was evident but it has been said, by some of our number, that if you were not good at sport you were considered useless. But there were exceptions. One of our number, Leslie Hayes was inept at sport. He was tormented and called "Hatter Hayes" but after leaving St. Mary's without any qualifications he secured, in due course, a scholarship to Oxford University. Perhaps if the academic subjects had received the same attention as sport maybe, just maybe, Hayes would not have been the only one to get to university in those days. Things did improve as the years passed. John O'D, one of our group, managed to go to university and no doubt there were others.

Keep On Keeping On.

(Delvin) John

RE: STORY

Dear John,

Excuse me for writing out of the blue. It is possible that we may have spoken/corresponded in the past because I worked for over thirty years for Cabrini (Formerly Catholic Children's Society).

I had lunch recently with Teresa, a colleague at Cabrini over many years and I also worked with Irena who is also known to you.

I am retired now and doing a Masters in Creative Writing at Exeter University. Teresa and I were discussing this the other week and she mentioned that you and your friends, who had been in a children's home during the war, were still in touch. She suggested there was a really good story to tell about your evacuation from the home during the war and that I might like to meet you to find out more.

If this is something in which you may be interested in exploring, I would be really pleased to meet. Teresa says she is happy to join us for such a meeting. Teresa and myself could both make the afternoon of Thursday 12th December if that was convenient for you. If not, we could look at other dates.

I look forward to hearing from you.

Terry Connor

Terry,

I remember a youthful Terry being appointed to The Children's Society but we never met. I think it would be great to have a meeting. I have been keeping copies of emails to and from the group for quite some time but have neither the skill nor the time to collate them into an interesting account covering the year from the 1920s.

In our group there is a wide span of ages from two or three in their eighties and some like Terry McKenna who is a mere stripling – a callow youth. I have mentioned to the group on more than one occasion to indicate if they have any objection to their emails being included in a book or article and none have objected. It would be like unscrambling the eggs. Not all of the members contribute on a regular basis but the mood music is very good when occasionally I speak with any of them by phone. They say things like 'I don't write but love reading the emails.' So there you are!

Caroline Whitehead who is an enthusiastic contributor has published her account of the days when she stayed at St. Anne's Orpington and left in the 1940s.

Speaking personally, I would love to meet you. I have met Teresa and Irena on a couple of occasions and the feedback has been beneficial to both them and us.

I am going away until Tuesday but you can pencil in the 12th December.

Kind regards,

(Delvin) John

ORPHANAGES

Hello Ann,

There were two orphanages at Orpington opposite the hospital. The St. Anne's was the orphanage for girls, then there was the church, and then St. Joseph's for boys. I can't recall anyone mentioning Doddington. Again, I can't recall knowing the names of the boys mentioned but there are some older members of the group who may remember those names.

Pat's mother was one of the kind ladies from the town who treated boys from St. Mary's. I was not lucky to be picked by anyone at Gravesend but was selected to stay with a family at Whitefoot Lane, Catford. But more on the subject of people treating boys for outings. There was a very kind man. I believe his name was Jack Harris. He was good to bunchs of us kids using his own money to treat them.

I remember an incident when were talking in the usual crocodile mode when a kind lady gave the nun 10/- to buy the thirty of us an ice cream. This just conceivably could have been Pat's mum. I think the Ice Cream shop was called Papa's. In those days ice cream was 3d a cornet. There were thirty of us kids and I often wonder what happened to the change.

Talking about names and places: when I occasionally look at the Gravesend Facebook, I always hoped that St. John's Secondary Modern School, Denton may get an airing for the period covering 1950's. I have mentioned it but had no takers. Just a tiny few of our lot went to the Technical School in the '50s but I suspect they are older than Roger Simmons who has mentioned the Tech School.

Keep smiling

(Delvin) John

OUR NEW TOY

Giday there, John,

I though I'd send you a few pics of new boat Tony and myself have bought. Why you may ask? Well, all I can bloody say is the bloody price was right, and it'll give us buggers some thing else to do. It's a bit over 30 ft long and a bit over 3 mtrs wide. Has a 4cyl Ford diesel motor, steel hull which is very sound, a freezer that I can stand up in, and as you can see it needs a bit of cleaning up and a good paint job. Now that'll keep us occupied for a bit, a, were looking forward to getting it all done and going out to fish the reef. I guess our pockets will have to get a lot deeper.

Hope all is well with you and your family. Tony is well. Take care. Regards.

Paul Orszanski (Australia)

Paul,

The boat looks great. I can remember a kind soul taking us scruffs on the Thames. The beauty of it was that it was a very small boat not much bigger than a tow boat and the feel of the water running through my fingers as I dangled my arm over the side, is something I will never forget. Maybe, just maybe, I will cadge a lift off an owner of a similar boat in the future. Great pictures, Paul, and Tony looks good.

KOKO

(Delvin) John

'morning John,

Colourful dialogue with Paul and his super new boat. Just hopes he hangs on tight to his beer mug when sailing to avoid the inevitable slip and man overboard!

KOKO

Caroline

RON'S GAZETTE

Dear All,

Please find attached the current issue of Ron's Gazette which is compiled by Tuart Place, participant Ron Love.

Wishing everyone a wonderful Christmas & New Year.

Kind regards,

Sue Stafford, Administration Officer,

Tuart Place, 24 High St, Fremantle, W. Australia 6160

INMATES LATE '50S

John,

Your contact details were given to me sometime ago by Terry McKenna who said that you may be able to help with information about the above when I was an inmate in the late-ish '50s. It was when Sister Monica was the head.

Regards,

Glen Cawdeary

Glen,

Nice to hear from you. Rather than adopt a scatter-gun approach I would suggest you ask any questions you have in mind and I will do my best to answer them.

Some of our number give a potted history of their time at St. Mary's such as when they arrived and other relevant information.

Regards,

(Delvin) John

John,

Many thanks for your prompt response. I arrived at St. Mary's aged seven in 1957 with my older brother, Alan. I went into Standard 2 which was "managed" (for want of a better word) by Sister Mary. I can remember some of the other boys – Michael and Eddy Toal, John and Joseph Kasporitch, Roland and Paul Tchikovsky, Robin Kerr and Stephen Mortan. I know that I was fortunate in that fate led me out of the institution into a prep school followed by a secondary education at a public school.

Without that change of fortune I don't know how things would have turned out. I would love to know how life ensued for any of my contemporaries at St. M's. Perhaps I'm laying a ghost - I have a few happy memories of my time there but I would be overjoyed to hear of others who came thro' relatively "unscathed".

Should you require any more information, please let me know.

Your help is much appreciated.

Glen Cawdeary

BOOT ROOM

John (Michael) Murray,

You had a brother who was separated from you and joined you for a holiday in St. Mary's. How very strange. Some might say that St. Mary's was a strange place to have a holiday.

Bromley is just a short bus ride from where we lived.

You must have had real potential for the nun to take the trouble to teach you to play the piano. We had a piano in our hobby room and many of the lads could play with the right hand and vamp with the left (I think that is what it is called). These lads could play any tune they knew by ear which makes me believe that there was so much talent which was never developed. We also had a fine snooker table and again imagine the talent that could have come to the fore with some coaching.

When you think we were captive 24 hrs a day seven days a week it was a lost opportunity for many of our lot. Eton and Harrow get results when they hold their boarders captive for that length of time. And of course the parents pay in excess of $30,000 for each child per year. Perhaps it is the teachers they employ which makes the difference or by not returning home each evening it prevents the parents undoing the good work that was done during the day.

I'm sure we all remember the "boot room" and how you regret your misguided attempt to knock Mr. Smith out. You were not the first to attempt this. When Mr. S. first arrived, his physique didn't command the respect due to his status and he had difficulty in managing the boys. Perhaps had we known he was previously a Physical Trainer in the navy during the war, we might have been a bit chary in confronting him.

One particular surly boy would shrug his shoulders in contempt when ordered to do something. It all came to a head when Mr. S. ordered this trainee thug to leave the "boot room" and instead of obeying the order a fist came from between the coats and smacked Mr. S. in the face. Mr. S. invited the lad to continue the disagreement elsewhere in the building. Some time later we saw the result. The boy was paraded in front of us in the big refectory and was a sorry sight. In deference to his daughter who is a member of our group and whose birthday party you once attended, I will not expand on what I have already said except to say Mr. S. had a very easy job from that date and we all knew he was not a man to be messed with. On a personal level I always had the greatest respect for him and considered him an ideal role model. As for the boy, he was always difficult and didn't completely fit in with the rest of us. Years before the incident, just described, I was the victim of being struck by a lump of boiler house clinker that he threw and someone had to mop up the blood from my injury.

I liked serving Mass. It was theatre; especially on a Sunday in front of the whole school. As for Benediction another name for the thurible was "stink bomb" and Tony Sayers, like you, would enjoy abusing the privilege and overloading it with incense and then try to swing the thing in full circle. All these antics were carried out at your own risk as Father Baker was not called Backie Booter for nothing. Backie was to do with his pipe smoking and booter was the part that connected with our backside if you couldn't get out of the way fast enough. About the Stations of the Cross. Yes, it was a real drag but the language was beautiful. On one of the stations the words went something like, "The blows were struck, the blood gushes forth and He the Holiest of Holy stood exposed to the rude and scoffing multitude". I'm not a master of English like someone who is educated but there is a kind of poetry in that language. As kids we had to stifle our laughter when Fr B. read that out. That was our lavatorial humour. And again "weep not for me but for yourselves and for your children".

As you say, John, that was the only way of life that some of us knew. I was signed up at the age of two years of age after being in the care of a baby minder. We were clean, we were warm and we were clothed. But were we loved?

John, keep up the good work or as I say – keep on keeping on.

KOKO

(Delvin) John

MY OWN RULES

To Everyone:

I may have overstepped my SELF IMPOSED RULES on which I write and I send to the members. I try to avoid: Religion Politics Sex. It is not my intention to offend any of our members and if I have done so by any of my writing by breaking my own rules, I apologise.

Remember KOKO

(Delvin) John

POLITICALLY-MINDED

Hi (Delvin) John,

I'm sure everyone agrees with your three stringent policies. Likewise, I might add! It brings to mind a situation at a writer's group meeting which became so political I decided it was not for me. It is one thing being politically-minded, which I am and have been since the age of 17, but to have another member's ideals thrust down my throat did not bode well. I actually had the courage to tell the co-ordinator of the group the reason for quitting.

Sex, well! Can't elaborate on that subject. Society being what it is today, anything goes with the younger generation so protocol is thrown out of the window. To each his own, I guess, would sum it up.

Hope you and Josie are keeping well. Lovely thought with all the house painting done last year you are not looking at either the expense or upheaval this year.

Caroline (honorary member)

Caroline,

Good for you. Mind you – you were the wrong person to leave the group as you were the victim. So you have been politically-minded from a young age – me too. I often wonder what makes us the people we are.

Everybody likes to look down on somebody. It reminds me of a story of a patient who went to the psychologist saying he had an inferiority complex and wanted a cure. The psychologist reached his conclusion and relayed this to the patient. He said, 'it's not complex, you really are inferior but don't worry, when it come to an election vote the same as the rich. You will still be inferior but you will feel superior.'

The rich often blame the poor for being poor. It helps to assuage their guilt as to why they are paid so much while the poor have so little. They often claim they got on by their own efforts. Nobody threw them a rope. But sometimes to blame the poor is like to blame a person with no legs for not joining the race.

Thankfully we all have different talents and as you said in a previous email our group seems to have done all right for themselves.

We have two Michael Monaghan's in our group. One lives in the UK and the other lives in Tasmania, Australia. The London Michael popped in to see us yesterday. He has a very good memory about his childhood at St. Mary's. The other Michael visited us when he was over from Australia a few months ago.

The Australian Michael joked about how when they were looking for volunteers to go to Australia, the London Michael lifted up his arm. It could have happened since nobody seems to know how they picked who was to go. Perhaps they put all the names in a hat.

Anyway Michael joined us for lunch at the local Wetherspoons, which I believe was founded by an Australian. Ok, so it's not haute cuisine but it was either that or the greasy spoon. The greasy spoon sells on drinks that refreshes but does not inebriate so they lost out. It was a good day in Michael's company.

KOKO

(Delvin) John

Hi (Delvin) John

You're dead right in thinking I was the victim when I left the local writer's group. Actually, I never looked at it this way until you mentioned it.

Your question what makes us the people we are is not hard to comprehend when you understand the path most of us have taken in our lives to determine the best route to go to shape us into the people we are today.

I think we live by our own principles that come from early training; albeit, realising some of our (and I use the word loosely) compatriots have strayed the narrow path. Narrow meaning we did not have parents to guide us and it was up to the individual to find his or her own way, which often led to compromised situations.

With the Michael Monaghans, each living in different parts of the world. Are they related in any way?

Good that Michael (London) was able to pop in and see you. I am interested in his memories of St. Mary's and wondered if he would like to join the author's page of the book by contributing anything he remembers of his childhood. Dates of events are always a good start.

I recently heard from a John Michael Murray who emailed me with the news he has written five/six chapters of his life at St. Mary's under the title "Laundry Boy" and is willing for me to incorporate his story in the book. He is also sending me a photograph of himself eight or nine years old. Would he be a group member?

As you know, John, the more material I can gather prior to setting up the manuscript would be most helpful. Also, I am putting it to the group to come up with a title of the book. Something appropriate, eye-catching, of course. The cover of the book won't be problem as in my view the old picture of St. Mary's would hopefully encourage the reader to read on.

To have the social history of St. Mary's known as The Manor of Parrock Gravesend 1383 period provided by Ann Phyall, gives us an insight to its original beginning going back to Abbott and Convent of St. Mary Graces.

KOKO

Caroline

ST. MARY'S GRAVESEND

Caroline/Terry McKenna

I believe but it is no more than a guess that St. Mary's and St. Mary's Bay Holiday camp ceased to exist in the seventies.

Changing the subject, can anyone remember the odd stock that Father Baker held in the tuck shop? Things like shredded wheat and weetabix minus the milk. There were other weird things by today's standards that our members may remember.

KOKO

(Delvin) John

John F,

It's the Irish humour that pours forth when you give answers to questions. You enlightened me: shredded wheat and Brillo pads are useful for pot scrubbing. Never tried that one! But nothing ventured, nothing gained, makes any challenge worthwhile.

Message sent on Brillo pads I haven't come across that one before. Rather humorous, to say the least!

Good or bad memories of Glen's, it would be interesting to hear of his short stay at St. Mary's. Photographs are of course welcome.

One thing I would like to know is if the summer camp at Dymchurch still exists.

Any idea of the date St. Mary's camp Dymchurch was demolished for a housing estate?

Keep well.

Caroline

Caroline,

I searched the Internet for the Brillo Pad tablet without success so I assume Glen is being humorous. Brillo Pads to me are the same as shredded wheat; both used for scrubbing cooking pans.

Alas, St. Mary's Bay holiday camp has ceased to exist. It was converted, like St. Mary's, to a housing estate many years ago. I believe Glen has a story to tell. More than that I believe he has the ability to tell it.

KOKO

(Delvin) John

FRANCIS FRITH SITE

Hello Delvin,

Why does St. Mary's keep on bugging me? I have been on the Internet again today to find out when St. Mary's was built and have found the following which you may already know about. It is possible the buildings were originally known as "The Manor of Parrock". Have read two entries, one on Discover Gravesend: entry 1383 Abbot and Convent of St. Mary Graces rented Manor of Parrock to Sir Simon Burley (Lord Warden of Cinque Ports). (Lord of the Manor of Parrock of Milton next to Gravesend).

On the Francis Frith site it reads: St. Mary's 1902 & a write-up by the then Michael Murray from 1946-1957 – a lovely photo of St. Mary's.

Ann

Ann,

Perhaps you already know more than me about St. Mary's building. As I wrote previously we had a great time celebrating the Jubilee of the taking over of the building by The Catholic Children's Rescue Society now renamed Cabrini. At the time I didn't even know the meaning of the word Jubilee but I have tried to educate myself since those far off days.

KOKO

John & Josie

John, hi.

The details of the original St. Mary's from Ann are much appreciated. I have noted the entry 1383 Abbot and Convent of St. Mary's Graces rented the manor to Sir Simon Burley.

Irena, Cabrini forwarded Tony Larkin's address to me so I can ask him for historical dates relating to the old school. As you know, every little helps, preferably before I start on the manuscript, along with lots of old photos some members may still be holding. I can't download the computer so have to hand-write emails. But I don't find that a big problem.

Perhaps as the year progresses more details of St. Mary's will come to light.

Caroline.

Hello Delvin,

In putting our "book" together, I invited "our lot" to write with "I remember when...." Some of the contributions were really good, especially from the Staff, and some were too silly. I wonder if there is a site in Gravesend for past pupils of St. John's school. There is for most schools and I think they're found through Friends Reunited.

Just saying!

Ann

Ann,

In reply to your earlier question I am not aware of any site dedicated to ex St. John's Denton, Gravesend other than "Friends Reunited". Friends was a really good site in the early years and I made some useful contacts from that source but I believe they were bought out and since then they seem to have lost their way. They obviously forgot the adage 'if it ain't broken, don't fix it.'

I also went on a fishing trip on the Gravesend site, the one which you obtained some good photos of St. Mary's asking if any of the members were ex St. John's but didn't get a bite.

Ann, don't let me get away with not answering questions. Questions are an indication of interest and I can always elaborate on anything asked; it also ensures that I am not just peddling my own interest but respectfully responding to the writer.

KOKO

(Delvin) John

Delvin,

The difference a short time can bring. By 1956 everybody in St. Mary's was going out to school. For those in primary school it was a school in the centre of Gravesend and we all marched off every morning rain or shine. For those who had passed the 11-Plus it was a grammar school in Sidcup and that meant a train journey every day and for the rest it was a secondary modern where you marched across a large field to reach it. Girls were therefore known from an early age.

Yesterday in Sainsbury's I was looking at sugar-reduced baked beans. That triggered a memory of the near strike or refusal to eat the beans in tomato sauce prepared in the kitchens. We wanted our baked beans out of a tin. Who were the leaders and why did the nuns respond in a positive way, because thereafter it was "proper" tinned baked beans.

As small boys you never considered that the nuns were under strict instructions not to show emotion. By the late sixties it was different for those children in care in family type homes. I remember when at university volunteering to work in the Hull Crusade of Rescue Home, which was a large institution and very much like St. Mary's. Nothing had really changed. But in homes run by the Hull Seaman's Mission it was completely different. There the children had house mothers and were in family type homes. I remember talking to one of the House Mothers about affection and being told of course you have to give it. How do children develop?

John M. O'Donnell

MEMORIES

John,

Really enjoying reading your memories. Terry McKenna, one of our members, has got to grips and written an interesting account of his young life and I am sure he would encourage you to write a book. Your memories are so vivid. Your writings are so fresh as though the events described were only a short time ago. As I continue to read your emails it triggers off memories of my own which have been submerged in my unconsciousness far too long.

Have you been in touch with your erstwhile laundry worker Michael Monaghan or vice versa? I have had the pleasure of meeting both Michael and Terry at our home. Caroline Whitehead who is a member of our group has published two or three books about her time at St. Anne's, Orpington and has already indicated that she will collate our memories with a view to publishing our life and times. Caroline lives in BC, Canada and was looked after by Terry Mc. when she made a trip over here recently. It is possible that she is our oldest member at eighty-seven years old but I have a feeling there are one or two who may dispute this. I have one or two pictures I will send by separate email which I hope will bring back more memories for you.

Back to your email. Barbara sent me a lovely picture of herself taken when she moved to secondary school. She seemed shy as a child and as you say we were also shy since we were not used to girls. I recall her standing back from her mum and dad in a picture which included her younger brothers. I have written before how I would liked to have met her father but he left St. Mary's soon after me and tracing a man with the name of Smith would be hopeless. BUT blow me down! One day I received a strange message from a girl on the Friends Reunited Social Network. 'Was I John Flynn etc. from those far off days?' The message was from Barbara the little girl now a grandmother, who invited you to her party all those years ago. In short time we were down in the Portsmouth area where Mr. S. originated and met up for a chat about her father and mother. Needless and sadly to say, her father and mother had died some years before but I believe Barbara was pleased to learn how much I admired her father.

Were we loved at St. Mary's? Many years after leaving I broached this delicate subject with the lovely Sister Magdalen RIP and she at that time referred to all of us lads as her children and my children as her grandchildren. But her love at St. M was strictly on the secret list. She told me that the order of nuns were instructed not to get too close to the children to avoid favouritism also they could be transferred to another address with a mere 24 hrs notice and this wrench for the nuns and the children was something the Order could not countenance. However, her obvious affection for those of us who visited her over the years was self-evident. That said it does not invalidate your comments about how we were treated in the giving examples. Iodine!! Gosh, I remember that. To me it was synonymous with germ free hospital environment unlike today with MRSA and other killing germs. Doctors in clean white coats and nurses with crisp starch uniforms. Today they look like a bunch of car mechanics.

When I think of it I cut and pasted your colourful description of "Kindness to Strangers" on the Facebook site covering Gravesend and it received almost an immediate response with question number one. 'What was it like?' I pointed out that it was a long story and how we tease out our memories with our writing club. Clearly I was unable to go into any details since Facebook is not necessarily secure and of course I kept your name out of it.

As to why you were picked as suitable material to mix with a family, I couldn't say. Someone must have considered you had a bit of class. But of course the same question could be asked of me. I was placed with a family in Orpington who already had five children and I made up the number of three boys and three girls. Settling in was difficult as the children were bright and I was dull, thick and shy. Nothing changes. I'm still the same.

Before I went to live with the family at Orpington, the Head Office felt that I should be kitted out with a reasonably decent outfit as, like action man, I was immune from growing. The Head Superior took me down to the clothes shop and I picked out the sort of clothes my role model Mr. Smith would have worn. The HS ordered me to try on the trousers and without more ado I dropped the trousers I had on then and there in the middle of the shop. The HS was mortified and hissed in my ear what I was going to get when she got me back to St. M. What did I know about changing rooms.

Later while staying with the family, the good lady of the house said my shoes needed to be soled. I pointed out that I hadn't had them very long and who would buy them? Of course she pointed out that meant repaired. Again, what did we know about these things? I had the wrong impression that I had to behave myself at all costs with these good people. I felt whether I was right or wrong – in the final analysis I would be wrong and transferred to the boys hostel at Blackheath. With hindsight I now believe that was wrong and I am still attached to that family to the present day.

The coronation. A big yawn. It rained all day. I couldn't wait for the day to end. Now, today I love that sort of thing. Great theatre. Any big royal occasion is to me the epitome of the top rank of show business. I don't stop at that – a new Pope, or Cardinal or a new Archbishop of Canterbury or new Prime Minister is top rate theatre. The lot of them are like actors on a stage and don't actually touch our real lives. But then again, I love Shakespeare's plays – at least the tragedies? Now I am getting carried away.

That was some achievement tracing the "kind lady". I've done a bit of exciting tracing myself so I know what a thrill of success it can bring in that regard.

Those of us who didn't make it to Australia were bitterly disappointed but we learnt years later that many were cruelly treated. We never learned by what method they used for choosing who should go and who should stay. Again we have representatives of that number in our writing group and we even traced the liner that the boys sailed on from Tilbury in February 1953 together with the passenger list. I believe there may have been more than one party of boys sailing as I noticed the absence of some names when examining the passenger list. A couple of the lads have made it back to the "old country" to research their family history with varying degrees of success.

Well, as the BBC used to say: 'That ends broadcasting for today. We will be on the air again.'

Keep on keeping on

(Delvin) John

HEAVEN SENT GROUP

Hello Delvin,

First of all thank you for the photograph of St. Mary's Bay. I loved it. It really took me back; the children in it looked like real urchins.

The only picture I have is one taken of me at the junior school. I look a proper picture. I was interested to read your memories of Mr. Smith. Like you I had a healthy respect and liking for him after being "straightened out".

I am pleased his daughter in is the Group; if she reads this I would like to thank her for the birthday party invitation. It was very nice.

I was not used to being around girls and was probably very shy. I hope I did not give a bad impression.

You posed the question: 'were we loved?' That is hard to answer. I cannot recall any affection given out by the nuns. If you hurt yourself and were crying you were told to stop or you would be given "something to cry about". If you grazed your knee you were given iodine which stung like hell. (I believe it is banned now). It was not until later in life I realised the healing properties of a cuddle. I do not ever recall receiving one from the nuns. I think I grew up being a bit "unfeeling" and often unsympathetic to moaners and wingers. I know I find emotion hard to show; perhaps that is my legacy from St. Mary's but I am not complaining. I often feel I am a better person for having been there, warts and all.

I often look back at my time at St. Mary's and ask was I really there. At nearly 70 I was unable to talk about it with the other boys who were there, that is why finding the Group is heaven sent. I am now living in Cardiff with my lovely Welsh wife and I find that when we are in the pub with her brother and friends they are able to talk about their schooldays and people they knew then who they still see.

However, back to the "Kindness of Strangers". I would be interested to hear if any other boys have similar experiences. I have never been able to understand why the following events happened to me. I was not an orphan. I had a mother, brother, grandmother, aunties and uncles who lived in Bromley, Kent. My mother told me I was in Gravesend because the Catholic Priest said I had to go because both my brother and I were born the "wrong side of the blanket". Who knows? (Father was a Canadian soldier who went back to Canada at the end of the war.)

The first instance that I now find strange was that I was invited out to people's homes for tea or parties. I enjoyed them as any kid would, but why me; was anybody else invited? I remember going to a big party and winning a competition to pin the tail on the donkey. I was picked up from the entrance hall and brought back there, when it was all over.

Remember the Coronation. I was taken to somebody's house to watch it on television. The house was near a pub called "The Battle of Britain". The house was full of their family and friends and I felt a bit of a freak because they kept asking questions about St. Mary's, a new experience for me. Still, the food was good, though I soon got bored of the Coronation ceremony as I did not really understand it. Was anybody else taken out to see it?

On one occasion a nun said to me somebody is coming to see me tomorrow (Saturday). Next day I was washed and scrubbed and given clean clothes. I had to wait in the hall (remember the big grandfather clock?) until eventually a young lady turned up. Her name was Jose and she took me out for the afternoon. We walked into Gravesend and went to a café and had beans on toast. I remember her putting a thrupenny piece under the plate. Jose came to see me a number of times and eventually I spent weekends with her. She lived in London in Old Brompton Road. I spent Christmas with her on at least two occasions. Eventually she married and went to live in America.

Through the power of the internet I managed to trace her and in May of this year (2013) we met up in Bath. She is in her late eighties now and getting a little infirm but we had some marvellous long chats. She told me she was an Air Hostess for BOAC and used to have long breaks between flights so she decided she wanted to do something with her time. Her Parish Priest suggested she contact Southwark Catholic Rescue Society and hence her appearance at St. Mary's. She said she was not vetted or checked and did not know who she was going to see till she got there. Again the question: why me?

There were lots of boys there who had nothing and were more deserving. My wife says it was because I was the first boy the nun saw. She could be right. Did something similar happen to any other boy?

Jose was twenty-one years when she was allowed to take me out. No Social Services in those days.

Were any other boys told they were going to Australia and didn't go? I was told by one of the nuns that I was going to Australia in the sunshine; as I recall there were a few of us.

When the time came I was told I was not going; imagine my disappointment. In hindsight I think it might have been a lucky escape. I discovered some years later that my mother had stopped it. I remember having to get up early one morning and looking out of the bedroom window and being told to wave. You could see the Thames and the docks as well as the ships which I assume was the one the boys were on or was it kidology?

So, at St. Mary's I did meet some good people who showed me kindness, which to me was unusual. I am not complaining. I enjoyed it. I just hope I was not the only one who had such experiences.

John (Michael) Murray

Hello John,

I've been sending emails mainly from my ipad lately and I'm not sure if you received my last three emails to you, as I've had no reply. We've been receiving emails from you and Caroline. They were – One a suggestion for a title for the book on St. Mary's. Two for an address for Caroline to enquire from Human services, Australia for tracing her relative. Three an email about the recent heatwave we had in Melbourne.

Thankfully, we had a cool change yesterday and the temperature dropped from 42 degrees to 23 degrees today. There's been a lot of bush fires in

Victoria. Seventy-eight were still out of control yesterday, and it will take a few days for the firefighters to get on top of them.

Mavis & Pat Heffernan

Mavis,

Sometimes I get confused. Have I replied to an email or not? If someone takes the trouble to write I feel strongly that their effort deserves a reply. Also, for posterity, I like to keep copies of my emails on the Apple word processing which they call "Pages" (now who has delusions of grandeur? Me?)

A few of our number are compiling an account of their early years at St. Mary's and in this respect I am keen to assist them in any way I can by letting them have emails received and old black and white photos. You met Caroline on one of your trips here from Australia. Caroline has already published a couple of books and is gathering information for another. Caroline is an enthusiastic writer but as I said there are other gifted writers among us who are researching those years.

Terry Connor, who was the main man at Cabrini, as successor of the priests, has retired and is now at Exeter University and he plans to research the early years and write the results in a book. I hope I have got that right, Terry? I have sent him a memory stick with loads of stuff and photos which I hope will assist his efforts.

All for now.

(Delvin) John

ARCHIVES

Delvin and Josie,

Thank you for both of today's emails. This one in particular which seems to have jolted my memory! I can't think why I didn't think to say something before – it just did not come to mind!

Are you aware that Liverpool University Archive Dept. holds all records of all Childrens' Homes/Orphanages in the UK? I had reason to ring them when I discovered quite by chance from NCH Archives that this is where our "history" is stored. I was given a contact number at the time but am blowed if I can find it, or the name of the chap who ran the department. Initially, he was very reluctant to speak with me but once I explained I was anxious that MY records were not on view to Tom, Dick or indeed Harry, he assured me everything is kept on microfilm and there is no possible access by T,D, or H. Or anyone else. He was, however, very interested in knowing details of my childhood by giving an account of our day-to-day lives in the Home; how we were cared for, punishments etc. He begged me to write an account of my time in the Home, but of course, I never did!

He was of the opinion that today's Child Care was doing far more harm than good and it would produce the "monsters of tomorrow", and was of the view that the clock would go back to provide the type of "institutional" care we had received. And so I wonder, Delvin, is this where some of Caroline's history is stored and that of others?

Ann

Ann,

Thank you for that information. If Caroline does not already know she may make some use of it. The others that are collating their history might also find it another source of facts.

Take care.

(Delvin) John

Hello,

Am not sure, Delvin, if there's a connection between St. Mary's and Milton Mount College, so just in case, here's an "oldie". Ann.

Ann,

I believe that was the original name of the building before it became St. Mary's.

(Delvin) John

Ann,

Thanks for update re Catholic Church, Parrock Road, Gravesend. It was my understanding that the St. Mary's boys had their own chapel for services, as confirmed by John F. The pews in the picture come up a blur, so nothing amiss here in your description and them being well worn.

KOKO

Caroline

Caroline,

I sent the picture of the Church to John F. thinking he and his contemporaries at St. Mary's had been regulars there, but he said, 'not so' as St. Mary's had their own chapel; duh! I'd forgotten that! I was being facetious about the pews being well worn. The red phone box is outside the church which is at the end of Parrock Street in the town centre.

Ann

TIMES GONE BY

Pamela,

Good to hear from you. I know what it is like to want to meet someone who conjures up good memories of times gone by.

You could first of all contact Cabrini which is the current holder of records over the years for children who were at St. Mary's. Their phone number is: 8668-2181 (Irena is very helpful) They also have a website.

Another avenue you may go down is the General Records of Births, Marriages and Deaths. Phone: 0300 123 1837.

The odds are that Rodney married and had children. It is a bit of a slog but it can be done. I found my mother using this method. If Rodney married he would probably have had children and they in turn years later may have married and had children. Each stage of the searching process brings you more and more up to date with addresses.

There are professional organisations that can undertake a search for you but using an agency can be expensive. In each case you will have to know Rodney's surname and hopefully, Cabrini will deliver this to you.

(Delvin) John

John,

Picking up your suggestions to Pam re searching for family with the possibility Cabrini might be able to throw some light on her inquiry, I wonder also if Pam is able to contact the Liverpool Archives to see what they come up with. This information via Ann is worthy of time spent and may possibly give answers to clues. Any avenue is worthwhile searching. I might add to Pam – the very best of luck! In past journeys had this news come my way the expenses of researchers with the exception of the late Genealogist Angus Baxter, could have been minimized.

KOKO

Caroline

METAMORPHOSIS

Hola todos,

Having digested the missives going back and forth 'twixt yourselves I can only surmise that St. M's must have undergone some semblance of metamorphosis sometime between the early 50s and 1957. In my time "in residence" many inmates had a parent or other relative who would visit them. Quite a few children had parents who were in the throes of separation. Very few if any of my contemporaries had been there since infancy.

Were the Sisters of Charity in charge of the place when you were there? Does anyone remember Sisters Monica, Mary, Clare and/or Benedict?

Confused of Ross.

Sent on my Brillo pad.

Glen Cawdeary

Glen,

I think you are right about St. M's going through a metamorphosis. When I met one of the nuns many, many years, after I left St. M's, if she had known that long word beginning with "M" I think she would have used it. I asked her if things had changed since my day. She said there had been an enormous change but not for the better, and that it was far easier in our day since most of the children, like me, were left in their care without the interference of the mothers who were making a new life for themselves without the worry of being a single parent. She went on to say that the children in care, at the time I was asking, did have mothers who were often women of dubious repute or/and suffered from addictions. Often the good work carried out during the week was undone when mothers would take the children out at weekends and spend time telling them their rights but not their obligations.

The email from Tony says something about the nuns who were there when he was a guest. That was a terrible incident of the boy falling over the bannisters. Afterward chain link fencing was used as a safety net with protruding bolts hammered into the rails discouraging the boys from sliding down.

The Sisters of Charity renamed Daughters of Charity in due course because of modernisation, were thanked for their good work over the years and were made redundant.

KOKO

(Delvin) John

Tony,

That was funny about the haircut. Haircuts were perfunctory exercises carried out by the nuns along with toenail cutting and other personal services. There was no such thing as style in those days, at least not for us.

KOKO

(Delvin) John

Glen,

I have always maintained that lads who arrived at St. Mary's always travelled an emotional road which was a tougher road than someone like me who was taken into care from the age of approximately six months. Lads like me didn't know a different way of life whereas children like you were snatched from freedom to an institution, to join a herd. Over the years I remember when young lads arrived at St. Mary's. The ploy was to leave them with some sweets and then the person, probably their mother, would slip away. Night-time was traumatic for the new arrivals who would invariably cry themselves to sleep while the rest of us would in the intervening period be calling out to them to 'shut up.' The sweets would have gone by night-time so there was no longer an incentive to cultivate the new arrival.

The usual adage applied: "kids can be cruel to kids".

I am thinking that you may be one of the youngest of our group; if not the youngest but never mind I doubt if things had changed that much from when I left St. M's in 1954 to when you arrived in 1957. A major change had come about five years before in 1952 when us kids went outside the building to go to school at St. John's. St. John's in those days was a collection of buildings scattered over a wide area and depending on your age determined what building your introduction to a "normal" school would take place. The ultimate plan for our age group would be to transfer us to the main school which was located at Denton. Denton school was known in our day as the Senior Department of the Primary School, Denton was amazing! We were, for the first time, in close proximity to girls. I fell in love in a matter of days – it was wonderful!

This is more than I can say for our education. We never failed an examination but then we never sat an examination so when it came to leave we were I suppose - "uneducated".

Looking at a couple of names in your email makes me wonder if perhaps they were the result of the Hungarian revolution, which took place in 1956. You talk about your change of fortune which I suspect was to do with you leaving St. M's. Happiness? Is it a relative thing? To be unhappy or happy at St. M's would suggest you knew some other way of life. If ignorance is bliss then it is foolish to be wise and in respect of my stay at St. M's I suppose I was ignorant. My wife Josie tells people that I am happy so, like you, I don't believe I was damaged by my upbringing.

Now what to do? If you are in favour I could send a memory stick with lots of letters from our group which has been going for sometime now. My role is mainly that of a facilitator or record keeper of letters but I try to reply to emails which gives me a chance to include my own memories in my replies. I always emphasize that it is not obligatory for our members to write but we have only had positive feedback. We have heard that while some never write they do enjoy reading what goes backward and forward.

Keep On Keeping On.

Delvin

MYSTERIES

Hi John,

Good to read the messages between Glen and yourself.

I can't ever remember a child coming to St. Anne's and given sweets to allay fears of being separated from a parent or to stop the crying. The only time we had sweets was on a feast day. Sparingly doled out from a tin bucket with a tin spoon and usually sticky hard rock cut in pieces. We loved it!

Rowland (my brother) remembered being dressed in a sailor's suit, clutching a bag of small apples he was allowed to keep while he bawled himself to sleep, when taken to St. Jos. Littlehampton in 1921. We still haven't a clue to this day who paid for his upkeep or took him there. Mystery upon mystery. Despite no record of him going through the channels of the Catholic Society.

Since Ann gave us the knowledge all records of children in care are on file at Liverpool University Archives I feel at times it's worth the effort to get in touch with them to see what Pandora's box reveals. The temptation often is too, too much!

Mavis and Paddy think the title for our book, "Living in The Wrong House", sounds good. Still waiting on other members with their ideas. I do want to get cracking on the manuscript and while your good self and

Terry Mc. forward your thoughts and suggestions on a memory stick, any other memories from members would add spice to the story.

You mentioned the Hungarian revolution in 1956, the year I came to Canada on a Greek ship that should have sunk it was so badly maintained with a German crew who spoke only German and none of us understood a word. Imagine being on a 7-tonner tosser that groaned and moaned the Atlantic Ocean with each surfacing wave. To cap it all, it was later known when stepping off safely at Wolfe's Cove, Quebec, the lifeboats were screwed to the decks.

The ship was filled with Hungarian refugees. I often wonder how they fared in their new life in Canada.

Glen was one of the lucky ones to have further education provided. To use your phrase, John: 'You've (me) been educating yourself since the age of 14.' How true! It never stops!

I don't believe any of the girls who were put in St. Anne's, as myself, at an early age could possibly comprehend there was another lifestyle outside the orphanage. It comes as a rude awakening to learn when sent "out in the world".

The many pitfalls we experienced would not have been the case if taught otherwise. We could carry on this saga endlessly and still not come to a conclusion how the girls might have reacted had they discovered there was indeed a different life outside. But of course had we known, there was little we could do.

Keep well.

Caroline

DITTY SANG AT ST. MARY'S

Mummy, mummy, take me home

From this dirty, dungeon home.

I've been here a year or two,

And now I want to be with you.

Eggs and bacon we don't see,

We get no sugar in our tea.

Now we are gradually,

Fading away.

– Colin Bedford

TEACHERS TO REMEMBER

What was the caretaker's name? Does anyone remember? He had a nice daughter and she and I had a few nice times out and at the movies on Saturday. Then he found out and called me into one of the cleaning rooms and told me in no uncertain terms that his daughter was not going out with some St. Mary's boy.

She was a nice girl and lots of fun. She had a great sense of humour. Guess he did not like me as I would bring mice into the school and leave them in the desk for the next unsuspecting student who came in to the class.

Hawkett was a great teacher. Had many a good conversation with him. I guess Grimes was the one with the paunch and the top button on his pants always undone, and the bamboo cane handy.

Was Rawlinson the one who taught us about the digestive system? We boys all found that one quite funny. All about food and water going thru the body. We had a great laugh talking about that. I thought that he also did not like Biro's, stating they did not allow us to write properly.

Tony Kelly (unsuccessful man in Canada)

John M Murray

Thanks, John, for your enquiry. I have looked again at the list of entries for the intake into St. John's, Denton in 1951 which in our days was called the Senior Department of the Primary School and the age is from 1936 to 1940 so the information that would help you would be a list of Primary School encompassing 1943. Now the thing is where are those records kept? Possibly with St. John's church or elsewhere. May I suggest you contact St. John's, Denton and ask if they have the entries for children born in 1942/43/44. I hope the information below will help. I welcome questions as it enables me to respond to an interest rather than just rowing my own boat.

Mr T. Cahill, Head Teacher.

Mr S. Maher, Head of School

St. John's Catholic Comprehensive School,

Rochester Road, Gravesend, Kent. DA12 2JW

Take care. KOKO

Delvin

OLD BOYS' NETWORK

John,

The general consensus from all those I've spoken to about how the Old Boys "Network" began is that it all started with you, John. Judging by what I found on your file, it looks like the Old Boys' Network actually started in July 1988 when you wrote to our then director saying you had read an article published in "Child" and would be pleased if you would put me in touch with any of the lads who left St. Mary's Gravesend to start a new life in Australia. I imagine things moved rather slowly at first, due to snail-mail, etc. but as we all know they picked-up, especially once computers became commonplace and email contact so much easier. Hope this tallies with your memories, John.

Best wishes to you both.

Irena Lyczkowska, Social Worker,

Cabrini Children's Society,

49 Russell Hill Road, Purley, Surrey, England.

Glen,

Patricia is married to an ex-St. Mary's boy (Ken Dutton). She is mostly visible on Facebook which is a social media that I rarely use but I think she may find our group interesting. As you are aware, many of our members are more in an observer capacity and don't write, but I do have knowledge that many read the messages.

Seasonal Greetings to you and yours.

KOKO

John

John,

The news of Patricia married to an ex St. Mary's boy (Ken Dutton) is good to know. I feel sure she will find our messages from the group interesting to a point she may want to add something of her life with Ken. Does anyone remember him?

KOKO

Caroline

SLICE OF CAKE

Ann/Caroline

That certainly is a good, bad news letter. Ann, how do you produce those gems of information and Caroline you must be thrilled that Ann is able to do so.

I left St. Mary's sixty-years ago this month (August 2014) and what a cultural shock that was learning to live among civilised people and not the law of the jungle.

I remember an example of the difference between living at St. Mary's compared with a family. On Feast days at St. Mary's, like Christmas or Special Saint's days, we would have extra treats and in the latter years, --- like birthday cakes, were supplied. The cakes were expertly cut up into wedges and disposed of in double quick time.

Now, at the family, I was in for a surprise. I was offered a sliver of cake and after the lady of the house assured herself that I liked it, she grandly announced that I will be having another slice later. Big deal!

I thought between us kids that we were going to demolish the lot, but I think I am civilised now.

Delvin

CHRISTMAS DEADLINE

Hello Mavis & Pat,

Trust you are both keeping well. Not sure how the climate is your end as it seems to fluctuate differently to that of the UK and Canada. We're having a hot summer and hopefully it will continue well past the Fall.

As you know, I am working on the "Keep On Keeping On" manuscript for the old St. Mary's boys from Gravesend. What I would like to ask if you have anything you can remember of the past we can put in the book.

Ron Mulligan, Antony Hayman, Terry McKenna have come forward with well-drafted manuscripts – all interesting. Ron has still yet to complete his final chapter on his Childhood at St. Mary's and other memories he wishes to have published.

John Michael Murray is currently working on "Laundry Boy".

Terry McKenna's "Welcome to Your New Home" is also mentioned.

Antony Hayman's "Memories of St. Mary's Before and After" are well-documented.

John (Delvin) Flynn has been instrumental in sending details of historical school events, School masters, Father Baker and his tuck shop, and other school memories.

Colin Bedford sent a drawing by a 10-year-old lad that was published in "Fragments" magazine. "Our Journey Back to Gravesend after the War". It is a detailed drawing and remarkable for a lad of his age.

These contributions towards the compiling of our book will enable the St. Mary's boys to have a voice. It is hoped next year (2015) to make a trip to England and have a book signing event in a book shop, perhaps Smiths at Gravesend, and enable those interested contributors of the Group to enjoy a common share in a reunion.

Our fund towards publishing costs stands at $795.57. Great support from a small group of worldwide members. Thank you for your generous donation.

Without John and Terry Mc's on-going support to ensure all material is made available to me, the publication of KOKO would not be possible. My goal is to have the book out by Christmas. This of course depends on further material I have yet to receive.

Take care.

Best wishes,

Caroline

CHRISTMAS POEM

We have a list of folks we know, all written in a book

And every year when Christmas comes we go and take a look

That is when we realise these names are all apart

Not of the book they're written in, but of our very heart.

For each name stands for someone whose life touched ours and then

Left such a print of friendship that we want to touch again

And while it feels fantastic for us to make this claim

We really feel we are composed of each remembered name.

And while you may not be aware of any special link

Just meeting you has shaped our lives a lot more than you think

For when you're met somebody the years cannot erase

The memory of a pleasant word or a friendly face.

So never think our Christmas cards are just a mere routine

Of names upon a Christmas List, forgotten in between

For when we send a Christmas card that is addressed to you

It's because you're on the list of friends we are indebted to.

For we are but a total of many folk we're met

And you happen to be one of those prefer not to forget

So whether we have known you for many years or few

In some way you have had a part in shaping things we do.

Now every year when Christmas comes we realise anew

The biggest gift that life can give is meeting folk like you

So may the Spirit of Christmas that forever endures

Leaves its richest blessings in the hearts of you and yours.

– Author Unknown

Sent by (Delvin) John Flynn

MY TRAIN RIDE

To John Flynn

This is very beautiful and I am honoured to have received it. On to you, my friend!

At birth we boarded the train and met our parents, and we believe they will always travel on our side. However, at some station our parents will step down from the train, leaving us on this journey alone.

As time goes by, other people will board the train; and they will be significant (i.e. siblings, friends, children, and even the love of your life). Many will step down and leave a permanent vacuum. Others will go so unnoticed that we don't realize they vacated their seats. This train ride will be full of joy, sorrow, fantasy, expectations, hellos, goodbyes, and farewells. Success consists of having a good relationship with all passengers requiring that we give the best of ourselves.

The mystery to everyone is: We do not know at which station we ourselves will step down. So, we must live in the best way, love, forgive, and offer the best of who we are. It is important to do this because when the time comes for us to step down and leave our seat empty we should leave behind beautiful memories for those who will continue to travel on the train of life.

I wish you a joyful journey on the train of life.

Reap success and give lots of love. More importantly, Thank God for the journey. Lastly, I thank you for being one of the passengers on my train.

By: H Ward.

SCRUMPING APPLES

Hello Caroline,

In the past, I have sent (Delvin) John some emails about me memories of my time at St. Mary's. One was the occasion of having a choice of dear Sister Patricia or the horrid Sister Gerard as the new Reverend Mother. The other was the time when I was caught scrumping apples and pears and being taken to Sister Gerard's office by Sister Catherine. I also mentioned the time I sneaked into the Nuns' dining-room while they were in the chapel. It was one of the Nuns' birthdays and they had plenty of cakes and goodies. I was very busy helping myself when one of the Nuns returned. I had to duck under the table, to escape being caught.

Also, I am unable to remember the full details, but, in the refectory, one table of boys used to be rostered for a month, to do all the washing up and cleaning the room after each meal. (I believe that kitchen duty also came under the same umbrella.) Cleaning out the large steam vats used for cooking porridge and soups, was hard labour!

Another onerous task I can remember was the moving of the beds in the dormitories, sweeping and putting floor polish onto the wooden floors, then having to buffer them with a heavy polisher on the end of a long pole, pushing and pulling it backward and forward. (Hard work for nine and ten-year-old boys!)

Out here in Aussie land, we are just into our first few days of Spring. We are both doing Okay. I have a lung problem, caused through serving on Royal Navy ships and submarines in the 1950s and 60s. A lot of asbestos was used to cover all steam, hot oil and refrigeration pipes. When the cladding on the pipes deterioriated, we just tied the breaks and painted over the tapes or ropes used. We have to remember back then the asbestos health problems were not known. I do get a small disability pension from the British government. I would much prefer to have good lungs. I receive free medical treatment for my condition, including a lung specialist and my doctor.

I am attaching copies of some emails I sent to (Delvin) John, in case you don't have them.

Best wishes.

Pat & Mavis, Australia

Hello Pat & Mavis,

To say I was delighted to receive your newsy message, is to say the least! Much appreciate having these past memories of youthhood and the many experiences you mentioned is reminiscent of chores undertaken by me at St. Anne's. I know curiosity kills the cat – hence when seeing a contingency of "shoppers" scurrying here, there and everywhere, carrying large tin buckets, it was only when I was caught by Sister Vincent did I have a clue what it was all about. This episode is mentioned in "Surviving the Shadows". The girls, unfortunately, had to "skate" or go down on our hands and knees to wax and polish floors. I remember my knees were always red when I undertook this chore; the refectory was the worst – the stainmarks of slime evident after scrubbing the large floor. I don't remember such a luxury as using a heavy polisher to shine the dorm floors.

I loved the bit about the Nuns' dining-room and can imagine the look of horror on your face when tucking into goodies only to be disturbed by a Nun who decided to return to the scene of the crime, that caused you to hide under the table.

An incident in the Nuns' dining-room at St. Anne's reminds me of something similar. Dorothy, the girl in charge of this area, one day asked if I would take over her duties (not sure of the reason), which I gladly did. The next morning I was hauled "over the coals" by the headmistress Sister Attracta whose head I felt surely would fall off through her screaming, pointed her finger at me in front of the whole class I was a thief. Apparently, a girl had sneaked into the Nuns' dining-room, helped herself to a chunk of bread and smothered it with butter. Hearing a noise, she fled the scene leaving behind half-a-chunk with big teethmarks. I knew who it was, but like most of the girls we were loyal to our friends and never "snitched" on them.

Such are the tales of delight from our group of "cousins" in London. Both my brothers were in the Navy – one Royal – the other Merchant, and suffered with lung conditions due to the asbestos in ships.

Happy to hear Spring has arrived in Aussieland, and that you are both doing okay. My new computer works to a degree but I have yet to master the art of downloading attachments. I will succeed!

Take care.

KOKO

Caroline

Dear Caroline,

It was a really lovely surprise to get your email this morning when I switched on my computer. Yes, you struck lucky, I am indeed Bernard's younger brother. I'm now eighty-two years old, and keeping in the best of health.

Sadly, Bernard passed away about twenty years ago. He was a lovely man, but his years in St. Mary's Gravesend took a dreadful toll on him and he was a very sad and bitter man, and I don't think he really got over the type of regime at that school. He was two or three years older than me, so he was much more affected at losing his Mum at the age of four or five than me, as I was only three. He was the right age too, to be conscripted into the Army (still a very simple lad – I say this in the nicest way).

He was wounded twice before he was nineteen and the rest is a long story which sadly embittered him. I remember him talking about your brother Bill and I know he cared for his (your) sister Betty. He didn't get married till quite late in his life, and the few years he had with Elsie before he died were I think, very, very happy.

Our time evacuated in Wells, Norfolk 1940/1941 were happy for him, as the couple with whom he was billeted took on a maid solely to look after him, and this was the girl who he became reunited with many years later, and then married. Just a few years of married bliss!

I looked up your book on the internet, and then dashed out to the library and have ordered a copy. I look forward to reading your memories and also how the experiences affected you in life afterwards. As you said in your internet blurb, we were brought up absolutely ignorant of the outside world, and then cast aside into a life that we just didn't seem to fit into. I could go on for hours in this vein, but I am just happy that you have contacted with me, and I don't want to bore you.

I really hope that you will mail me again, as I would like to learn more of you and your impressions of our years "in captivity" (mine were 1933/1943).

Best wishes,

Ron Mulligan.

THE BONGARTZ BROTHERS

Dear John,

Having my daily dose of your emails (extremely efficacious by the way), the name Bongartz leaped out at me. I was at St. Mary's until November 1943, and we had a Douglas Bongartz in our class. I'm afraid I can't tell you much about him (Brain cells v Anno Domini) though I remember he had a younger brother. Strangely, I can remember a visiting School Inspector asking him (Douglas) to spell aeroplane which he did correctly but made the mistake of pronouncing it "airzeplane" for which he was given a right mouthful later by our teacher. You can see that my brain can recall an enormous amount of useless information, whilst the good stuff goes straight through one ear and out the other!! Anyway, I think Douglas was younger than me, as he was still at Ugbrooke when I left. Incidentally, my two sons took me on a trip down Memory Lane two weeks ago (Sept. 2014) to Wells-next-the-Sea for a few days. Considering that episode of my life was seventy-five years ago, I was able to wander round like a native.

Keep up the good work!

Best wishes.

Ron Mulligan.

Hi Caroline,

I left St. Mary's in November 1943, and I well remember the two Bongartz brothers. Douglas was in my class and I am sure he was still there when I left. I am unsure because each boy left the School as soon as he reached the age of fourteen, so one or two of the lads were always going off to Blackheath or to see their Mum or Dad.

I would like to contact Douglas's sister, if she is willing. My middle son Michael has an Engineering firm in Billingshurst, He had a house there until a few years ago but moved to a nearby village.

Re: my brother Bernard, he was about three years older than me, but he died about 20 years ago. He was in the war at eighteen, wounded twice and came out of the Army a very different man. He lived a very sad and lonely life until he met up with a lady who had been employed to look after him whilst we were evacuated in Wells-next-the-Sea in Norfolk. Bernard was about twelve or thirteen, and Elsie was 16. A Mrs. Tuck who had taken him in, owned a shop, and employed Elsie to look after him.

We tried to locate her for many years and by the purest chance, a workmate of Bernard's stayed at a caravan site in Norfolk owned by Elsie's sister. By convoluted methods we eventually tracked down this lady and after a lifetime, they were reunited. Then they got married, moved back to Wells and were like two lovebirds. Sadly, they didn't have long together, as he had a heart attack and died just as our whole family five brothers and Dad went the same way. I took a trip down Memory Lane two weeks ago to Wells and attempted to visit his grave but sadly all the graves had been levelled, as it was easier for the Church maintenance team.

Hope this letter wasn't too boring, but it's lovely to read all your emails to the group. I would be pleased to hear from you if you have the time.

Best Wishes,

Ron Mulligan (now 85)

REMEMBERING DOUG. HARRIS

Hello John (Delvin),

Yes, I think I remember Doug Harris correctly as the maintenance man. Doug was able to do jobs that needed to be done! Carpentry, painting, inside the building or outside. Making new doors or window frames. No problem. Repairing the cords in the sachet windows and securing the lead weights. Done. Whatever job needed doing Doug was able and willing to do it. I remember Doug had the job of cleaning the gutters on the grand old building of St. Mary's and he used to carry the extended ladders to each part he was dealing with. Imagine the height of St. Mary's?

In my last few months at Gravesend, I was assigned to Mr. Harris's workshop. I was put on painting some doors. I don't remember where in the building but Doug showed me how best to paint doors and do the finish with brush strokes in the same direction.

In discussing my future, Doug thought I could go into Sign-Writing. In those days most signs were hand-painted.

I did enjoy the big mugs of tea Doug provided in tea breaks.

The photo is not the way I remember Doug as I mostly saw him in cloth cap and blue overalls. But he made a great impression on me that work was worthy. Clean up after every job, and that he was personally a good caring man and interested in me as a person to encourage to excellence.

Does that sound like Doug?

KOKO. All the best to John and Josie and all our readers.

Michael Monaghan

FOOTBALL TEAM

Hi Caroline,

I came across a newspaper article from the *Gravesend Reporter* which was basically about the St. Mary's football team, which was famous before the War. Some of it however may be of interest so here are the relevant bits. No story of SM would be complete without mention of Mr. Roche. Five foot six, slightly built, bespectacled is Sportsmaster Richard Roche, the idol of the boys of St. Mary's and the most unassuming man one would wish to meet.

Also this piece about the Boys who were swept into the maelstrom of War. Johnny Barzee, American born, wounded in France and awarded the Purple Heart before he died. Joe Anderson who went to Dunkirk along with Jimmy Warren, Joe Izzio and Louis Buckthorpe. Jackie Read, Louis Izzio and Jimmy O'Keefe also made the supreme sacrifice in 1944. Tell you what rather than giving you bits and pieces I will mail the cutting to you. I will also include a collection of postcards. While these are just requests from my brother to take me out for a few hours, the stamps may be of interest, especially the Edward VIII.

One of the problems, I think, when telling the story of SM is that there is a world of difference between pre-War and post-War. As you know I left SM on the outbreak of War. When I went back in 1946/47 the School was totally different. Fewer boys and those were being educated in the town of Gravesend. They were also attending the Church of St. John's rather than the School chapel. So there were no Teachers and no Sisters of Charity. None that I saw anyway. The war changed many things, including SM. How many of us pre-War boys are still alive to tell the story of life in the Thirties?

Antony Hayman,

Sent from my iPad

PERSONAL FILE

Hello Caroline,

When I visited Cabrini last year (2013) and was given my "file" I had to sign an undertaking not to publish or disclose any of the information contained in the documents without their consent.

In the first part of my "writings" (some 2000 words) I tell of how I came to be sent to St. Anne's in Brighton. Most of what Cabrini had related to the correspondence between my Mother and various people within the Southwark Catholic Rescue Society, Social Services and the Canadian Army, I have used some of that information. I will add that I was very unhappy at the amount of information that had been removed (blanked out as "Third Party") particularly as it was me to whom they referred. My thinking was that by clearing this hurdle at this stage it could avoid a problem later on, and hopefully not ruin it for anybody, else.

At the moment Irena has read it with one observation and has passed it to her boss. I should hear in a day or two. If the decision goes against me I intend to challenge it most strongly. The bulk of what I have written relates to the time I was at St. Mary's, which apart from a few letters in the file from my mother to SCRS, does not concern Cabrini.

If you like I could send you the "offending" document if you can receive attachments.

Keep smiling. Kind regards,

John Michael Murray

John,

Thank you so much for your concern with Cabrini and with whom I understand you had to undertake an agreement not to divulge some of the information in your file without their consent.

I am appalled after all these decades to realise the audacity of these people who continue to dictate in our lives after leaving the long-defunct institutions who today have no right whatsoever to determine what can or cannot be published about your family's history. What can they do in this day and age to deny anyone to publish the right of their Biographies, for social history?

If it ever appeared in the courts you had "infringed" upon their contract when releasing personal documents to you, it would not stand up in court. In any event, John, you would have the backing and full support of our group members who understand fully the story you wished told.

The big question: What is it THEY have to hide? I think enough shanningan has gone on long enough and that "free speech" to which we are entitled, will prevail. That they blanked out certain details is questionable.

By all means challenge their decision if it is opposed to you releasing certain details. Do send me the offending document. I will let you know if I was able to download. In any event whatever documents you have and WANT to have published in "Keep On Keeping On" – The Boy's of St. Mary's, I will keep on file until your decision is made to publish or not.

Yes, keep smiling.

KOKO

Caroline

Hello Caroline,

I sent you a reply to your last email but I think it has got lost in all the excitement of Barack Obama flying over our house during the NATO Summit (Sept.2014).

Regarding what I have sent to Cabrini I had to sign an undertaking not to publish any of the information received from them that was in my "file" without their permission. The work I have sent them relates to the machinations between my Mother, the Church, Social Service and the Canadian Military authorities that led me being sent to St. Anne's in Brighton.

Irena has read it and has suggested a minor alteration but she has passed it to her boss for the final say so.

Be assured that if the result is that I cannot use the information contained within the "file" I intend to challenge most strongly. I thought that by doing it properly now it could avoid future conflict or problems. I should add that I was "not best pleased" and the amount of information that was denied me being marked as "third party". This was the information of the faceless people who made decisions that affected my life. The document sent is

2,000 words of my memories, limited though they are, of pre-St. Mary's. If all else fails I will move the start point.

I hope all is well with you.

Will be in touch soon.

John Michael Murray

Sent from my iPad

John,

The email I have now sent covers what you have written in this message. Well, the excitement of Obama flying over your house during the NATO Summit is history indeed!

When you have the outcome of Cabrini's decision and you send me a copy, let's take it from there. What is the connection to the Canadian Army – or do I need to ask? Anything to do with Canada of course in particular the Army, those records could be made available through Veteran's Affairs. If you need to investigate, do let me know. Always happy to help a comrade.

You know, John, life before the days of being institutionalised are as important to record as those after. It is a birthright to know the truth and while the powers that be think otherwise they have no right whatsoever to deny that information to which we are entitled.

There isn't any challenge we cannot face!

Caroline

Antony,

I like your matter-of-fact style of writing. You tell your story in an almost conversational self-deprecating way rather than pandering to fake literature. Sadly, with our lack of education, we boys were unlikely to rival Charles Dickens in the literary stakes. But when we write we do our best to communicate – that's the main thing.

I was surprised that although you were at St. Mary's a few years before I arrived some of the people mentioned by you were still around in my day. Certain things you wrote brought back memories that I thought I had forgotten – winter and summer clothes, new boys crying themselves to sleep in the night because they missed their mothers, boys wetting the bed, the closed community. Sister Patricia, the plain unappetizing food, boys doing the housework, bath time, Sister Vincent, Christmas at St. Mary's, religion, the medal of Our Lady, Latin Mass, pure theatre, the choir, the retreats, the football team with Mr. Roche, Billy Keirnan, cricket, throwing the sweets and bread into the group of children, Bertram Mills Circus, holidays at St. Mary's Bay, Dymchurch, evacuation, names you may recall.

We thought if we were naughty in the town we could get away with it. We didn't realise the clothes we wore were in essence a uniform that marked us out from other children, the boots, the corduroy shorts, the socks and as you say we changed over to Khaki shorts and sandals with the white crepe soles, they were white when they were new, minus socks for the summer months.

After your time when they stopped throwing the sweets but not bread into the crowd of us boys in the playground, bread that missed the grappling hands would be trodden into the asphalt and although filthy would still be eaten. Instead of "sellings" or throwing sweets into the crowd, we started to get pocket money. Pocket money, what did that mean? We didn't have pockets in any part of our clothing. Our crodge (personal possessions) were stuffed up our jumpers with the 'S' buckle belt securing everything in place. Clothes were made on site so there was not the luxury of pockets or fly button on the shorts. Hitching the trouser leg was what we did if we wanted to do a pee.

I can remember Father Arbuthnott arriving at St. Mary's and announcing to a gathering of boys that we would in future be receiving pocket money. The amount each child received would be in accordance with their age. I think it started, at least for me, at 4d then rose until the maximum of 2/6d for boys working for Doug, the handyman, pending being placed at either the training farm at Bletchingly, Surrey or the hostel at Blackheath, South London. But some, as was in my case, for reasons unbeknown to me, were placed with a family.

We were, at least in the early days, a closed community. School was in-house with strict discipline but we didn't learn much. Then for the first time my generation went out of St. Mary's and enrolled en mass at the local Catholic school. The school was described as the Senior Department of the Primary School and there were girls there. I enjoyed my first puppy love, as I immediately had a crush on one of the girls in my class. It was wonderful hugging my pillow in the dead of night, the pillow being a substitute for my girl.

But sadly it was all too late to catch up on the academic subjects and I and others left school hardly being able to write.

Wetting the bed by some of the boys was seen as pure laziness. Lazy boys had to be punished and part of the punishment was for the offenders to parade through the length of the dormitories with the wet sheets draped over their heads. Sometimes the nocturnal emissions had not long taken place and not only the offenders but the rest of us were punished by the awful stink of urine.

Most of the food served up was not to my taste. Potatoes had more eyes on them than Miss World. Peas clotted together in some amorphous mass. Lumps of meat fat would be unsuspectingly delivered to the mouth only to be gagged up. I recall when staying at Lord Clifford's stately home at Devon, where we were evacuated during the course of the war and I was slow at finishing my dinner. Not to worry. Without more ado the person in charge pushed the unwanted dinner to one side and poured the milky desert on to the same plate. I was told I had better eat the lot as there were starving children in Africa.

Everyone loved Sister Patricia but while I was in the infants' refectory it was announced that she was to leave St. Mary's after being there for over fifteen years. She was a big round Sister who was lovely. She managed to instil discipline without being cruel. We were all rather sad to see her leave. Sisters were not encouraged to get too fond of the children as they could be moved without notice to another caring job. We had gained the impression, not necessarily true, that Sisters who left St. Mary's were replaced by not-so-nice Sisters. Sister Patricia would have been the same Sister to whom Antony Hayman referred.

Letters in or out of St. Mary's were censored. Any letter written in a "libelous" way would never reach its destination. "Interesting" letters written to children by their mothers would on some occasions be read out to the whole class.

Some of us whose parents had left the scene and were no longer in contact had what we called "bodge up aunties". These wonderful ladies would take the children out and at Christmas time would buy presents. Letters would be written on the blackboard for the boys to copy thanking the "bodge up aunties" for last year's presents and letting them know what was wanted this year but ensuring the phrase "if you can afford it" was included with the request. "If you can afford it" must have been perceived as a sort of challenge to the recipient of the letter as often our wish would come true. One year I received a lovely Conway Stuart fountain pen.

Christmas at St. Mary's was good. Christmas Eve we would be sent to bed at the normal time and be awakened in time to attend Midnight Mass with carols, then into the refectory for a warm drink, then back to bed. Next day was presents day. Piles of brown paper parcels would be piled on to a long refectory table then names would be called out at random. We waited in trepidation. What if there was no parcel with my name on it? But my fears were always groundless. In due course my name would be called and the parcel ripped open to reveal sweets and fruit. As at other feast days the discipline would be relaxed. And of course over the Christmas period, like you Antony, we would go to Bertram Mills Circus. Christmas was always a happy time.

One year I stayed with a "bodge up auntie" and Christmas was definitely not a happy one. The relations popped round with presents for the children of the household but all I received was a pat on the head and pitying looks for orphan child.

Antony, I agree your description of our religious services and surprisingly I have been using the word theatre for some time. Like you I loved the Latin Mass and Benediction. Pure theatre!! I stumbled upon a film of "the installation of the new Archbishop of Philadelphia" on Youtube. It was so good that I have watched it six times. The service wasn't in Latin but there was such dignity in the ceremony that it brought back memories of how things used to be. There were six cardinals and over sixty bishops and countless number of priests, seminarians and other dignitaries. The music was heavenly with a young singer giving a rendering of a version of Beethoven's Ode to Joy backed up by the choir and as you say, it was pure theatre.

When you compare the Catholic Church services today with days gone by the services seem so sterile and lacking in solemnity. Now we have girls serving on the altar and as someone said 'when the girls go on the altar, the boys come off.' They say you have to change with the times and I believe there is truth in that. We loved the Latin but let's be honest unless we looked at the translation alongside in the missal we didn't know the meaning of what was being said.

I remember Mr. Roche as a very successful football manager, also our most famous "old boy" Billy Keirnan who played for Charlton in 1947 and 1948 winning the FA Cup. I wonder if you knew William "Bill" Marshall who was the brother of Caroline Whitehead and is a member of our group. He was born in 1924. Then there was Ron Mulligan who with his brothers attended St. Mary's. John Coduri another ex St. Mary's boy. Also one of the "old boys" returned as a PT teacher but was later sacked for allegedly sexually interfering with some of the boys.

Holidays at St. Mary's Bay "the largest camp for boys and girls in England" was much the same as in your day. Discipline was relaxed and we were given so much more freedom. Many of us had girlfriends. The girls travelled down from the orphanage at Orpington in Kent. I contacted the sister of my ex-girlfriend but she made it clear that her sister wanted nothing to do with anything or anyone from those days. She had apparently married a man who was well off. I pointed out to her sister that my only reason for wanting to contact her was because when I left St. Mary's I went to live with the family in Orpington but was too embarrassed to tell them that I had a girlfriend at the orphanage. I thought they would tease me about it so I backed off. I never ceased to care for this girl and I told her sister it was my lack of backbone which made me so cowardly to hook up with her again. I am happily married and have no wish to get involved with any other woman even if she was an ex-girlfriend. Still I am pleased it all ended well for her with a prosperous lifestyle.

(Delvin) John F.

THE BOYS OF ST. MARY'S: OUR FOOTBALL INSPIRATION

ARTICLE IN REPORTER LTD.
WRITTEN BY "THE TOWNSMAN" *UNDATED*

THE BOYS OF ST. MARY'S

When, at a quarter to seven tomorrow night, eleven young lads troop from the green-painted wooden pavilion on the Imperial Paper Mills sports ground at Milton on to the football ground a roar will go up from upward of two thousands throats: 'Come on, St. Mary's!'

'Who are these lads who so capture the hearts of the local football public?' a stranger might ask. He would not be long in getting a reply, and well it could go something like this: 'The best boy's team for their ages in the county.'

The dazzling displays these youngsters have put up in the days before the war are talked about wherever soccer is discussed in the town.

Came the war.

Evacuation. The lads' orphanage home standing on the hill overlooking the town at Echo Square, requisitioned. No more football. The boys go to Suffolk, Norfolk and finally Devon.

Others, too old now for school, are swept into the maelstrom of war. The services take them. Blood, sweat, toil and tears. Let's look around.

Johnny Barzee, American-born, formerly an inside-left who also had a left hook. He reached the Great Britain schoolboys' boxing final at the Stadium Club, London. During his earlier American Army career he gave exhibition bouts to the boys in khaki in company with Joe Louis and Billy Conn. But the war was not fought with fists. Johnny wounded in France, was awarded the American Purple Heart before he died.

THEY SERVED

Then there was Joe Anderson, the goalie and centre-half. He went to Dunkirk in company with three of the others: Jimmy Warren, Joe Izzio and Louis Buckthorpe, Jackie Reade, Louise Izzio and Jimmy O'Keefe made the supreme sacrifice in 1944.

Ron Sullivan, too, a brilliant outside-right, went down with his bomber in the Bristol Channel – 1945. Billy Gibbons (centre-half), Gordon Kane, George Buckland and Jimmy Fisher were killed two years earlier. Jackie Boddington, also of the R.A.F, lost his life in 1944.

To the Navy and the country this proud little school gave the lives of Dennis Brooke, Walter Graham and Jackie Coogan.

Of the others of that year you will, dear reader, recall Billy Kiernan, the little left-winger who played for his county. He is now soldiering in India, a lieutenant in the Army and an amateur on the books of Charlton Athletic. Manager Jimmy Steed keeps in close contact with the now not-so-little Billy.

But let's get back. Last season, after the boys had returned to their hilltop home, schoolboy football came to the town once more.

Out of less than forty boys, most of who had never seen or played football before, became the nucleus of the team.

Who is behind this remarkable little side? Five-foot six, slightly built and bespectacled is sports master Irishman R. Roche, the idol of the boys of St. Mary's and the most unassuming man one could wish to meet.

HOW IT'S DONE

On the hard concrete playground, with shirts down for goalposts, he trains his boys, using at times only a tennis ball. A lad who never looked likely to kick a ball is slowly, carefully welded into the vacant position to fill the side. He had goalies playing half-back.

Tomorrow his regular goalie is inside left.

How does he do it? Let Mr. Roche tell you: 'Football,' he says, 'is essentially a team game. We play a series of minor games which are intended to teach them one of the important, if not the most important, things in football: to move into the correct position to take a pass.

'All the players realise that they are units in the team. Individual ability is very important but it must be used for the good of the team. They are also taught that it is much easier and more to their advantage to make the ball do the work.'

TEAMWORK

'The ball is pushed into the empty spaces and players are running forward to receive it. By doing this younger and lighter players can go through a game doing very useful work and yet they rarely come in contact with their opponents.

'Boys are taught that they must never question a referee's decision. We do not congratulate the boy who scores a goal. Goals come from teamwork and the credit goes to the team.

'I always impress on my team

that I would much rather see them lose playing good football than win by playing what is commonly called kick and rush. Lastly, the most important thing for boys and men in football, as in any strenuous game, is to keep oneself mentally and physically fit.'

Tomorrow these boys will show their paces for the first time this season. This will be their team: C. Hayes, C. Bedford (aged 11 and the youngest player), N. Hearne, P. Rose, R. Hedges, C. Stewart, D. Dutton, N. Shaw, R. McGuinty, R. Walsh, C. McGillicuddy.

Proceeds go to the boys' holiday fund camp at Dymchurch from Friday next to September 19th. Dartford East Central provide the opposition.

The boys who trained with a tennis ball, play games without a referee or linesmen and use shirts for goalposts will, I guarantee, give you a display of football worth going a long way to see.

'Are you going?' I am.

S C H O O L B O Y
F O O T B A L L

SATURDAY, 7TH JANUARY, 1950
ST. MARY'S V ST. JOSEPH'S, ROTHERHITHE
STONEBRIDGE ROAD GROUND
(By kind permission)

ST. MARY'S
A. Fisher
B. Baker   G. Gillin
J. Duffy   J. Desmond   M. Desmond
B. Wooldridge.   R. Beddice.   C.McGillicuddy   T. Shaw.
M.Lewis

ST. JOSEPH'S
J. Donovan.   D. Buckley   J. Herd   B. Pearcy   G.
Richardson
J. Wright   P. Messenger   P. Bonney
F. Livermore   B. Buck
C. Donovan

Reporter Ltd. Gravesend.

GATHER UP THE FRAGMENTS

Drawing by a 10-year-old boy of this historical event sent by Colin Bedford.

ST. MARY'S GRAVESEND.
SILVER JUBILEE NUMBER. 1926-51
EDITORIAL

Our readers will understand if this number is devoted very specially to the Silver Jubilee of St. Mary's, Gravesend, which is to be celebrated on Saturday, June 9th. It is felt that those who have played the chief part in its foundation and subsequent success should tell the story. The first boys, not a few of whom gave their lives in the last war, entered the school on March 24th, 1926, and we have chosen this anniversary rather than the formal opening on May 31st, 1927. Father Joseph Crea (now Monsignor Crea), Sister Bernard (the first Headmistress) and two boys of the School, together with Mr. Roche, who has been closely connected with sports and scholastic achievements for 25 years, will develop the story for our readers.

Monsignor Crea writes: 'Although the Southwark Catholic Rescue Society was founded in 1887, St. Mary's School, Gravesend, opened in 1926, was the first of its own Homes. Prior to that it had been a long and hard struggle to pay for the Voluntary cases boarded out in other Homes or with foster parents, and to meet the deficits on the Diocesan Homes for Poor Law and other State-aided children. For years the society received 3/- and 5/- per head per week for the maintenance, clothing, and education of these boys and girls. Now that the State boasts of being the unwanted child's champion and friend and talks glibly of the Children's Charter, its former meanness and neglect should not be completely forgotten nor should a tribute be withheld from the Catholic and other Societies which for so long did heroic work for countless thousands of little ones.

'Milton Mount College, Gravesend, had been founded for the education of the daughters of Nonconformist Ministers. It was evacuated during the First World War and later came into the markets; the owners having decided not to return. Though insured for 78,000 pounds it was purchased for 7,750 pounds. Modern equipment throughout and complete furnishing cost approximately 12,000 pounds and so for 20,000 pounds we had a splendid Home readily sanctioned by the Ministry of Health for 230 boys.

'We are grateful to Mr J. Tolhurst for drawing our attention to the property and advising us. Only seven acres of grounds went with the property but a generous gift of 20 acres from the Milton estate of the late Mrs. Callaghan provided us with much needed playing fields nearby.

'The late Mr. Bernard Tolhurst gave the adjoining property, "Glen View", used as a Receiving Home for new arrivals and also the Chaplain's residence.

'The new venture attracted the attention of Miss Agnes Foley, who became a great supporter of the Society especially later on when the Training Farm at Bletchingly was opened. Generally, support for the new Home was most generous and widespread, and within two or three years it was free of debt.

'We fitted the dining hall with finely carved oak altar and Rood Screen purchased from an "Anglo-Catholic" Church in East London which had been closed down.

'The Sisters of Charity under the first Superior, Sister Bernard Kelly, moved in on March 24th and on the feast of the Annunciation March 26, 1926, the first Mass was offered. The first batch of boys arrived in the following afternoon for Benediction. A year later the formal opening took place and so the Silver Jubilee is being celebrated this year. 1926-1951.

'With the blessing of God and under Our Lady's care the new School flourished. It became most popular with the Town. The boys' splendid football teams contributed greatly to this. Often they were invited to represent the Town in Charity matches. Alec James, Arsenal and England International, then in his prime, came down to referee and backed them against any schoolboy team in England.

'A Board of Education Inspector (who had given a most laudatory report on the standard of education in the school) later admitted to winning a fiver from a colleague who had rashly stated that he had in his official district a boys' team which could beat St. Mary's, Gravesend! There were of course difficulties.

'A retired Thames Pilot had a garden adjoining the School Playground. Sometimes the boys, impatient of delay, would climb the wall and enter his garden to retrieve a ball. The Pilot's literary gifts were considerable. He wrote a furious letter of complaint. After a page or so of vitriolic efforts his tone changed. He was sorry to write so; he knew the grand work being done in the School, they were exceedingly fine lads, etc., etc. But he was a great character. Every now and again he would come to the School beaming upon all and carrying a bag which contained the cricket and tennis balls he had confiscated. These he returned with generous gifts of sweets and off he went full of goodwill... until he broke out again! But in spite of all, the School had no more staunch supporter in the Town than the River Pilot. And, after all, boys can be trying! So, St. Mary's prospered. There was a fine spirit amongst the boys. They left with happy memories and were proud of their School.

'The initial success of the Society's land scheme owed much to the Gravesend boys. In the War too they had a fine record, many of them becoming non-commissioned and commissioned officers and winning distinctions. Some, alas, did not return.'

Sister Bernard writes: 'On 25th March, 1926, St. Marys Boys' School, Gravesend, opened with Holy Mass, offered by Rev. Father Crea, now Monsignor. Two Sisters of Charity were present. The Sisters of Mercy with some of their pupils attended, and sang hymns. Later the same day, six Sisters arrived with between fifty and sixty boys from two to eleven years, from Mottingham House.

'During the week the Stations of the Cross were erected by Fr. Crea, who must have vivid recollections of amusing scenes during the Ceremony – solemn though it was.

'The boys were thrilled with the largeness of the place, and next day got busy throwing rubbish into some neighbours' gardens! The said neighbours were hostile to having a school of boys come to disturb the peace and harmony of the district.

'The House was beautifully fitted up but the grounds needed attention. A landscape gardener was employed, and under the direction of Rev. Father Pritchard, the place was soon transformed. A kitchen garden, greenhouses, hen runs, and piggeries were soon in order. The lawn in front of the House was beautifully laid out in flower beds and surrounded by flowering shrubs and herbaceous borders.

'After a month, boys were admitted from other Schools, Eltham, West Grinstead, Littlehampton, etc. until the numbers were 240 and the Sisters increased to twelve.

'In 1927 Mr. Roche came as House Master and instructed the boys in games – the football team was one of the best in Gravesend and rarely lost a match. Later on shortage of a teacher led to the appointment of Mr. Roche as teacher and he is still at his post.

'The boys' club in which the older boys were very interested was started. The prefect system was a special feature. The School was divided into "Houses" and prefects were responsible. They did their work well, and were a great help in maintaining the discipline of the School.

'The boys left at 14 years and were transferred to the Working Boys' Home, then at Clapham. It was custom to give the leavers a great send off by having a club party the night before. Club concerts were frequent, and a source of great amusement. A play shed, which was a great boon, was erected.

'Every year there was a Flag Day in the town in aid of St. Mary's and the people were most generous.

'The Dymchurch Holiday Camp was the event of the year, and was looked forward to with genuine delight. During the holiday various places of interest were visited.'

Mr. Roche writes: 'When Mr.Pocock, H.M.I., visited the School in the latter part of 1946 he remarked on the intelligence and all-round ability of some of the boys. I commented that it was a pity that they could not enter for scholarships. There and then he said that they were to sit and all the necessary arrangement were made.

'Since then twelve boys have taken Technical Scholarships and three boys have passed for the Grammar School.

'At the moment nine boys attend Gravesend County Technical College and two boys are at Blackheath Academy. In September 1949, arrangements were made for thirty boys to have woodwork lessons. In September 1950, the number was increased to between fifty and sixty. These are divided into three sections. One section attends on Monday morning, one on Monday afternoon and one on Thursday morning.

'Internal education will end in September 1951, when St. Mary's boys will attend the local Catholic School. The Managers are very grateful to Fr. McNally, P.P., for his co-operation and interest in this extension of his school. He has been a good friend always to St. Mary's.

'In the early 1930s there was a School Football league in Gravesend, but there was a rule forbidding Homes, Orphanages, etc. from taking part. Several times we applied unsuccessfully for permission to take part. We had to be content with any friendly games we could get. In April 1934, we staged our first big game with Alex James, then Captain of the Arsenal, as referee. Over 1,000 people who came to see Alex were soon remarking on the high standard of football. In our following games the attendance kept on increasing and within a season or two the rule forbidding Homes, etc. to compete in School Football was done away with and our lads got the chance of being selected for County and representative sides. We feel that we were instrumental in abolishing that rule.

'Since then we have consistently held a following of from two to four thousand, according to the state of the weather.

'Besides Alex James, Arthur Rowe (present Manager of Spurs), Bernard Joy, Ted Ditchburn, Dr. O'Flanagan and several other famous players refereed games for us and still take a keen interest in the team.

'BOXING: Before the war our standard was very high. Each season we consistently produced a few County and Divisional Champions. But our crowning success was the reaching of the final of Great Britain by Johnny Barzee. Johnny joined the American Army during the war and was killed in France.

'This year we again took up serious boxing and one boy won a County Championship. We have a very good side for next season and we hope to do really well.

'ATHLETICS: Before the war we had several boys who were up to County Standard particularly in the High Jump. We have some very useful runners and jumpers at the moment and given another year or two in age and a little more beef they should do very well.'

TWO BOYS' CONTRIBUTIONS

A TYPICAL DAY: 'A typical day during the summer. Our day begins when we get up at a quarter to eight in the morning. We then have breakfast and those who have a job to do, do it afterwards.

'We usually play football, cricket or rounders during the morning. Dinner is at 12.30. We always have a good variety of dinners during the week and there is no shortage of meat or other food.

'In the afternoon we are allowed to go where we like within reason. As many of the senior boys can swim, the swimming bath is usually the destination for most.

'"Tea or supper" as we call it, the last meal of the day is at 6 o'clock.

'After supper, and if the day has been too hot for football, we may go to the playing fields for a game. Otherwise we go to the playground for a game of something or other until we go for a bath and then bed at 8 o'clock. In bed we are allowed to read until 9.30, when we have to go to sleep (if we can).' — *D.W.*

SUMMER HOLIDAYS: 'During the summer holidays we can go out in the morning and afternoon. In the morning we had a game of cricket.

'On some afternoons we go out for a ramble to the warren. When we get to the warren we pick blackberries to bring home. We spend the afternoon there. We eat most of the blackberries on the way back. The rest go to make a pie. Other times we go fishing in the afternoon. There are two places for fishing, Tilbury and Chalk. Tilbury is on the other side of the River Thames. We go across in the ferry. We can go swimming too. We bring the fish to the aquariums in our grounds. Chalk is another good place for fishing. We spend many afternoons there.

'Another time we went to Shorne for the day. We have plenty of fun. Then we have lunch near the woods. We have a game which is very good.

'The other part of the summer holidays is spent at camp or in other words Dymchurch. We have fun on the beach and swimming. Sometimes we go fishing, or pay a visit to the fair. We like to go to Hythe for shopping and on the boats in the canal. We also saw the bones in the old church.

'About once a week we go on a trip to Hastings or St. Leonard's Bay or maybe Dover. In Hastings we have lunch on the beach, and go for a swim.' — *T.S.*

'The Society can never repay its debt to the Sisters of Charity who have exercised such a profound influence on each generation of boys. Achievement is not measured only in successful scholastic and athletic events. The shaping of character comes first and the inculcation of the Catholic Faith. Hence to the religious staff attaches the most important contribution. They have fully justified the confidence placed in them. Many local friends have supported the Sisters – the Doctors Outred (father and son) have been at the service of St. Mary's day and night and have helped in ways which go far beyond the sphere of medicine with extraordinary devotedness. The Tolhurst family never relinquished their interest from the day on which they initiated its purchase. Others there are too numerous to mention. No one will mind if we single out Mr. Harrison – a non-Catholic friend whose kindness to the children is well known in Gravesend.

'Dr. Healy (as Secretary of the Society) carried the School through the difficult days of evacuation and war and brought it back (against terrible odds) to St. Mary's. Sister Bernard, Sister Vincent, Sister Patricia, all served the School in their special and individual way. Now Sister Gerard is opening a new chapter of its history. Fr. Baker combines so many and such useful roles as Chaplain that we fear his promotion to a Parish. The celebration of Jubilees at Orpington last year and Gravesend this year indicates the stability of our work. Are these Homes becoming obsolescent in the light of new ideas? We believe that they have established traditions which must not be destroyed or lost. We believe also that there must be development in the character of their organisation. Large Schools can be broken up and rendered less impersonal by establishing "family groups". Thus St. Mary's and the Schools at Orpington may have reached a turning point in their history. Much thought and possibly heavy expenditure will be required. Already the introduction of adequate pocket money and the necessary contacts with the normal household have removed much of the institutional character of both. Education outside the Home has associated the boys with the community.

'All will wish St. Mary's a happy journey to its Golden Jubilee whatever may be the modifications of the future. No one will wish that its many good features should be imperilled.'

— Catholic Rescue Society Publication

RON'S STORY

Me as a child, July 16, 1933, the day I was taken to St. Mary's; age 16, eighteen months after leaving St. Mary's; and, in 2012 at age 85 with sons Mike (53, on left) and Andrew (51)

BY RONALD MULLIGAN

A VICTIM OF CIRCUMSTANCES

The "Roaring Twenties" and the "Hungry Thirties" were two very harsh decades for the poor in England. Ex-servicemen and women returned home after a brutal First War to a "promised" land fit for Heroes. How they were misled. Mass unemployment became the norm and good honest families were reduced to a level of poverty and despair. Men who had seen untold horror in the trenches and in the Arctic Convoys, survived with little or no help from their government. Many took to the bottle or sought comfort from their wife. This was an era of large families which just added to their hardship.

My two brothers, Stanley and Bernard and me (they were also in St. Mary's). Picture taken by my Dad on one of his visits to the school at Gravesend, Kent. Year unknown.

My father was such a victim. Seven children were born into our tiny two-room flat and number eight was on the way. Sadly, as was common in those days the baby died inside my mother and the result killed her too, at the age of 38 years. There was no help available in spite of appealing to the authorities. My father was forced to sign away the three youngest children into the care of The Catholic Rescue Children's Society. His rights to communicate or remove any of us until the age of fourteen years of age, were drawn up in a legal document and thus we were taken into the Children's Home in Gravesend, Kent. My dad tried to soften the blow by telling us we were going to the seaside, but we were taken instead to this very large forbidden building and given to care of the Sisters of Charity nuns. Thousands of children had been abandoned in this way, but thanks to a dedicated number of caring Christian organisations, we were taken in, clothed and fed and given a happy childhood.

St. Mary's, Parrock Road, Gravesend, Kent, was a Children's Home for boys. A large grey stone building, administered by The Southwark Catholic Rescue Society in London, was a home for about two hundred boys from the ages of two-years up to the age of fourteen, looked after by the team of The Sisters of Charity nuns. We were there for a variety of reasons. Many of the boys were orphans, but mostly it was because of difficulties within their families just unable to cope with the terrible economic times of the 1930s. But the reasons did not really matter to us. We were all in the same boat and we all learnt to cope with this new environment, whatever the circumstances, and we had a very large group of ready-made friends.

EVACUATION YEARS (1939-1943)

September 3, 1939. Who could ever forget that date? This was the day that World War 2 was declared. But on that Sunday morning the boys of St. Mary's Children's Home in Gravesend, Kent had other things on their minds. "EVACUATION". The entire school, all Two Hundred boys, eleven Nuns (Sisters of Charity) were being sent to the countryside for safety from the expected air raids. We had already been fitted with gas masks; we had heard the sound of an air raid siren alarm, and we had practiced forming groups to march to the Air Raid Shelter. The older boys had been helping Sister Josephine in the workroom to make a little "hessian haversack" for every boy to carry a change of clothes (all marked with our name) to their new homes. Labels had been made to identify each and every one of us, and tied to our coat and to our haversacks just in case we got lost.

I was only ten years old and had been in this Home since the day before my fourth birthday in 1933. But this was the day I came to LIFE! So, after our usual visit to the Chapel for Sunday Mass, our lightweight rucksacks on our back, gas masks over our shoulders (ready for the expected gas attack, which thankfully never came) we marched to the docks in crocodile fashion, singing our school song "St. Mary's Boys". Quite a few people lined the streets to wave us goodbye, and we sang even louder.

We arrived at Gravesend Dock and boarded the pleasure boat "Royal

Daffodil" and sailed down the Thames, and headed up the North Sea. At 11 o'clock (over the tannoy system), we heard the Prime Minister, Mr. Neville Chamberlain, announce that Great Britain had declared war on Germany. This momentous occasion was lost on us younger boys, as we tucked into sandwiches, cakes and drinks served out by volunteers accompanying us (to help with keeping any of the children from falling overboard). Quite a few of the boys were seasick but most of us just wallowed in these unexpected treats and made the most of the freebies!

We arrived at the Port of Lowestoft in the County of Suffolk. A quick headcount (nobody lost at sea), down the gangplank, and we were welcomed by another army of helpers. The sirens were blaring when we landed, and with our small rucksacks on our backs, we were lined up and taken to a disused cinema. All the seats has been taken out and a bedding of straw covered the floor. We slept on this, and we were fed by the good ladies of the town. I think we spent a couple of days there, and eventually we were issued with emergency rations and then we were bused into nearby Beccles. (As an aside, Lowestoft, far from being a safe place and being a Port, it was severely bombed during the war, and much destruction was caused.)

On arrival at Beccles Town Hall, we were paraded in front of the citizens of the town and nearby villages, where, like in an Egyptian Market, we were all scrutinized, poked and prodded, and eventually chosen to be billeted with these patriots. I was very small for my age and as usual, was left till the end of the bargain basement.

But then, a stroke of luck. A latecomer, Mrs. Dowding, arrived and took the last four of us boys, and two of the Nuns. We were shepherded outside to her chauffeur driven car, and we drove in style to her large stately home, known as Reddisham Hall Estate. A tied-cottage near the House was put at our disposal, and with the two Nuns, we became a happy little family; set up home there to a life of bliss. Every day Mrs. Dowding visited us with one of her gardeners, and she would bring a basket of vegetables, fruit, salads and other goodies from her large walled garden, and for a time, we lived like Kings.

After our spartan fare at Gravesend, food we never knew existed, became the norm. Mrs. Dowding's chaffeur, a Mr. Mean (a lovely man) would take us around the estate in the "shooting brake" just for a ride, and once a week we were allowed to have a real bath in the House. Waiting in the gun room until it was our turn. Pictures of "Big Game Safaris", Shark Fishing, and Holiday Cruises lined the walls. Fishing rods, guns, pistols, spears, etc. in cases all round the room. This was the life! Luxury indeed!

Each Sunday, the ballroom was converted into a chapel, and Mr. Mean (with two of us on board our "shooting brake") scoured the surrounding villages, St. Andrews, Ringsfield and Gillingham looking for St. Mary's boys so we could bring them to Mass. How we Lorded it over them as we picked them up. It was so easy to become a snob!

But all good things must come to an end and one day, for no apparent reason, we were sent away to another billet. A very sad time for me as I had become accustomed to that life of grandeur. I learnt later that the House served as a Military Hospital for the duration of the War, but I still feel miffed!

Anyway, what a comedown! Back to the Billeting Office, and with one other boy and my older brother Bernard, we landed up with a Mrs. Clarke in Gillingham. She had one son called Douglas, about the same age as us. He did not like us being there, and we in turn hated him. There was no piped water, and all water had to be pumped in by hand. We each had to pump one hundred pumps a day for our needs except of course (yes, you've guessed it) Douglas who crowed and smirked with delight at our efforts. The whole area was surrounded by celery fields, and to this day, the lovely smell of celery takes me back to my temporary home at Valley View, Kings Dam, Gillingham, Suffolk.

After a while, we were on the move again; this time to Wells-next-the-Sea, a fishing village in North Norfolk.

A new billet was with a Mrs. Doyle on the sea front. A strict little old lady, always wearing a long black dress, who frightened me just to look at her. There was no electric light, no gas, and water had to be taken from a communal pump outside. We had to take a candle to bed, and we boys saved up the matches, candle grease, and periodically would have glorious bonfire in our room. How we never set the house on fire, remains a mystery.

The primitive outside toilet was shared by the six of us and our neighbours, and every other night "the scavengers" came with horse and cart to empty out the buckets. Mrs. Doyle had real courage to take in and look after six of us boys, all under twelve years old. (What a heroine she was!)

But one night, her patience snapped. During the night, when one of us boys (not me, guv.) could not make it to the outside "loo" and left his "visiting card" in the kitchen sink. We were all punished, until the culprit owned up, and then, my brother Bernard (it wos 'im) and I were speedily dispatched back to the billeting officer with a black mark on our record.

My next home was in a combined fruit and vegetable shop. Mr. & Mrs. Tuffs, a really nice cuddly couple who already had a son and daughter, they became father and mother to me. I shared their second bedroom with Poppy (nineteen) and John (fourteen). This was my second taste of heaven; plenty of meat and plenty of fruit and veg. And lots of love from Mrs. Tuffs. They had a pony and trap for their deliveries, which they allowed me to harness and drive when we came to a quiet road. I became quite rich with the tips I got from grateful customers: tuppence here, threepence there, and I learned how to doff my cap and smile brightly (It worked too!). A glass of lemonade and a pat on the head. Absolute bliss, until I got my marching orders again. I never knew why (I was only eleven years old) so I had not knowingly blotted my copy book.

A very stern Mr. and Mrs. Crowe were waiting in the wings to take me in. They had one daughter, Phyllis. Their pet name for her was Girlie. She was twelve and I was eleven. Girlie was taller than me, and had a very superior manner and she knew just the right buttons to press to make me cry. I was reasonably happy here, but Friday Bath Nights were torture. The Nuns at Gravesend were prudish, and we all had to keep our nether regions covered at all times. Glimpse of flesh led to temptation! (And one of our oft repeated prayers was "Lead us not into temptation"). Thus exposure was forbidden. Even in the bath we had to wear our bathing gear, "clingy long shorts".

But of course, Mrs Crowe would have none of this. I had to strip naked and get into the tin bath in the one and only living room. Girlie sat in the corner of the room reading her comic, but kept peering over the top and smirking at me. Utter humiliation! Of course, I was packed off to bed straight away afterwards, so I couldn't do the same to her. Was there no justice in this world? I had to wait many, many years for a glimpse of the female flesh.

Mr. Crowe was a big man, who was an engineer at a firm near the Railway Station. Sometimes I would have to go there to take a message to him and he would describe all the intricacies of his job, which was to keep all the moving parts lubricated. So, with an oil can in one hand, and a piece of rag in the other, he would be scanning a large console deftly pumping a squirt of oil here, a blob of grease there, having a swig of his tea, and repeating the process "ad infinitum". How I admired his dexterity and also his patience in explaining the importance of his job.

But my admiration came to an abrupt end one day when he came home from work, slapped my face hard, grabbed me by the ear and propelled me outside into the road and marched me to his garage door. Somebody had chalked in large letter "Ronnie loves Girlie Crowe". A wet cloth was thrust into my hand, and I was made to wash away these offending words. All this, I might add, was accompanied by a tirade of abuse and more clumps round the ears until the door was clean. No supper for me that night, and the humiliation of smirking at me, rubbed salt into the wound. The galling part was I hadn't chalked these words on the door. I was only eleven years old, and I didn't even like the girl. From that day on, it was WAR, but the worst thing I ever did was kick her bike and poke out my tongue at her. That showed her!

The greatest benefit living with this couple, was that my friend Michael Bannister was billeted next door with a Mr. & Mrs. Powley. Mr. Powley was a train driver, working from Well Railway Station, and Saturday mornings he had to shunt the carriages and goods trucks ready for the following week's work. Michael and I were allowed to ride with him on the footplate and shovel coal, blow the whistle and help to push the engine turntable round. We both had a railway man's cap and we felt the real McCoy. Saturdays have never felt the same since, and Steam Trains have always held a fascination for me.

Our education suffered somewhat during this time as we had very few books and no writing desks or facilities. We met daily in an old cinema, and Sisters Vincent, Patricia, Augustine, Mary, Josephine, Cecilia and Veronica vainly tried to keep our young minds on the straight and narrow. An uphill task as there were so many distractions to be had and learning boring old sums, etc. was not on our list of priorities. I learned to ride an old bike during this time, and I suppose I began a love of cycling from that day which in later years, took me thousands of miles.

Amidst all these wonderful adventures Michael and I were having, fate was plotting to take us again from this El-Dorado. Again the powers that be were planning to get all the boys together under one roof. They (the Nuns) were losing control of our minds and souls, and it was necessary for us to be gathered under their religious umbrella.

So, we were on the move again. This time to Devon, glorious Devon. A certain Lord Clifford of Ugbrooke Park, Chudleigh, Devon, 250 miles away, was the very place to curb our sinful ways, and so another chapter was to unfold, and we packed our bags.

The good people of Wells-next-the-Sea brought us their charges to the railway station and waved us "Goodbye". Many, many tears were shed on both sides. Lots of these lovely people had grown to love us and they were genuinely sad that we were leaving them. The feelings were mutual and it was an unhappy time for us all. Our train took us to London, where evidence of the bombings were plain to see. Then, on to Paddington Station and onto a train to Exeter. Coaches met us there to take us on to our final destination.

UGBROOKE PARK – CHUDLEIGH

We arrived at Ugbrooke House late in the evening, and after some welcome grub, were shown to our dormitories. Next day we were let loose to explore this vast 400-year-old turreted building set in about 600 acres of parkland, owned by our new Landlord, Lord Clifford of Chudleigh. The family, who were Roman Catholic, had survived a few hundred years by devious means, and owned this lovely estate. The house was enormous; God knows how many rooms, and we were given the run of the place. Many of the rooms had been stripped of carpets and furniture, and had been converted into dormitories, classrooms, a refectory and playrooms.

Because of storage problems, many of the rooms still had their ancient oil paintings, large gilt mirrors and tapestries left hanging on the walls.

A beautiful winding staircase rose 20 to 30 ft from the stone-flagged Great Hall, leading up to the landing and first floor rooms. Its elegant polished banister rail was an open invitation to us high-spirited boys to slide down. Inevitably, one of the boys, Leslie Cobbet, fell over the rail on his way down, and was badly injured on the flagstone floor below. He was taken to hospital and I can't remember ever seeing him again. The banisters were roped around all the way down, and from that day, the staircase was out of bounds, and we were banished from using this staircase, and had to use the back stairs.

There were a couple of old retainers, Mr. & Mrs. Davey, living there, who I would think went grey overnight at the antics of these "Gravesend Boys" especially when one of the valuable oil paintings was used as a target practice for the lads' bows and arrows. Many years later I was asked by Lord Clifford when I visited Ugbrooke, 'was I the culprit?' 'Not me, Guv,' I said, 'but I know the boy who did it!' (No names mentioned, I hasten to add. Nobody likes a snitch.)

Soon, some of the old routine was established as we settled down. Enormous rooms overlooked the magnificent parkland (designed by renowned landscaper Capability Brown). Our dormitories were upstairs, and one of the dorms I was in, was the Library, in which there were thousands of books, floor to ceiling. Some of these books weighed a ton, and we handled them disgracefully. Mostly, they had been written in some long forgotten language, but some of them were quite revealing to young and inexperienced eyes, and naturally we all took an avid interest in them.

The door at the end of the dorm led through to the Private Chapel, and it was a breath-taking sight to gaze down on the Altar and its surrounds designed by Adams, hundreds of years before. There was an enormous Pipe Organ in the Loft, and each Sunday a Mass, attended by the locals, was celebrated. The Organ was the type that had to be pumped continuously, and our Boys were shanghaied for this task. Boring, boring. Many times the lads dozed off, pumping ceased, and the majestic sounds of the Organ faded into a pitiful wail. 'Pump, you beggar, pump,' called out Mrs. Mowksom (the organist) in a stage whisper, and eventually normal transmission was restored.

Classrooms and playrooms were downstairs. Our Headmaster, Mr. Roche, resumed where he left off in 1939, and once again the boys took up football, cricket, boxing, shinty and even gardening. How I loved that time there. Walking into Chudleigh, or Newton Abbot for swimming. Teignmouth. It was a paradise. Some times we were taken out to Bovey Tracey and Dartmoor to harvest the potato crop. Vast fields, in all weathers, the potatoes were turned over by great big cart horses pulling a "spinner". We learnt to admire and appreciate those lovely patient and docile creatures. Our reward for this backbreaking work? We were paid tuppence per day, which was paid into "our Bank for sweets and treats". Still, it was worth it just to miss classes.

Music played quite an important part of our lives. A very young looking Nun called Sister Teresa played the lovely old Grand Piano, and taught us songs (some of which I still remember). I think, as a twelve-year old, she was my first crush! And my very first experienced of unrequited love.

Of course, religion was very much on the curriculum, and the wonderful "in house" Chapel became our second home. During our stay there, the Lord Clifford, who lived in Kent, died, and his body was brought back to Ugbrooke to be buried in the vault under the Chapel. I was lucky to be chosen to lead the funeral procession, and I carried a large high cross. Another group of boys, acolytes, carried Incense Candlesticks and Holy Water.

The Clifford family followed us down the narrow passageways to the burial chamber sited down in the underground cellars. An eerie circular dungeon with spaces all round the walls, many occupied, but still quite a few vacant, square holes awaiting the next member of the family to shed this mortal coil. On a more cheerful note, I and the other boy acolytes were paid 2/6d for our efforts. Another fortune!

The parkland was full of deer and other game. Sometimes we were employed as beaters for shooting parties arranged for His Lordship. Once again, we were paid 2/6d for our services. One day, during school lesson, we could see a plume of smoke coming from the woods. A serious forest fire had broken out, and we all rushed down to the woods to help put out the flames. The sun, shining through a broken bottle in amongst the dry bracken had caused the blaze, though there were suspicions that "those vaccies from Lunnon" were to blame. Much damage had been done, but we were all thanked by 'Sir' for our bravery, and selflessly, giving up our lessons for the afternoon.

There were always Saturday trips to Chudleigh to spend some of our wealth. Jars of fish paste 2d – Oxo cubes 1d – bread 2d. We were always hungry, and those with money were popular. Trouble with the "Chudleigh Boys" was always a threat, and it always paid to go about in pairs. Once we played them at football, and I'm pleased to say we thrashed them. That learnt them!

Sports Days were always a big occasion. All the boys were divided into four Houses so competition was sharp. After all the athletic races, egg and spoon, thread the needle for "The Grannies", the climax of the day was "The Chariot Race". Three boys would link arms behind them, and two robust boys would bend down at their rear and hold on to their wrists. A rope would be tied to the arms of the two outside boys up front and used as reins. Lastly, a smaller boy (the jockey) would stand on the backs of the two bent over boys, holding the reins, and as one unit, would gallop down the 100 yards course to the ecstatic cheers of the rest of the boys, as this result often determined the total points of "Sports Day". A footnote to say, that on the last Sports day that I was at Ugbrook in 1943, me being "vertically disadvantaged" (a short arse) I was chosen (I was Captain, anyway) to be the jockey for our House Chariot. We managed to stay upright for the entire length of the course, and we came in first. No Olympic Winner could have been more proud! This was probably my only claim to fame for the next 68 years. (Well, ever, really).

The last few months of my time at St. Mary's was a particularly happy time. I became a prefect and was able to sleep in "The Four Poster Bed" in our form. Some of us had pet rabbits plus a vegetable plot. I grew radishes, carrots and lettuces and it was one of my favourite lessons. But there was a thief about, and our produce was mysteriously disappearing from our plots. Us prefects were secretly commissioned to climb a nearby tree and keep watch, but we were "sussed", but the pinching suddenly stopped and the produce from our plots were left to grow to fruition.

St. Mary's School was, for me, a wonderful experience. The Nuns, though distant, on the whole were very kind to us. They gave us a good basic education and kept us fed and healthy during the 1930s and early 1940s when life on the outside was certainly not a bed of roses. It had been home to me since I was four years old, and I learnt many valuable lessons like loyalty and esprit de corps. My love of sports was nurtured there, thanks to Mr. Roche and my love of music blossomed with Sister Cecilia. Even now, I can remember words of songs she taught in class and I think very fondly of her smiling face.

But now I was fourteen years old, and St. Mary's decided that they could live without me, and let me loose on the outside world. I was apprehensive of what was to come, and with a heavy heart, was fitted out with long trousers and a jacket, two shirts and a pullover. When dressed in my new gear (with label attached) I looked just like a Rumanian refugee.

I left Ugbrooke on the 5 November 1943 and went to live with my Dad in Wandsworth, SW18.

After the full life at Chudleigh with all the boys that I had grown up with, my life changed drastically, and I was very, very lonely in this new environment. Though I was with my Dad he was a stranger to me, and I spent many lonely hours whilst he was working in London. The days seemed endless. Brother Bernard was leading a very sociable life before he was called up for the Army.

So my life was put on HOLD until my Dad could find me a job. I was a very unhappy bunny…. But, there was light on the horizon, and on to the next four years (leading to my joining the Army), I became an apprentice engineer and started work on 2nd January 1944, and I began to learn some of the wicked ways of the world.

1943-1947 – FINDING MY FEET

Dad met me at Paddington Station (I didn't recognise him after so many years) and he whisked me away along the platform, down the steps and onto an underground train. This new experience, so noisy, and speedy terrified me and I was glad when, much later, we came up into the fresh air of Southfields, SW18.

Arriving at Dad's flat on that first evening, I was disappointed to see how tiny and spartan it seemed. Number 162 Heythorpe Street. A house that had been divided into two flats, with a Mr. & Mrs. Murphy living upstairs, and Dad living downstairs. Dad had fallen out with the Murphys years before, so there was a state of war all the time I lived there.

Our flat consisted of one bedroom, one sitting room (never used) and a scullery which served as our main living room. All cooking, eating, washing was done in this room. A single tap (only cold water) served all purposes, i.e. washing and washing up. We had no bathroom, but there was an outside toilet which regularly froze in the cold weather. No power points, and the doorless gas oven provided our heating. I had to share the double bed with Dad, and brother Bernard (who was about 17) had a single bed in the same room.

The first weekend was an eye-opener. We caught a bus to Wandsworth High Street to get the shopping. Long queues to buy our meagre rations; bomb damage everywhere. Home again for our lunch, from a large saucepan filled with sort of stew to which every day more vegetables or meat (when we could get it) was added. I don't think I ever saw the bottom of that saucepan! Then down the Pub, again.

Sunday morning Bernard (under duress) took me along to the local Catholic Church in Wimbledon Park and waited outside during the Service. He had become very anti- religious since leaving the School, probably because of the over-emphasis of that subject by the Nuns, all the time we were there.

Bernard was very good to me, sensing my bewilderment, but he was now working and had a very busy social life. He worked in a local factory which made, among other things, chocolate bars. Sweets were rationed, but he somehow managed to acquire his own supply and his private cupboard was like an Aladdin's cave. Once or twice a week he would open it up and I would drool at the sight of so many goodies, then he would donate some of the more mutilated ones to me. I never complained!

Dad took me out and about to start with at weekends, to see his old cronies, and most of the time I spent waiting, standing in the doorway of a pub with a packet of crisps and glass of lemonade. Now and again, he would emerge from the bar with a pal, who would look me over, and disappear back into the smoky Public Bar. Then, near closing time, he'd come out of the pub, more crisps, and then like a racehorse, would gallop along to another pub where the whole process would begin again. He took me to meet his brother (Uncle Joe and Aunt Mimi) who lived nearby. They had no children of their own, and had wanted to take me in when my Mum had died ten years before. All my five brothers had had the chance to be taken in by well-meaning family members, but because of religious reasons Dad declined all offers and he decided that Stanley, Bernard and I should be brought up in a Catholic Children's Home.

Joe and Mimi were a lovely couple, who really did try to help me to settle. They too had a tiny flat, but they welcomed me every Friday to have a bath in their one and only room. Mimi would put out their tin bath, and laboriously fill saucepans and kettles, which, then after my ablutions, we would bale out the water and pour it down the sink. This went on for a year or so, until I discovered the Public Slipper Baths in the High Street. Only 3d a time, but worth it for a towel, soap and an abundance of hot water. Well worth the long wait.

Monday morning Dad would travel up to his work in Covent Gardens, and get back about 6pm. He would unload his pockets and bag which contained carrots, parsnips, potatoes and mouldy old fruit. These were cooked and added to our stockpot. The days were long, having nothing to do all day and knowing nobody around. I was very lonely and yearned to be back at St. Mary's. I had been ten years at the School, and I had never felt lonely before.

So for the eight weeks up till Christmas, other than Mimi and Joe, I hardly met a soul until Dad or Bernard came home from work. Having said that, my brother Arthur came home on leave from the Navy. I didn't really know him as I had not seen him since I went into the Home and then, I was only four years old. He made a real fuss of me, and cooked me lovely meals, or took me to a café for a meal. I came to idolize Arthur, but sadly he died quite young after having had a heart attack. He won the DSO whilst hunting submarines in the Atlantic, and he just loved being a sailor. He was married to Edna, and later had three children. He spent a lot of his leave taking me out and about. He lived in one of the first Prefab houses in Wandsworth which, at the time, were considered the last word in modern living, with a bath, inside toilets, a refrigerator, and built-in cupboards in the kitchen. Luxury at that time.

It was two or three years before I met the rest of my brothers, as and when they came home from the Forces. My only sister (who was the eldest of us all, whom I'd also never met) lived miles away in Haslemere, Surrey. Dad took me on the train to visit her. She had three children, lived in a tiny cottage. We got on really well and she made a great fuss of me, and from then on, regularly wrote to me. While all this was going on, Dad and Uncle Joe had decided that I ought to serve an apprenticeship and to learn a trade in Engineering. So, after a few interviews, they settled for me to have a five-year stint with a large local firm called SPV which made Milk Pasteurising Plants. I was too young at fourteen to start in the workshop, so the management kindly allowed me to start in their main office in Wandsworth SW18.

So, 1943 passed, and on the 2nd January 1944, I presented myself to Mr. Crosby, the Managing Director. He took me to an office along the corridor and introduced me to a Miss Fowles who was in charge of the Printing and Filing Room. In turn, she introduced me to the other two girls, Betty and Jean who were to be my instructors. They were about sixteen and seventeen, and I had to call them Miss Santos and Miss Phenns. I think I was really surplus to requirements, and so I became a general Dogsbody. I was very willing to do well, but was excessively shy and very naïve, and it amused them that I blushed a vivid red whenever they spoke to me.

The Draughtsmen, and the lady Tracers upstairs in the Drawing Office, took great delight in phoning our office and asking for a 2H pencil, or a couple of drawing pins, and I had to take the articles up to them in the D.O. I would clump down the long length of the room, vainly looking for the person, getting back to the Filing room, only for another body wanted some nibs or rubbers to be taken up. It was a long time before I realised they were "having me on."

Miss Fowles was extremely kind to me, as she recognised that I must have had an unusual upbringing. She used to invite me to her home to tea, and would take me on the bus to London to Lyons Corner House and to Museums; and in a way she became a sort of Mother figure. Though I never lost the embarrassment of blushing when spoken to, I enjoyed the work, especially getting a pay packet every Friday. 18/4d came my way each week, but I had to give Dad 10/-, bus fare 30d, and also pay for my lunches. Dad told me I had to buy my own clothes, so my economic situation never did improve and I was always broke. Purchasing of clothes was strictly rationed during the war years and Clothing Coupons were issued for this purpose. Since I couldn't use mine, I was very popular among the ladies as I dished them out to anybody who asked.

Before I left the school the Nuns at Ugbrooke had rigged me out with one shirt, one pair of pants, one pair of trousers, one jacket and one pair of shoes, and so my one set of clothes got shabbier and shabbier. Mr. Crosby would send me out on errands for him, to his home in Kingston-on-Thames. His wife always invited me in to their home, for biccies and lemonade and on one occasion, she gave me three silk shirts that once belonged to her son.

Frequently, Mr. Crosby sent me up to Bush House in London or to a photographic firm in Kingsway, giving me 2/6d for fares, etc, always making sure I gave him back the correct change. But one day, I succumbed to temptation and stopped in a café and had a cup of tea and a bun, total cost 3d. Later in the day the roof fell in as I was summoned to his office to explain where all the money had gone. I burst out crying as I thought I would be transported for this heinous crime, but I was let off if I promised to repay this large sum. As I didn't have any money at the time, I had to promise to repay the following payday, which I did, and he ostentatiously put the money into his Petty Cash box, carefully noting that the sum had been repaid.

'Don't do it again,' he warned me.

I slunk back to the office thoroughly ashamed of myself.

I gradually began to learn the system, mastered the printing machine, and even answered the telephone. (I was terrified of this gadget.) There were enormous filing cabinets which contained all the Technical Drawings that were ever made there, and we had to locate any that were required upstairs at the drop of a hat. Sometimes, a few of the younger members of the Drawing Office staff would go out together in groups, and one weekend invited me to join a Working Party at a derelict Youth Hostel near Leatherhead.

We helped repair the roof, dug out trenches for drains, and put up fences, and were responsible for the other bods who came to help. Normally a Warden supervised the domestic arrangement, but as the place was virually uninhabitable, we had to look after ourselves. Separate dormitories in the YHA were usually strictly observed, but it was no holds barred this weekend as everybody let their hair down. I had only been invited to make up the numbers on paper. I was only fourteen so I was really just a wallflower. But my innocence and purity were put to the test when one of the young ladies approached me, and I could only manage, 'Good Night, Miss Anderson.' I don't think she ever forgave me!

June 1944, World War Two was still raging, and on the 6th of that month, English troops and its Allies landed in Normandy. D-Day.... Still a long way to go, but the beginning of the end!

My fifteenth birthday on 17th July 1944, Mr. Crosy sent me to another office over the Road. This was the Planning Office, which was to be my home for the next twelve months. The man in charge, a Mr. Browne (spelt with an E) gave me a Drawing Board, Tee Square, pencils, etc., but I didn't have a clue what I was supposed to do. He treated me as though I was useless (which of course I was) and I didn't draw a thing the whole time I was there. I just sat doodling or practiced printing, or running errands, so really it was a waste of everybody's time.

There was a very nice young girl in our office, called Pam. She was only sixteen, and would always wait for me to cycle back home after work. Her elderly parents would be at their garden gate waiting for her, and I got to know them quite well. One day, she had to get home early, and left without me. Sadly, as she crossed over Wandsworth High Street, a Fire Engine, answering an emergency call, jumped the lights, knocked her off her bike and killed her. I arrived at the scene just minutes after the crash to see her lying in the road and the fire engine buried in a shop window. Such a tragic and unnecessary loss of the life of a young beautiful girl. I really did miss her very much, and life in that office was never the same again.

Every Tuesday I had to attend lessons held in the firm's clubrooms nearby in Wandsworth High Street. Surprise, surprise! I was considered quite a bright pupil and passed all the tests ever given to me. I was lucky, as many of my classmates had had little schooling because of the war. St. Mary's at least had taught me the rudiments of the three Rs. And so in "The Land of the Blind, the One-Eyed Man was King"! I passed the RSA exam, and so they sent me on to Wandsworth Tech. Bad move. I floundered from start to finish. I just could not grasp these new-fangled "Laws of Acceleration", "Hookes Law" and the "Laws of Resistance". It was all Greek to me. My exam results were atrocious, and so they sent me back for another try. I did improve slightly. Many years later I developed a real love for these subjects but, sadly, it was too late for my exams then.

At home, I had found a wreck of a bike in Dad's shed, and I decided to have a go at getting it going. Though I knew nothing about the mechanics, I soon had it on the road. Really it was a death trap, with only one brake, no mudguards, and the chain kept coming off. There was a bike shop in our road, but in those days there was a shortage of just about everything, and it was a triumph if the shopkeeper would let you have just one cotter pin instead of two. Getting a chain link or a bicycle bell would depend on how politely you asked.

'Don't you know there's a war on?' was the reply, if you dared ask for a pair of brake blocks as well!

But at last, it was ready to go, and it saved me about 18d a week in bus fares; and but more importantly, introduced me to the world of cycling, which changed my life completely.

As I had now been at the firm for over a year I was given a week's holiday, so I decided to revisit Wells-next-the-Sea on my bike. Wells was 150 miles from London, so I joined the Youth Hostel Association, which would entitle me to stay at very basic lodgings anywhere in England. The journey was to be done in two stages, the first leg, through the East End of London, up through Essex and onto Stowmarket in Suffolk, which was 100 miles away. The next day would be on to Wells, Norfolk, a further fifty miles. So I booked to stay in Stowmarket, and set forth at 6 am. I had all sorts of trouble cycling through Whitechapel because of the cobbled streets and the tramlines, and my luggage kept falling off the back of the bike but, eventually, it got me to my destination. I had one puncture, and since I had no puncture outfit or pump, I had to push the bike the last eight miles into Hadleigh in Essex. There a good Samaritan (on a bike) recognized my plight and gave me his home address with a message to his wife to "look after my problem". Her motherly instinct came to the fore when she saw this dishevelled figure at her door, and learning I had just cycled from London, made me sit down and eat two bowls of rice. She then noticed my torn trousers (yes, still the same ones), made me take them off and she repaired them for me. I told her all about the constant air raids and how we had to spend a lot of our time in the air raid shelters. She then helped me mend my flat tyre and sent me on my way, waving to me till I was out of sight. What a kind lady she was.

No more mishaps, and I arrived at Stowmarket, and stayed with a Mr. & Mrs. Hose, who were the Wardens. They lent me a pump, which I returned later in the week on my journey home. One had to pay the 3/9d per night (bed, breakfast and evening meal) in advance in those days, so at least I was all paid up. Jolly good grub it was too!

Next day, only fifty miles to go, and I pedalled with renewed vigour and reached Wells in good time. I had written to Mrs. Crowe, inviting myself, but I am not really sure she wanted me back. I had absolutely no money to pay for my keep, but I promised to send a contribution later. (I travelled all that way without a penny in my pocket.) It was really lovely going round to see all my old friends, and I had achieved my ambition. So, after a week there, I cycled back to Stowmarket. Mr. & Mrs. Hose were pleased to see me again, and I gratefully returned their bicycle pump. The next day, after an enormous breakfast, I cycled back to London without mishap and arrived back home with 300 miles on my clock. Not bad for a first time trip.

So back home in Heythorpe Street, life continued as before. Dad couldn't believe my adventurous spirit and he saw less and less of me as my bike took over my life.

Meanwhile, Dad had a letter from the War Office to report that

Bernard was missing in action. Luckily, it was a mistake and he eventually came home after the war, a very changed man.

When I had settled back into the old routine, I decided to join the Sea Cadets. I was kitted out with a uniform, and learnt all the knots, Semaphore and Morse Code. They asked me to join the Band and gave me a bugle, urging me to practice daily as a big parade had been planned.

Looking back, I must have been Mrs. Murphy's (upstairs) worst nightmare as I blithely and discordantly played "The Last Post", "Sunset" and "Come to the Cookhouse Door". Learning to row on the Thames near Putney Bridge in a Naval Whaler every Saturday afternoon was one of the highlights, especially when Fulham Football Club was playing at home as their ground backed onto the river and we were subject to many ribald remarks as we passed by. Joining the Cadets had opened up a new world for me and I made some very good friends.

Fancying my chances, I even volunteered to enter the London Boxing Championships which were to be held at Regent Street Polytechnic. A famous actor and comedian at the time, Will Hay, refereed my first match, but unfortunately, he couldn't stand the sight of blood (my blood – I had a nose bleed) and he stopped the bout in the second round. Being a glutton for punishment, I tried again next year. I lasted nearly three rounds, but once again, my sensitive conk let me down!

I volunteered to go on a Training Course to Portsmouth, and spent a hectic week on a ship HMS *Foudroyant* out in the harbour. This was one of the last wooden sailing ships. They used it for target practice soon after I left, and sunk it. I really enjoyed all the activities, which included a visit to "Whale Island Gunnery School", where I learnt to fire all sorts of weapons (never hitting a thing). The week ended with a visit to HMS *Victory* located in Portsmouth Harbour, where a broadcasted service was held to commemorate Trafalgar Day. Very moving as we all sung "For Those in Peril on the Sea".

1945, and I was nearing my sixteenth birthday. My Aunt Mimi and Uncle Joe decided to take me to Wimbledon Theatre to see "Die Fledermaus". On the big day, I discovered that they had also invited their next door neighbour and her daughter along as well. Jean was sixteen, and for me it was love at first sight. For the next twelve months we went everywhere together. Up to London to watch "The Victory Parade", to theatres (up in the Gods, 1/-), cycling, etc. We were like Romeo and Juliet. Life was good, that was until her father came home after being abroad in the Army for six years. He had left England in 1940, leaving his ten-year-old baby, and now she was being courted by this sixteen-year-old spotty face lout. By fair means and foul, he put a stop to our going out, and she gave me the "elbow". A big black cloud enveloped me, and I mooched about like a perfect misery. I decided to end it all, and dreamed up all the different ways of achieving my aim. There was a steep hill coming down from Wimbledon Common, and I sadly pushed my bike to the top with the intention of racing down and crashing into a tree. It was a Friday evening and as I mounted my bike for its final run, I suddenly realised that tomorrow was Payday – Saturday morning. Too good to miss as I had recently been given a raise, so, with nobody looking, I coasted down the hill, applied the brakes and stopped and lashed out 3d at the chip shop. Lovely chips. Life was worth living after all!

Two of my Sea Cadet friends, Frankie and Johnnie, and I, decided to go on a tour of the Wye Valley on our bikes. We stayed at Youth Hostels and had a fabulous time. Johnnie took his ukelele, and wherever we went we would have a sing-song. We must have cycled about three hundred miles that week, and enjoyed every minute. Oh! The simple pleasures of life!

Later that year, Frankie and I went on an Agriculture Working Holiday in Suffolk. Because so many farm workers were still in the Army, the government organised volunteers to spend a "holiday" bringing in the harvest. We had to pay 28/- a week for our keep, and we were paid 1/- per hour for our labour. The accommodation, strictly separated, was in Bell tents and it was said they blew a bugle at 6 am to remind the campers to get back to their own tents. During the time we were there, they announced the end of the war in Japan.

Much earlier, before our breakup, Jean had had a girlfriend called Eileen. We introduced her to my friend Frankie to make up a foursome. They got on well together; in fact too well, and suddenly, at sixteen, she became pregnant. Panic stations, as in those days, in that situation they had to get married. He had to give up his apprenticeship, and trained to be a Prison Officer just to earn extra money. I used to visit them in their tiny flat in Balham, and later when I joined the Army, used to take them food to help them out. It was a sad situation, which just could not last, and sadly it ended badly when they decided to split up.

By now, I had started my apprenticeship in earnest in the main workshops. Mr. Wilson, foreman in the Machine Shop, took me under his wing and put me on a Capstan Lathe. I soon mastered the easy tasks he gave me, and quite enjoyed the work, though it was very repetitive. Looking back, the machine shop was very Dickensian, with overhead leather belts driving the machines. There were about forty men working in this department all on "piecework" so there wasn't much training, or help forthcoming, as they didn't have the time. But like all groups, they soon spotted a gullible naïve rookie. Being sent to the Stores for a "long weight" or a "candlewick" rubber spanners, or to the Manager for "the Apprentice's Free Tea Tickets" created smirks all round especially when the foreman discovered that I'd been missing sometimes for an hour or more....

One day a week I'd go to Wandsworth Tech. to learn Maths, Technical Drawing and Engineering Science. Each subject was complete Greek to my brain, and I struggled from Day One. I must have been a late developer, as in later years I became quite a whiz kid on these subjects. But at that time, I was quite miserable as I just could not cope with these subjects however hard I tried. The exams at the end of the year were a disaster and the Works Manager decided I should go to night school as well. I think I improved a bit, but really, I needed a private tutor, or at least, a brain transplant.

Still nursing a broken heart, I cast around and decided to join a local YHA Group. This was my salvation in a way, as their activities included cycling, walking and many social activities. I met up with some lovely characters and did midnight rambles over Box Hill and Wimbledon Common, besides going on working parties to Chalden, Tanners Hatch and High Halden. One Bank Holiday weekend, four of our group Tom, Jack, Johnnie and me, cycled down to the Isle of Wight, starting out at 8 o'clock on the Friday evening, and kept going most of the night.

We stopped at a Fun Fair in Guildford, had a ride on a very speedy roundabout (Tom was sick, and the rest of us couldn't stop laughing). We managed to persuade him back on his bike, and we continued our journey. (I think Tom just wanted to lie in the field and die.) Later he became my brother-in-law. He had borrowed a thermos flask (a rarity in those days). Tea, to be enjoyed at precisely one o'clock in the morning. Finding a small road menders hut by the side of the road we winkled our way in, and were really looking forward to this forthcoming treat. Unfortunately, Jack knocked it off the bench in his haste to get in, and the flask shattered into a thousand pieces. Jack, who had a weird sense of humour, was highly amused at Tom's rage, and what with him still feeling unwell, was not a happy bunny, and I don't think he smiled the rest of our trip.

Our YHA group, consisting of about ten lads and girls of about sixteen, seventeen, eighteen, went out and about all over the county. We frequently volunteered for working parties repairing some of the older Hostels. There was a YHA Farm at High Halden, Surrey, where we would spend long weekends out in the open air working the fields. I was introduced to the joys of camping down at Cobham where we observed all the niceties like digging out toilet facilities (male and female), a group kitchen, and tents with strict lines for Male and Female. How innocent we were in those days. Lord Baden Powell (Chief Scout) would have been proud of us.

Thursday evenings were always special, as we would take turns to meet up at each other's houses and play records and have sing-songs. Gone, gone are the halcyon days of our youth.

Meanwhile at work, as I was nearing seventeen in 1946, it was time for a move. I was sent to work in the Maintenance Department. My first stint was with the Electrician called Jack. I became his mate, carrying his steps, test lamp, and a coil of cable, around. It was our job to make sure to keep all the machinery going, mend fuses, repair electric cables, and if necessary, wire in new machinery. Jack was a man with a lovely sense of humour, and nothing would hurry him, and he would talk incessantly about his garden. I think I learnt more about flowers during those months, far more than about electricity. He was a very popular man, and whichever department we called in, there would be always a cup of tea waiting for us. Sadly, he developed Parkinsons Disease quite early, and had to take early retirement.

After six months with Jack, they moved me into the mechanical side of the Maintenance Dept. A Bob Yeaxly became my mentor; a totally different character to Jack. I trundled round the factory as before carrying ladders, crowbars, sledgehammers. (Anything to make us look important. Never go round empty-handed was his motto). Our main job was moving heavy machinery, repairing broken down equipment and generally keeping the factory running smoothly. I learnt the importance of giving every job a "severe looking at" before make any rash decisions (like make a start). This was the First Principle of the Maintenance Department.

Still attending Night School, and Wandsworth Tech. on a Tuesday, I could not take in the mysteries of Maths and Engineering Science, and as I was having difficulties at home, I agreed to be conscripted to do my National Service. I had itchy feet, and had visions of travelling the world. The world was to be my oyster, and I avidly studied the Atlas.

So, on 18th September 1947, I joined the Army. The authorities sent me to Invicta Lines in Maidstone, Kent where I met up with about 100 other rookies. We were kitted out in khaki uniforms, given rifles, and for the next six weeks, our feet didn't touch the ground. We rushed about like whirly dervishes as the sergeants tried to mould us into potential fighting machines!

'God help the British Empire,' was his more quotable remark!

Footnote: After our Primary Training, the Army decided they needed me close to hand in England, so they sent me to Brize Norton, a RAF Station in Oxfordshire. I languished there for the next two years in a REME workshop attached to the RAF helping to make things for the speedy discharge of freight from their planes.

So much for having itchy feet!!

TALES OF A LAUNDRY BOY

BY JOHN MICHAEL MURRAY

EARLY MEMORIES... AUGUST 1943–OCTOBER 1950

I was born on 5th August 1943 in Farnborough Hospital, Kent and baptised in the Roman Catholic Church of St. Mary of the Angels in Liverpool on 21st August 1943.

How or why, in the space of sixteen days I moved from Kent to Liverpool I do not know.

My parents were Margaret Joan Veronica Murray, a Bank Clerk for Williams and Glynns Bank in the City of London and George Hotzon, a serving Canadian soldier. I do not have any good memories of my father; neither do I have any bad ones. He came for the war, when it was over he left. I met him once in the mid-nineteen sixties; he married my mother, took her money and returned to Canada. He had the appearance of a member of the Mafia.

My mother, at the time of my birth was married to Norman Murray, a photographer serving in the Royal Air Force. They married very young and were probably caught up in the madness of the time that affected so many. They were separated while he served away; she carried on working in the City. During the week she stayed at Osterley Park, North London with other bank staff, going home to her mother's house in Bromley at the weekends. She told me of the good times she had in London when she met up with her brothers, Johnny and Dickie, when they were on leave from The Royal Signals. Her elder sister, Eileen, was in the ATS in Nottingham so they did not meet very often.

In the house in Bromley lived my grandmother, Edith Maud King and her daughters Cis and Maureen as well as my mother at weekends.

What I know of those times is as told to me by both my mother and Cis, my aunty. Before my mother died we had long conversations about this time of her life. She could not understand her mother's apparent hatred of her and her siblings; a hatred I was to witness first hand when I finally went home to live.

My grandmother was fond of drink and often spent time in the Crooked Billet pub on Southborough Lane. Nearby was a detachment of the Canadian Army who also spent time there. Liaisons were formed and parties often followed back at the house. My grandmother was not backward at pushing her newfound friends in the direction of her daughters. Cis told me of the many occasions when she had to lock herself and Maureen in the bedroom to resist the advances of the drink-laden soldiers.

My mother would come home to this and was not exempt from the advances, even though she was married. Because she resisted she was "stuck up" according to my grandmother, who even went to visit Norman's parents and told them what a "loose woman" she was, in an attempt to end the marriage.

The situation became so bad that Cis took Maureen away and lived in lodgings. Mother was now alone with my grandmother and her

THE BOYS OF ST. MARY'S   127

friends, one of whom was George Hotzon who my grandmother intended that he and my mother should become "friends". My mother refused, angering my grandmother who promptly informed Norman's parents she was having an affair; this had the desired effect. Norman and my mother separated on a trial basis.

George and my grandmother were often waiting at Bickley Station for my mother when she came home at weekends.

The inevitable happed, and I was the result. A few years later, my grandmother the worse for drink referred to me as "a bastard who was conceived on Bickley Station". Norman was informed of the situation, he offered to continue the marriage if I was adopted, my mother refused and divorce eventually followed.

George and my mother continued their relationship, my brother Brian coming along in April 1945. The war ended, my father returned to Canada leaving my mother with two children and the promises of a new life to come. It never happened.

It did not take my mother long to grasp the gravity of the situation, two children, no husband, no job, no money.

She went to work scrubbing floors, paying a child minder 18/- per week to look after us children. This did not work as my mother found that we were not being well looked after. Often when she came to collect us we had soiled our pants and had not been fed. She ended the arrangement. In desperation she contacted the Catholic Church.

Her local Parish Priest, a Father Scarborough, who was by all accounts a kindly and caring person, took up her case. I think my mother was expecting some form of financial help from the Church; instead he contacted the social services of the time. He convinced my mother that the best interest and well being of both my brother and myself would be met if we were placed in a church-run home. She refused. Father Scarborough was persistent.

In January 1946 he wrote to the Southwark Catholic Rescue Society (SCRS) requesting assistance, stating, 'she had no means of support but if her two children could be accommodated in a home under their care, she would be able to go out to work and support herself and her two children. She is living at home with her mother, three sisters, a brother and her own two children.' The Society was unable to help at this stage. My mother was advised, 'as she was destitute she should approach the Relieving Officer of the Public Assistance Authority to see if a home could be found for her two children.' This she was reluctant to do as her mother had previously approached them without success. (My grandmother had approached them without my mother's knowledge or permission to have my brother and I housed in one of their homes).

Mother was now advised she could contact the Canadian Military Headquarters (CMHQ) in London and through them seek financial assistance from the father. This was done; the reply coming back was 'This man (George Hotzon) is not in a position to provide any financial assistance and the CMHQ could not divulge any information regarding the life, conduct, etc. of George Hotzon, the matter is now in the hands of the Society for National Defence.' They advised my mother 'not to take any further action until she heard from them and that if she was in need of immediate financial assistance she should approach the District Administrator of the Canadian Overseas Children's Fund.' Eventually she heard from them but the answer was negative. (Whatever happened to "Suffer the little children to come unto me?")

My mother had by now found a job as a cleaner in an Opticians in Bromley. While she worked in the evening, my brother and I were looked after by a child minder, my mother paying 18/6d per week which was half her weekly wage.

On 9th July 1946 my mother signed an agreement with the SCRS handing me over into their care in exchange for a fee of 15/- per week. On 28th October she was informed, 'John Murray is right on the top of the waiting list at three homes.'

On 17 November 1946 my mother was told that a place had been found for me at St. Anne's convent, Landsdowne Road, Brighton, an orphanage predominately for girls.

My brother stayed with my mother who continued working at the Opticians. She became a receptionist then studied, took exams and became a qualified Optician. She remained there for 30 years and eventually became the manager.

Your birth certificate is a record of when you began your life in this world. Your first memory is your record of the start of that life and with it the people and circumstances that influenced how that life would be led and the person you would become.

State and Church combined to begin my life with a walk up a gravelled drive, holding my mother's hand.

The former St. Anne's Children's Home

I do not have many memories of my time at St. Anne's but I remember quite vividly the day I was taken there. It was a bright day and I was excited at the journey on the train from London. We walked from the station and up the long drive to the convent.

A nun from the Poor Servants of the Mother of God met us; she exchanged words with my mother, who kissed me goodbye, then was ushered out of the door.

I remember there being two big statues of the Virgin Mary and the Sacred Heart in the hall. The nun took my hand and we climbed a long staircase to a room where other nuns were gathered. That night I cried myself to sleep; in the morning I had red marks on my cheeks.

I have often thought of that day and conclude that the nuns had a well-rehearsed routine for dealing with what must have been a very traumatic experience, a mother giving away her child. My mother told me how she cried all the way back home and for many a day afterward.

I was now an orphan in the care of the Catholic Church who would feed me, clothe me, and house me. I would be moulded, punished, but never loved, all for the contractual fee of 15/- per week. And so I remained for ten years, years in which the memories I have that define me, good and bad, were formed. That is when I, John Michael Murray, aged three on 17th November 1946, began my life.

TEN YEARS AN ORPHAN. THE BEGINNING

It is strange how things remain in your memory, but thank goodness they do. I recall my first Christmas at St. Anne's. How or why I was there I do not know, but I was locked in a cupboard. I could hear the other children singing and to this day when I hear the Glor-or-or-or-or-or-or-ia of the carol *Ding Dong Merrily on High* I am taken back there. Eventually somebody heard me and let me out. In a big room all the other children were seated round the wall, piled on a table in the middle were presents. Nuns were calling out names and the children collected their presents. I did not get one!

Like all young children of the time I had nits and had to suffer the "cure" administered by the older girls. The black Derbac soap was washed into the hair followed by the hunt for nits with a metal comb. Some of the girls were quite gentle and probably grew into caring mothers or nurses, others were harsh and became "Camp Commandants". It stung the eyes like hell!

On sunny days we were taken to the beach, sitting in a group between the Palace and West piers. The beach was stony and fine pieces of pebbles got into my homemade swimming trunks (a brown denim-like material) making my bottom very sore. Vaseline was later rubbed on to ease the soreness, as was Calamine lotion dabbed on my sunburn. (No factor 15 in those days.)

On one of the trips to the beach I saw my first banana. A family were sat behind us having a picnic. The mother took out a banana; I just stared and stared and stared. I must have embarrassed her, which was not my intention. She got up and gave me the banana. One of the nuns saw this and intervened, refusing to accept the kind gesture. I was told off and had to wait for my first taste of a banana.

I started my schooling at St. Mary Magdalen's Infants School which if my memory serves me well, was not too far from the orphanage. I can recall early lessons in reading and writing. I was not too bad at the start as some of the girls at St. Anne's used to teach us. Every afternoon we had to put our head on the desk and go to sleep.

I stayed at St. Anne's until I was seven. The Mother Superior wrote to my mother stating: 'She was rather upset that I was too old now to be with her and that she cannot keep me much longer.'

(Was she afraid for the girl's safety?) (They usually did not keep boys past 5 years of age.) My mother contacted SCRS and a place was found for me at St. Mary's, Parrock Road, Gravesend, Kent. On 6th October 1950 I left Brighton and started a new life in Gravesend.

OCTOBER 1950 – SEPTEMBER AGED 7 TO 11

As a seven year old everything looks big. I can still remember my first view of St. Mary's, how big it was, the ivy and the big front door. For the second time in my young life I was handed over to a nun; this time she had a huge butterfly on her head. A few words were exchanged and my mother left.

I spent my early days in the playroom near the toilets, adjacent to the "shed". Here I did all the things six and seven year olds did. I played, I looked at picture books, and I did as I was told. I think women rather than nuns looked after us at this age but I can't recall who they were. I was just at the tail end of being educated "in house".

I must have been about eight when I was moved to another playroom. This one was at the end of a corridor next to the "boot room". It was here with other boys of the same age, I was looked after by Miss Mary and Miss Martha. I think they were novice nuns. They were Irish, sometimes kind, sometimes not.

They were not averse to giving us a slap, with hand or stick. In their kinder moments we would sit round in a circle and they would read to us from the weekly comics. The Hotspur and The Wizard are two I remember. I looked forward to the weekly instalments of the serials; my favourite was "Wilson, tough of the track".

It must have been about this time that music came into my life. A nun, I believe her name was Sister Alphonsus, decided I could sing. In the playroom was a piano where she sat and made me practice the scales. Aaaah, aaaah, aaaah, aaaah, aaaah, aaaah, aah, over and over again. At first she was quite kind, but as time passed she became very strict, for every wrong note I sang my bare legs suffered.

She started to teach me the piano as well. Again for every wrong note my knuckles suffered a whack from a ruler she held up her sleeve. (Throughout my time at St. Mary's I lost count of the number of sticks, etc. held up the nun's sleeves.) I was told to 'project my voice to the back of the room.' While the other boys were playing I was taken to the chapel, up into the choir, to practice singing the "Ave Maria" and the "Adeste Fidelis", both in Latin, so I didn't have a clue what I was singing. One day she took me on the bus to St. John's Church in Gravesend. It was huge compared to the chapel I was used to. The choir was at the back up some winding stairs. Sister Alphonsus played the organ. I had to sing. I remember looking down on the church and feeling frightened being so high up. There was a priest and two nuns looking at me. They were Sisters of Mercy from the nearby infants school.

In hindsight I suppose that was an audition. I'll never know, for soon after the singing lessons stopped and Sister Alphonsus was not seen again. Perhaps she died, she was quite old, or perhaps she was moved on. It was not the end of my singing career though; I seemed to be earmarked to forever sing in choirs, but more on that later.

I made my First Communion about this time. There were weeks of practice learning about taking communion and making my first confession. As a seven year old, what did I have to confess? We were dressed nice and smart and sat in the front row of the Chapel; children from outside were there as well, including girls in pretty dresses and ribbons in their hair. The highlight for me was not the feeling of being "full of grace" but the fried egg we had for our special breakfast. I think that was the first time I had a fried egg. What a treat!

At this age we ate our meals in a refectory at the other end of the building. I can remember being given something to drink about once a week that was absolutely horrible. I think it might have been Epsom Salts. When the nun wasn't looking we tipped it out the window or used slices of bread to soak it up like blotting paper.

Can anyone remember the horrible beans we were given to eat and the little ditty: "Beans, beans good for the heart, the more you eat the more you fart"? Some things you never forget.

It was here that we had our birthday party. All the boys who had a birthday in the month were given a little party. I think we were allowed a guest. We had jelly, ice cream and cake. I had my first fish paste sandwich on such an occasion. I have not had one since.

At this age we were introduced to "borstal walks". We were all ushered out of St. Mary's and told to walk with a nun in charge. I can remember going to the waterfront quite often. I used to love seeing all the ships and can still remember the Hospital Ship permanently moored in the Thames. There was one funny occasion when it rained quite heavily and the nun's butterfly hat got wet and began to flop. A kindly woman took the nun in; we stood in the rain getting wet. When we were older Father Baker took charge of the walks and we used to go to the aerodrome or Robin Hood's tree.

The year 1951 was the 25th Anniversary of boys being at St. Mary's. The school was thrown open to the public for the afternoon and many of the boys were given the task of showing these good people around the premises. I was one of them. I took charge of a man and a woman with their young son and daughter and showed them our magnificent accommodation. I wasn't quite eight at the time so I had yet to develop my best travel agent patter, but I think they enjoyed it. They gave me a shilling for my effort.

I took them to the laundry where I worked. They were shocked; apparently, I was not supposed to take them there.

A performance was put on for our guests on the lawn in front of the building. The group of boys I was with sang "The Teddy Bears Picnic", in our grey shorts, white shirt, blue tie and brown sandals; our posh uniform. The grand finale of the day was a gymnastic display by Mr. Smith and the "big boys". It impressed me though I had no wish to emulate them.

When you are this young you have daft thoughts and ideas. On one such occasion myself and another boy whose name I cannot recall, decided we would climb up the ivy growing on the wall and get in through a bathroom window at the top. We noticed a window was opened so we checked no one was around and were about to begin our quest when we heard a sound. We looked up; a nun had closed the window. I am not sure whether we were relieved or not but I never had the urge to try it again.

SCHOOLING

In September 1951 we started to go to St. John's for our schooling. The infants school was in the town so we had to walk there and back every day. I cannot recall any supervision; we just walked, a scruffy bunch of boys in our short trousers and black boots. En route we passed a lane at the back of some houses call Love Lane; we called it Dog Dirt Lane for obvious reasons. It led to the barracks.

At school we came in contact with "normal children" and girls. Most of them were nice towards us but some were not. One particular girl, Mona Freeman, was very snobby; her mother often helped out at St. Mary's. Whatever happened to her? They were different nuns who taught here, all in black with a white bib, just like penguins. They were Sisters of Mercy; what a misnomer.

We were separated from the girls in the playground but we sat next to them in class. It was here I met my first love, Ann Hibben, a lovely blonde girl. She came from Bean and her father dropped her off every day in a car. I was given the cane for being caught kissing her through the playground railings. She was given a note for her parents. I only did it for a dare. At that age the kiss didn't seem to be worth the cane. I'm glad to say that changed in later life. I remember buying Ann a box of Liquorice Allsorts for her birthday, which I think was in September. It

St. John's Junior School circa 1951/52
Back row: Malcolm Horrigan, Raymond Napper, Douglas Dougal,
Derek Baldwin, Gerald Higgins, Carlo Ferrari, Peter Martin.
Third row: Geoff Daw, John Michael Murray (author) 5th in, Janet
Hodges, Michael Jeffreys, End of row: Keith Hyland. Second row: 4th
in Barbara? Maureen Aldridge. End of row: Bronach Freeman. Front
row: Michael Murphy, 3rd in John Wallis. Ann Hibben? Ann Lock.

cost me 7d and I had to plead with the shopkeeper as sweets were still on ration. Even then I knew how to give a girl a good time. If you are still out there, Ann, a big Hello.

The nuns taught me to read and write, add up and take away, but most of all "fear the Lord". Each morning the first lesson was Religious Instruction. That meant learning the Catechism. Can anybody out there remember standing round the walls of the classroom and reciting parrot fashion the responses to the questions read out by the nun. 'Who made you?' *God made me.* 'Why did God make you?' *God made me to know him, to love him and serve him in this world and to be happy with him forever in the next.* We learnt our times table by the same means, almost singing it, *five-fives are twenty-five, six-fives are thirty* and so on and so on. In hindsight I do not think our education at this age was too bad. We learnt poetry, which I did not understand at the time but now I enjoy. General knowledge featured as a lesson, I think it was Friday afternoon. I loved it; we got a star for every correct answer. I still enjoy quizzes, which I put down to these early lessons. A very important part of our education was the teaching of "manners". We were taught to say please and thank you, give up our seat on a bus for an older person, hold the door open for our elders and always to be polite. I once had to write one hundred times "Manners maketh man". I wish the youth of today had the same lessons.

I continued my love/hate relationship with music. Once a week we had a music lesson produced on the radio by the BBC. We each had a white song book containing such songs as "Bobby Shaftoe", "What shall we do with the drunken sailor?", "Linden Lea" and a song that I still cringe at every time I hear it, "Greensleeves". Henry VIII, you not only ruined some lovely churches and monasteries, you wrote the worst song ever. I could not get away from it. We had to sing it in class and in a competition for school choirs. Dressed in our Sunday best grey short trousers, white shirt, blue tie, white socks and brown sandals we were loaded onto a coach and taken to a big hall somewhere. Then we sang, "Alas, my love, you do me wrong". Little innocents who did not have a clue what we were singing about. We also had to recite, as a group, the poem "How the good news was brought from Ghent to Aix". It had to be recited at a fast pace to convey the urgency of the ride. I think some of the horses were faster than others as the nun who was conducting us had difficulty keeping us in check.

What started at a trot moved to a canter then a full gallop, then chaos. It was not the end of Greensleeves for me. I was taken by one of the nuns to a very big hall in London and had to sing it on a stage before a large audience. I wish I could remember more of that little outing; thankfully it was the last time I sang that horrible song. (Perhaps my voice broke.)

I can recall the day the King died. A nun came into the class and told us the news, followed by us all having to say a prayer.

We received a bottle of milk each day. I can remember in the winter the milk being frozen, sometimes solid ice, when it was delivered. We were allowed to put it on the pipes to thaw out. It was lovely when it was warm. The bottle tops were cardboard with a hole in the middle. We used these to make pompoms with old wool.

I took my 11 plus at St. John's, having to decide what pattern matched another pattern; a whole book of little posers. I am still puzzled by the results of this test. Two boys in the class, Patrick Nye and David Stoddard passed and went to the Grammar School in Sidcup. My mother showed me a letter years later from Kent County Council saying I had passed the test for the Technical School, but as there was not a Catholic one I had to go to the Secondary Modern School in Denton. At the time I didn't mind, I was with my mates. I have since seen the letters my mother wrote to the education authorities to have the decision reversed, to no avail.

After school we returned to St. Mary's, calling in to the "boot room" to clean our boots and change into plimsolls. There was always a large tin of polish and brushes on the floor. We cleaned our boots and had to present them to the nun on duty for inspection. She would take the boots off you and give them a good looking over before handing them back to put in your pigeonhole. One particular nun, who shall remain nameless, would bang the boots round your ears if they were not clean enough. I soon learnt how to clean boots. I found rubbing dust from between the floorboards helped get a good shine. Another skill learned at St. Mary's that served me well in the RAF.

I think we had black boots for school, brown boots for Sunday and sandals in the summer.

A BAD MEMORY

It was while at St. John's Junior School something happened that I can never forgive.

I was on my way to school one morning after the other boys, as I was delayed. Why I know not. It was autumn and the pavements were covered in leaves, which I used to love kicking. While I was doing this I saw a half crown. I looked around, nobody was watching so I picked it up. I clutched it in my hand till I arrived at school. I toyed with the idea of handing it in to one of the nuns but argued with myself that 'God had meant me to have it' so I thought that if I put it behind one of the toilets in the playground and if it was still there after a week I could keep it. (Remember the open-air toilets in the playground, very cold in the winter?) I checked on it every day and worried over the weekend. The week passed so I picked up the coin. Now my troubles began. I kept my find a secret, keeping it wrapped up in my handkerchief. I made the mistake of trying to spend it in Father Baker's shop. He took it off me, asking me where I got it from. I told him I found it; he didn't believe me. I was taken to one of the nuns, it may have been the Sister Superior. I was now frightened. At first she was nice. She asked me time and time again where I got it from. I gave the same reply, I found it. She accused me of stealing it and gave me the cane; first on the hands then on the bare legs, but I stuck to the truth. I was accused of breaking the eighth commandment, 'thou shall not steal.' I was told every time I told a lie 'it made God cry.' I never saw the half crown again. That night I was woken up by the same nun and Father Baker and again asked the same question, same answer. The following night it was just Father Baker who woke me. He didn't hit me, just asked me the same question over and over again.

I have never forgotten nor forgiven being called a thief and a liar. There is a moral there somewhere but I am damned if I can find it. Perhaps the reader can. Would you have done something different? Would you have handed it in?

A few years ago when I lived in Scotland I found a half crown while preparing a vegetable patch. It was dated 1943, the year of my birth. It is on my key ring now as a reminder of the incident. Such a lovely coin; such a bad memory.

CARRYING THE CAN

I am sure we have all done it; asked ourselves 'why me?' During these early years three things happened that have prompted me to ask that question. I relate to them: unsure of the sequence in which they occurred, so please forgive me if I have put them in the wrong order.

The first "why me" occurred whilst at the junior school. I was told by one of the nuns that I was to go to their convent at dinner time and bring back their dinner. I came out of class early, went to the office, collected my bus fare and proceeded to the 495 bus stop. The convent was on the road from Echo Square towards Denton where we used to walk to St. John's Secondary Modern School. Why I was chosen I do not know. I wasn't a particularly big boy. I do not know to this day what special qualities were required for this task. Still, it was a nice bus ride.

At the convent I was given dinner, which I presume was the same as the nuns ate. Meal over I was handed a contraption containing food, six dishes with lids supported in a frame with a wooden carrying handle. Off I went back to St. John's. I used to see the rest of the school snaking their way to St. Mary's for their dinner as I passed on the bus. One day it went wrong. Whilst waiting at the bus stop in Echo Square for the return journey some boys turned up, they were all bigger than me. There was always a smell of food coming from the cans and this attracted their attention.

At first it was questions, 'What's in the cans?' 'Let's have a look'. Then they thought it fun to grab the cans. Of course I resisted. I could see the bus coming but they still carried on, then they let go. I took my chance and swung the can catching one of the boys on the side of the head. He yelled. By this time the bus had drawn up, the driver and conductor had seen what had happened and chased the boys off. The cans were now displaying their contents as gravy and custard oozed out and ran down the sides. The conductor insisted I sit at the back of the bus on the bench seat near the door to minimize the mess.

I could do nothing about the smell of six or seven dinners coming from my direction. The conductor was very kind; he let me off paying my fare so I was a 1d to the good on the day. I think St. Mary's boys were well thought of in Gravesend, hence the kindness. On arriving at the school I had to explain to the nuns what happened to their dinner. I am not sure they believed me. I think I was taken off the task shortly after.

MY "BODGE-UP AUNT"

Jose and me on one of my weekends in London

My second "why me" relates to my "bodge-up aunt". (Bodge-up was our word for pretend.)

Some memories stay in your mind forever, and this one does mine. One day, near the "boot room" a nun said to me, 'Michael, someone is coming to see you on Saturday.' I thanked her and thought no more of it at the time, but that conversation has remained in my memory for well over 60 years. Saturday came, at lunch time a nun fetched me from the playroom, washed me, changed my clothes and took me to sit in the hall. The tall clock ticking away, for what seemed an age. The doorbell rang, a nun opened the door and in stepped my "bodge-up aunt". Her name was Jose. She was an Air Hostess working for BOAC. Even at such a young age I could see she was a stunner. I was introduced. Of course I was very shy and tongue-tied. She took me into Gravesend and we had tea in a café. I can remember having beans on toast, probably the only thing I could think of, and Jose showed me how to leave a tip. This time it was a threepenny bit left under the plate. I think I enjoyed myself that day.

She promised she would write, and she did. I started receiving postcards from all over the world as she was on "long haul" flights. This was fantastic to a youngster like me who collected stamps. (What a great hobby and a way of learning about the world.) She visited me many times and then I was taken to London to stay with her for the weekend. She lived on Old Brompton Road. We went to Regents Park where she knew one of the officials who took us behind the cages of the "Tea Party" chimpanzees. I also met some Orang-utan. They stank, but they were really gentle. I even had a ride on an elephant.

What a memory. On another occasion we went to the Festival of Britain Fun Fair. I had my first ride on a Big Dipper. I was both terrified and elated.

Jose was really kind to me. I spent Christmas with her in London then again with her and her sister in Glastonbury. Her sister and her husband had a large butchers business in the High Street. I can clearly remember all the turkeys hanging in the window and the rooms at the back where the birds were plucked and dressed, feathers everywhere. I saw Jose a few more time and kept receiving the postcards.

Then it all stopped! I later learned that my mother had got to hear about Jose and was not happy, hence the visits stopping. My mother did take me to see Jose get married. We stood outside the church in Kensington waiting for her to arrive. She did not know I was there. How my mother knew I'd never know. Jose got out of her car, in a full wedding dress. I was pushed forward to give her a present my mother bought. Jose was overjoyed.

That was that I thought, but not quite. About 50 or so years later, on a trip back from Dorset, I took a detour through Glastonbury. Whilst looking round the old abbey ruins my wife and I went to a demonstration of how the monks lived, particularly how and what they ate. A jolly looking monk was preparing a meal from home grown produce. We watched for a while then got up to leave. At the door I turned to face the monk, 'Dominus Vobiscum', he said, making the sign of the cross. Without thinking I replied, 'et cum spirito tuo.' My good Catholic upbringing still intact.

We decided to look for the butchers shop for old time's sake. It was now a Building Society. It was Sunday so it was closed. I explained to my wife what the building meant to me. I took the phone number of the business, planning to ring them when I arrived home. Monday morning I made the call. It went something like this. 'Hello, my name is John Murray. I think I spent Christmas in your premises some many years ago when it was a butchers shop. Can any member of your staff remember the butchers shop?' Silence. 'Pardon.' I repeated the question. I was asked to hold on. I heard her ask other members of staff and eventually a very nice old dear came to the phone. She told me she used to buy her meat there and was still friendly with the former owners. She was able to give the address and telephone number of where they had moved; they were running a Bed and Breakfast business nearby. I rang them, again a strange conversation but fortunately her sister remembered me. She brought me up to date on Jose who was living in America and had not long lost her husband. I sent her a letter with my email address if she wanted to get in touch. She did. I had a most wonderful email from her.

I have since met her three times when she came over from America. She is in her late eighties but still very active. She still is a truly wonderful woman.

In later years I asked myself 'why me?' Was it because I was the first boy the nun saw on that particular day? There was any number of boys at St. Mary's who had no one. I had a mother, a brother, aunties and uncles, but I can't help thinking of those who were not so lucky. Some boys had no visitors.

But Jose was not the only person who was good to me. I was taken to somebody's house to watch the Coronation. I was collected from St. Mary's by a nice lady and off we walked. It seemed a long way away but I remember a pub sign "The Battle of Britain". Is it still there I wonder? The house was crowded so I sat crossed leg on the floor. This was the first time I experienced real boredom and a numb bum. I am sorry Your Majesty but it didn't do it for me. The food was nice though. Then back to St. Mary's in the rain.

LAUNDRY BOY

This is my final 'why me?' Why was I chosen to work in the laundry? At the time of being "selected" for this prestigious job I was already gainfully employed working for Mrs. Grundy, cleaning the stairs. Mrs. Grundy was old, short and rotund, always wore black and stank to high heaven. I had to report to her on Saturday mornings where she armed me with a tin of paraffin and some wire wool and told me to clean the rubber on the stairs. I think it was only the central staircase, the one that started on the landing near the bathroom and Father Baker's bedroom and finished at the passageway leading to the side entrance of the Chapel. I can still see the red rubber covering on each stair. I do not recall how many steps there were other than "lots". I would spend ages picking bits of metal out of my fingers. (Can anybody else remember Mrs. Grundy, and did any other boy have this thankless task?) But then, promotion.

One day I was told to gather up the wet sheets from the "bedwetters" and take them to the laundry. I can tell you the bundle was quite heavy and it was a long way down to the laundry room. I used to drag them down the stairs leaving a wet trail behind me. It was here I met Michael Monaghan who proceeded to show me the ropes and taught me all I know about laundry work. First of all the sheets and nightshirts had to go in a colander. I think that was what it was called. Two huge cylinders, one inside the other, the inner door secured by spring-loaded bolts. We put in the soap powder, pulled down the inner door and locked the bolts. Monaghan and I were not big boys at that time so we each took a bolt, our arm span was too small to allow us to do it singly. We pulled down the outer door, again each taking a handle, then we turned on the water. We had to close the outer door otherwise we would cover the place with soapsuds. This door was heavy; how two small boys managed it I'll never know, but we did. The whole cycle was started by one of us pressing a red button. Then we waited for the wash cycle to complete. The next phase of the procedure was to remove the washing and put into a huge open topped spin dryer. As I already said, Monaghan and I were not tall lads and we struggled to reach in to empty the machine, our little legs dangling from the opening. Into the dryer, switch it on and round it whizzed. Monaghan was brave, he used to put his hand in whilst it spun at speed. Then came the "horses". Huge airers that fitted into the wall, we pulled them out, loaded them up and pushed them back. On my first day Monaghan said something had fallen off inside and as I was the smallest I had to get onto the "horses" and he would push me in to retrieve it. I did. He pushed me in, turned off the lights and left me. Inside was a network of hot pipes, and it was black. I called out, no reply. Monaghan had scarpered. Eventually he returned and let me out. I think I wanted to hit him but he was a little bigger than me. (Mick, I owe you one.) After school I had to go to the laundry, empty the "horses", bundle up the sheets and nightshirts and take them up to the dormitories.

On Saturday, under the watchful eye of Sister Brendan, we had to do the sheets belonging to the nuns. This entailed putting the sheets through the huge hot rollers to iron them. Monaghan at one end, me at the other, we fed the sheets through careful not to crease them. At the other end were Sister Brendan and Miss Blanche, who folded them neatly with a well-rehearsed routine. If they were not there, Monaghan and I had to run to the other end to receive them and then fold them. (Not very neatly.)

Huge drive belts coming down from the ceiling drove the rollers, sometimes they came off so we had to climb up and put them back. Health and Safety did not exist in those days. We had to put through the rollers the white squares of linen that were the nun's headdress. Once flat it was placed on boards and starched, then it was allowed to dry. The next time it was seen it was on a nun's head.

Strange things stay in your memory from childhood and one particular task of working in the laundry was cleaning out the gutters. Behind the colander and the spin dryer ran a channel (I think it was ceramic or something similar) which by Saturday morning was black with the scum of the weekly washes. Armed with a tin of scouring powder and a cloth we had to clean away the muck till it was white again. I can remember feeling extremely satisfied when we finished. This was a skill I was able to put to good use when I joined the RAF. During the holidays we worked in the laundry in the mornings, washing all the shirts, pants, socks or anything else that needed washing.

Working in the laundry was Miss Blanche. I remember her as a strange woman who read the *Daily Mirror* (no connection between the two) which she allowed us to read. I was introduced to Jane and Garth in the comic strips, which I loved. Allowing us to read her paper actually gives me a marker of the length of time I worked in the laundry. I can remember clearly reading about the FD2 breaking the world airspeed record, flying at 1132 mph. That was in March 1956 when I was twelve. I think this might have prompted me to join the RAF. It must have been about the time when boys were stopped from doing such work, and my time in the laundry ended.

Next to the laundry was the boiler room. A very kind man ran this little haven; I believe his name was Mr. McAuliffe. We could go in and talk with him. He would show us how the boiler worked, explain all the dials and pipes and open up the front of the furnace so we could see the fire. Can anyone remember the huge pile of coke that was stacked near the boiler house? Mr. McAuliffe lived in the gatehouse with a horrible woman who reminded me of the wicked witch of the west. She had ruddy cheeks and a sharp red nose. Sometimes she was on duty in the "shed" when we played. If we needed to go to the toilet she asked if we wanted a No. 1 or a No. 2. If it was the latter she gave us two sheets of shiny toilet paper. She kept us in line by pinching with her horrible long nails. I think she had a fair-haired son who was sometimes allowed to play with us. If my memory serves me well he was not liked.

BED WETTING

I was one of the unfortunate boys who committed the heinous crime of "bed wetting".

Why I did it I don't know. I didn't want to do it, but I did. Every night I would dread going to sleep. I would try to stay awake so I could go and have a "wee" when I felt the need. Some nights it worked but most nights it didn't. I would wake up in the warm wet sheets dreading the nun coming round to get us up. First it was morning prayers kneeling beside the bed. The wet nightshirt (bedwetter's wore nightshirts) now turned from warm to cold.

Prayers finished it was sheets off the bed and over the head and there we stayed until the other boys, the dry ones, came back from the washroom. Sometimes we stood by our bed, other times we moved to the landing. At this point, one of the nuns, whose name I will not repeat lest she still lives and is ashamed by her actions, proceeded to cane us with a piece of bamboo she kept up her sleeve. It used to smell under that wet sheet and it grew progressively colder. When it was our turn to go to the washroom we put the sheets in a bundle, took off our wet nightshirts, wrapped a towel round our skinny white bodies and shamefaced walked through the other dormitories to shower. Some mornings we were given a cold shower; not very nice. Can anybody remember the bars of pink soap that we had to cut into squares to use?

Back to get dressed. I cannot recall any of the other boys looking at us as we traipsed through the dormitories, neither can I recall any nasty name calling. There was a silent honour among us boys, perhaps they remembered being in the same position.

I think part of the problem was the lack of toilets. I remember a small urinal on the landing where Father Baker slept but the floor was always wet and cold on bare feet, and the dormitories were dark and quite frightening to a youngster.

Someone must have told me 'you wet them, you wash them,' and that was possibly why I finished up working in the laundry.

I have read other accounts from boys at St. Mary's who wet the bed and how it damaged them. I think I was a lucky one and remain unscathed from the experience. Today such treatment would be called "child abuse" and would fill the Red Top papers. It was not pleasant and those who were responsible for our welfare that instigated or condoned such practice should be ashamed of themselves.

When I relate this aspect of my time at St. Mary's to others I am often asked 'did it affect you?'

I always reply 'No, I knew no different; to me this was how life was lived.'

I found out later I was wrong.

A VERY LUCKY ESCAPE

My early life seemed to have been a sequence of nuns asking or telling me things. Like the time I was told about my "bodge up Aunt". I was asked if I would like to go to Australia.

Of course I said 'yes.' I did not go.

My mother somehow found out and put a stop to it. I remember one day being taken to one of the top dormitories and told to look out of the window and wave. We could see the River Thames and Tilbury docks and ships sailing from it. We were told that one of them was taking the boys to Australia. I don't know if the gesture was genuine or symbolic as I later learnt that particular ship had sailed from Southampton. There were a few empty beds that night.

That was January 1953.

One boy who was on the ship was Michael Monaghan, not the laundry one. Another one who I did not know existed. I was researching St. Mary's online and put in his name and found that he lived in Tasmania. I left a message for him on a University Message Board and eventually heard that he was coming over to the UK. He came to my house with his wife and we spent a very pleasant few hours together. He told me of the early days in Australia, how he and some other boys ran away. It made me glad that I did not go. He remembered Ann Hibben and said he fancied her as well. It took me over sixty years to find that out. You heart breaker, Ann.

Michael is now a fine Australian and embodies the "can do" spirit that typifies that marvellous country. It was through this meeting I discovered John Flynn and the network of former St. Mary's boys.

TO PLAY OR PRAY

For youngsters growing up play is important, but so too is prayer. Looking back I am not sure the balance was right.

We used to play in the Shed or the "hobby room". In the winter the Shed was cold and I recall being very young and very cold and shivering. If we complained to the nun on duty at the door we were told to run around to get warm. Never easy when you are small and the "big boys" are playing English bulldog and taking up the entire Shed. What a fantastic game that was, bending over and having the other boys taking a pot shot at your backside. Most times they missed, but when they hit your bare leg it stung like hell!

There was a wicket drawn on the wall so we played cricket. We were all budding Len Huttons or Donald Bradmans. Sometimes we played football; great fun but not easy with a tennis ball or even a bundle of rags. It was in the Shed that I had a disagreement with Mr. Smith. He was taking us for Physical Training (PT) and we had to do handstands. Most sports I can do; handstands I cannot. I was trying my best but Mr. Smith crept up on me and whacked my bare legs with a plimsoll. I reacted and punched him on the face. Big, big mistake. From somewhere he produced two pairs of boxing gloves. We put them on. He proceeded to hit me; I never laid a glove on him. I learnt a valuable lesson that day. Keep your temper though I did lose it a few times after that. Mr. Smith lived in Glen View and had a daughter Barbara who invited me to her birthday party. Thank you, Barbara, and I am truly sorry I hit your dad. I liked him and had a lot of time for him.

Whilst on the subject of "hitting" I can remember an occasion in the Shed when we were sitting on the bench by the wall when a boy called O'Leary started pinching my cold bare leg. It hurt. He would not stop so my temper took over again. I gave him a backhander right across the nose. It was splat and there was blood everywhere. He never touched me again. I do not want to give the impression I was a bruiser, I was not, but all the boys had to stand up for themselves in such an environment. Some were clever and could talk themselves out of trouble, I couldn't. Fights were commonplace and served to clear the air. Friendships were often formed after fights.

Play in the "hobby room" was good. It was warm. We had table tennis and snooker on a table with a tear in the cloth. A radio that was not always on but when it was we listened to "Journey into Space" or "Dick Barton" in complete silence. In one of the rooms was a piano and many a boy tried to play. Some were quite good. I could play one or two tunes reasonably well but I have always regretted not continuing with it.

I collected stamps and enjoyed learning the names of all the foreign countries. I had a good collection, thanks to my "bodge up Aunt", Jose. There was often long bargaining sessions with other boys for "swaps". Many a good negotiator must have originated from those times. There were some clever boys at St. Mary's. One particular boy, Alfred Odell, was not very sporty and often had his nose in a book. On one occasion he showed me how to make a photograph from a negative. I was amazed. Can anyone recall watching Quartermass on a small television and being scared stiff or being allowed to stay up late listening to Don Cockell fight Rocky Marciano?

In the summer, occasionally, we had the treat of going to the outdoor Swimming Pool in Gravesend. I cannot recall it ever being warm; in fact to me it was freezing. We were not allowed in the water unless we were wearing our Miraculous Medal, a small aluminium facsimile of the Virgin Mary suspended round our neck on a piece of string. On one occasion I jumped off the top board for a dare and an ice-lolly with ice cream in the middle. I had to be fished out of the deep end, which was 10ft deep, and I never got my ice-lolly.

Can anyone remember the Brylcream dispensers in the changing rooms? For a 1d you got a squirt of Brylcream. We used to suck it out as we rarely had a penny.

When we were not playing it seemed we were praying. Please do not assume I am anti-Catholic, I am not. I still retain a great love for the Church, but I can recall the sore knees from praying. I was an altar boy and learnt all the responses in Latin for the mass. When it was your turn to serve at mass you were woken early by a nun then you made your way to the sacristy. Sometimes there were two boys, especially if one was learning "the ropes". When it came to the part when the nuns took communion I used to be quite nervous holding the plate under their chin to catch the host if Father Baker dropped it.

I loved swinging the thurible to try to make as much incense smoke as possible when serving Benediction. Often Father Baker gave me a clip round the ear when we got back to the sacristy. When I wasn't serving on the altar I was up in the choir. Again I had to sing the responses when we

The Chapel as seen from the Choir. The Stations of the Cross can be seen on the wall. "Many hours spent on my knees here!"

had High Mass. At Benediction, which we had every Sunday evening, we sang a hymn in Latin called "Tatum Mergo" (I think that was it) which sounded very much like "Deutschland Uber Alles". The service always finished with a "Prayer for Russia". Did it work?

It was one Sunday evening on our way to Benediction as we came down the stairs from the "hobby room" one of the boys went over the banister. I think his name was Michael Jeffries. He survived and I hope and pray he made a full recovery with no after effects. Wire netting was put over the banisters to prevent it happening again.

May was the month I hated the most, not only did we have to say the Rosary every day but on Sundays we had the long procession from St. Mary's to St. John's. We assembled on the drive of St. Mary's, boys, nuns and members of the public, behind a Crucifix and a banner and off we went, singing hymns along the way. One hymn that still resonates in my brain, "Ave, ave, ave Maria". I heard it on Songs of Praise recently; it took me back to those days. About this time I was told that if I said a Novena (nine days of special prayers), God would grant my wish. I said the Rosary in secret every day for nine days asking God to bring back my dad so that I could live at home. He must have been busy with other requests as I stayed at St. Mary's for a few more years.

I never enjoyed the Stations of the Cross in Lent. They seemed to go on forever and you had to alter your position as you moved round each individual station. Kneeling really hurt the knees.

Can anyone remember saying the Angelus? I think the bell was rung twice per day and on hearing it we had to stop what we were doing and repeat 'The Angel of the Lord appeared unto Mary, and she conceived by the Holy Ghost,' etc.

The highlight of the year for us boys at St. Mary's was our annual holiday in August to Dymchurch, or St. Mary's Bay Holiday Camp to give it the full title.

It started with a coach trip in which I recall was a cream and blue coach with the name of AC Ltd. We fought for a window seat when it was time to board, and off we went, singing our little heads off as we passed through the Kent countryside. I think we had a packed lunch of jam sandwiches. The camp itself was a huge collection of huts; pictures today makes it look like a POW camp or worse but to us boys it was heaven. Sleeping arrangements were not exactly five star, low wooden frames with canvas stretched over the sides. At the end of each hut were washing facilities. In August the huts could be quite cold; concrete floor and bare feet do not engender a feeling of warmth. But we didn't care. We were all given swimming costumes, mostly homemade. The unlucky boys had woollen knitted ones and we all know what happens to them when they are wet. On one occasion I managed to acquire a pair of leopard print lace-up trunks. I felt like Tarzan in them.

The first dip in the sea was always eagerly awaited. We stripped off to our trunks and ran down the beach. Sometimes the tide was out for what seemed miles and even in the water we had a long way to go before the water reached our waist, but it was great. We held our breath as we waited for the cold water to reach our "privates". Sometimes we were plagued by jellyfish. I don't think they harmed us but they did not look very nice; best to avoid them. We spent most of the time on the beach when the tide was out and I remember having great fun exploring the rock pools and looking for crabs. We played cricket and rounders and did all the things healthy young boys did when given freedom. This was all under the watchful eye of one of the nuns. They must have been very hot in their habit, which I recall as being quite thick. Their bonnet kept the sun out of their eyes.

I must have gone on six camps whilst at St. Mary's but I remember clearly at one of them playing on the beach next to some foreign children. Somehow I got talking to one of them, a girl called Magda Zadrazil, she was from Czechoslovakia and she told me her parents had come to England to escape the Germans. She was a nice girl and we wrote to each other a couple of times. I remember her address as being Smith Square somewhere in central London. Needless to say, I was the recipient of a fair amount of "mickey taking" by the other boys.

The highlight of the holiday was always a trip on the Romney, Hythe and Dymchurch railway miniature trains. Small open carriages pulled by a perfect replica steam train with such exotic names as "The Green Goddess" and "Doctor Syn". After all these years the railway is still running, giving the same pleasure to a new generation of children.

In keeping with the holiday atmosphere we did lots of group walking, sometimes along the beach to the funfair at Hythe or out into the countryside. I have fond memories of one such occasion buying a tin of Golden Syrup and we all taking turns to dip our finger in as we walked along. Absolute bliss!

The food seemed to be better here than back at St. Mary's. I think the sea air played tricks with our taste buds. I remember the dining-room being huge and very noisy. It made the saying of "Grace" before meals difficult, but we did.

Once we were taken to Dungeness Lighthouse but were not allow to go inside and climb the stairs to the top; it was considered too dangerous and steep for our little legs. I made the climb a few years ago. They were right, except it was too steep for my old legs.

The camp had huge playing fields where we amused ourselves before bed. Being August we were often plagued by swarms of flying ants, but we didn't care.

There was traditionally a football match against other schools, played by the "big boys" who were quite a formidable team. I remember watching them and hoping one day to play in the match, but I left before I became a "big boy".

The end of the holiday was always a sad occasion as it meant that returning to school was not far away.

FINAL DAYS. SEPTEMBER 1954 – DECEMBER 1956

I had reached the grand old age of eleven and now received my schooling at St. John's Secondary Modern School, Denton, or the "big boys" school. Compared to the Infants School it was huge. Lessons were now different, the classrooms bigger, the teachers stricter and not a nun in sight. The Headmaster was Mr S.A.C. Bray. He always wore his black gown and had leather patches on the elbows of his jacket. That has always been a mark of authority to me. He was a good man but was still capable of swinging the cane if you were unfortunate to be sent to him for punishment. I can remember one poor boy receiving six of the best across the backside at assembly, allegedly for stealing carrots from the vegetable plot.

We were now taught woodwork and gardening as well as the usual subjects. The classes were mixed and there was an influx of fresh faces as it had a wide catchment area. I remember being amazed at the large playing field with two football pitches marked out. Games formed an important part of the curriculum. We had at least one double period per week of football in the winter and cricket and athletics in the summer. I was quite reasonable at games and played Right Half (mid-field in modern parlance) for St. John's at my respective age group. There were a few boys who were very good at football; two who come to mind are Alan Reed, a Welsh boy, a very good winger. He was the first boy that I can remember who could take a corner kick and reach the goal area with the ball high enough for us to head. Another boy who showed amazing talent was Peter Foley. Peter had a problem with one of his arms and legs, but he never let that deter him. He was as rough and determined as the rest of us when pursuing a football. He was also surprisingly fast. The only drawback playing football in those days was heading a wet ball and catching the lace. I headed a goal playing against a school from Gillingham and the lace cut my forehead. It was war after that!

We had a small garden plot where we were taught how to grow vegetables. During one of the lessons the inevitable happened; a boy pierced his foot with a fork. We learnt the art of "double spit" digging, growing potatoes, cabbages and carrots. It must have been a leftover of the "Dig for Victory" campaign during the war.

Woodwork was a new skill to us all. I loved it. Learning how to plane, saw, markout, making halving joints, mortise and tenon and when we were really good, dovetails. I still have an oak coffee table I made in that class and when I left I had to pay 2/6d to cover the cost of the wood.

The girls did Domestic Science or cooking as we called it. The smells that came from the kitchen were mouth-watering. If one of the girls took a shine to you she would give you some of the cake she made. One such girl was Pauline Napper. She was a year older than me but she used to give me bits of cake and sweets. A belated thank you, Pauline. I can remember being very rude to you, which you didn't deserve, but the "mickey taking" got a bit too much for an eleven year old.

In summer we played cricket and athletics. Playing for the school one day I was wicket keeper, not my usual position, and I was not wearing a "box". My eyes watered, need I say more. Sometimes we received coaching from Mr. Martin, the groundsman who allegedly played for Kent. The coaching took the form of us bowling to him in the nets and he hitting the ball all over the place. I did get him out once, a pure fluke.

Another part of his coaching was sifting soil. This comprised of throwing shovels full of earth at an upright iron mesh to remove the stones. He said it would build up our muscles. Liar!

Athletics was fun. I could run, not very fast but distance was no problem. One year I won the discus for my age group and received a medal, which I still have. From that I took part in the schools championship at Cray Valley Technical School. I didn't win.

We of course had music, or singing as that was all it comprised of. This was under the very professional tutelage of Mr. Grimes, a short, bald-headed Scotsman who ensured we reached the correct notes by whacking our bare legs with a cane or strap. I still have memories of the class lined up in rows with the second row standing on a bench and singing "Jerusalem" while he stood next to you listening for wrong notes, followed by the inevitable whack. He did teach us a lot of Scottish songs, very few that we understood.

We used to walk to Denton unsupervised. Part of the route was across a large field. There were bushes round the side and I spent many happy moments looking for bird's nests in them.

If I was flush, by that I mean having 3d, it would buy three pennyworth of broken biscuits from the grocery's shop in Echo Square.

FOOD, GLORIOUS FOOD

I cannot remember the food at St. Mary's being particularly good or even particularly bad. Breakfast usually comprised of porridge. Sometimes it was thin, sometimes it was thick, quite often it was lumpy. The best part of this delicate fare was being allowed to scrape the bottom of the pot; the burnt bits always tasted best. If we had bacon, streaky not nice back, the nearest thing to heaven on earth was being allowed to dip a slice of bread into the fat that remained at the end. I seem to remember having black pudding but I didn't like the white lumps of fat in it.

Sometimes on a feast day we had a boiled egg for breakfast. We used to play a little trick with the empty shell. The secret was to make the smallest hole possible when eating the egg, fill the empty shell with tea leaves and then bang it on the back of some poor boy's head. I had it done to me a few times by "big boys" and I am sure I did it when it was my turn.

We often had "toad in the hole" with very rubbery batter, lumpy mashed potato, and smelly cabbage. I never liked the "frogs spawn" or tapioca to give it its correct title, but I did enjoy the chocolate flavoured custard we sometimes had.

Tea time mainly consisted of bread and Echo margarine, raspberry or greengage jam and sometimes lemon curd that were served from large catering tins delivered by Kearly & Tongs in their big green van.

Sometimes there was cheese on the table as well. On feast days there was cake. We used to stand to say "grace" before meals. At this point, if there was a crust or a "cruny" as we called it, on the table, and if you were quick enough you would "dog" it or "huff" on it to make it yours. The tea we drank was strong and always had the leaves in it.

Eventually it was decided that I was responsible enough to become a "table boy". This entailed getting the meals for the other five boys at the table, washing up the dirty dishes and cutlery after the meal and laying the table again. The washing up process was always a scramble; if you got there too early the water was too hot, too late and it wasn't hot enough to clean off the grease. I don't think they used what we now know as washing up liquid but something called Teepol, which didn't froth up very well. (I later used it in the RAF for cleaning aircraft.) Added to this was the problem with the "big boys" who always pushed in. All of this extra work was rewarded with the princely sum of 6d per week extra pocket money, unless you lost or broke something then it was forfeit.

Whilst on the topic of food I have two confessions to make as I am now too old and too big to be punished.

The first involved the time when we were playing in the "hobby rooms". When the watching nun changed shift I would rush and ask if I could get the bread from the kitchen. This was usually about 3 o'clock. If successful I would fetch the tray of bread and on the way up the stairs I would pick out any crusts that I fancied and hide them behind a radiator, to retrieve when I took the tray back. I stuffed them under my jumper or shirt and shared them with my mates.

The second confession involved a chance encounter one Saturday morning when we were playing up at the "Square". I had asked to go to the toilet. Can anybody remember the open-air toilets at the bottom of the slope from the "Squares"? On my way down I noticed one of the "big boys" leaning into one of the open windows of the kitchen. I watched him as he pulled out first one, then another, then another sausage on a long stick. He turned and saw me. He threatened me with a thick ear if I talked but gave me a sausage. Shortly after I think he went to the "farm" and I inherited his sausage stick. From that day forth SOS meant Sausages on Saturday. I always shared out my booty, after I had my fill.

THE "SQUARES"

The Squares were the outdoor playing area away from the main building, opposite Glen View where Mr. Smith, the big boys' House Master lived. There were two, separated by a high wire fence, which also encircled their perimeter. Here we could run around and make as much noise as we liked. There were swings on which we used to go as high as possible before jumping off to see who could get the farthest; how we did not damage our feet I'll never know.

In the Squares was a pile of tyres. Judging by their size they must have been ex-army. Stacked one on top of another they made an ideal den. I do recall one or two of the "big boys" climbing in and having a quick drag on a fag while we shrimps kept watch on the nun or Father Baker, sat at the entrance.

Some boys were lucky and were given roller skates for their birthday by their parents or "bodge up aunts". We had such fun learning to skate, first on one, then on two, going round and round. The posh boys had rubber wheels on their skates, so much quieter and smoother. I think most boys at this time were quite generous and didn't mind sharing. When the wheels ran dry or there was a problem, Mr. McAuliffe, the boiler man, was always willing with a squirt of oil from his can or the use of a spanner.

Drawn on the wall was the inevitable wicket. I think most boys enjoyed a game of cricket or tip and run. We could only use soft balls but as I recall there were some nifty cricketers among the boys. One of the good parts of playing the game was trying to hit the ball over the fencing and going to look for it. There were a lot of trees and bushes around one side and rear end of the squares. Even if the ball didn't go there that is where we finished up looking. We used to look for bird's nests but the biggest prize of all was to find a male Stag Beetle. Some huge ones were found and brought back into the Square as trophies for all to see. I had one that I kept in my "crodge box" in the hobbies room; not surprising, it died. In the sixty-years plus since that time I have never seen another Stag Beetle.

As well as cricket we played football in the back Square, usually with a tennis ball. There were some pretty hard fought battles played out. The worst part of such games was the picking of sides. Two boys were captains; usually the biggest or best, and they took turns to pick their team. I always felt sorry for the boys who were last to be picked, as they were generally the worst players. Many acres of knee skin were left on that hard concrete.

The Square gave an easy way out of St. Mary's via a back dirt road. On one occasion one or two other adventurous boys and I had managed to get out, by asking to go to the toilet. We ducked down and sneaked out and headed for Windmill Hill. Here we would continue in one of our favourite pasttimes of bird nesting. I recall watching with another boy, I think his name was Michael Finn, a couple lying under a blanket. We lay in the grass intrigued by what they were doing. We concluded that they were doing "it" though we did not know what "it" was. Sex education was an unheard of topic in those days. The man saw us and got up. He was a soldier wearing what remained of his uniform, and chased us away, using language that was quite foreign to us delicate boys.

CLEANLINESS

We might have looked like urchins or rejects from "Oliver Twist" but by and large we were clean. It was certainly the case when we were attending the junior school. After breakfast we had to go and wash our hands and face, comb our hair and present ourselves for inspection to a waiting nun. It was hands out, turn them over, then a look at your neck and ears before giving the OK to go or not. For the senior school we were trusted to do it properly without inspection. Usually at this point our hair was given an expert assessment by a completely untrained, devoid of any skills, nun, to ascertain as to whether it needed cutting. If so we were subjected to what can only be described as a shearing as our hair was removed from our young heads by manual clippers in the hands of an over-enthusiastic nun.

Many a boy myself included displayed, like a badge of honour, bald patches where the clippers had caught and were released by a sharp tug, taking the offending hair with them. Occasionally, blood was drawn.

The cleaning of teeth was also a well-organised ritual. After showering or washing our face we retrieved our toothbrush from our pigeon hole, formed a queue in front of the waiting nun, dipped our tooth brush into the tin of powder and proceeded to clean our teeth. Most times it was tooth powder but I am sure on occasions it was bicarbonate of soda.

Saturday afternoons I recall as being reserved for bath time. We would sit on the benches in the bathroom, in nothing but a towel covering our modesty and wait our turn for a bath to become free. There were a number of baths, each with its own open cubicle. The first boys got the hot water, the next less so, and so on down the line to the poor unlucky individuals who had an almost cold bath. That wasn't the worst of it, as more boys used the water the thicker the scum was formed on the surface. If you were very, very lucky, and a kind nun was on duty, you could change the water.

Of course the last boys had to clean the bath after them.

LAST MEMORIES

The last years of my time at St. Mary's I look back on with a certain degree of strangeness. It was at this time I realised I was not an orphan, despite having been told to the contrary by the nuns. On one occasion my mother came to visit me and took me out for the day. I believe that was the time I learnt that I actually had a family outside of St. Mary's. I remember the day being very wet.

A few days later Sister Gerard told me my mother was seriously ill and I was to visit her. I think it was Father Baker who took me to Bromley hospital in his Morris car. She had double pneumonia and pleurisy as a result of the soaking she had received. Fortunately, she made a full recovery.

I began to be allowed to spend occasional weekends at home with my mother and my newly-found family. I was given 2/6d, being the return fare from Gravesend to Bromley Market Square, and caught the 725 Greenline bus opposite the statue of Pocahontas.

It was on the first such trip I realised I had a brother. He was twenty months younger than me and lived at home. I can clearly remember thinking how unfair it was. He did spend one summer holiday at St. Mary's, presumably because my mother could not find or afford childcare. I must be honest and say that I did not get on too well with him during his stay, so much so we had a ding-dong fight and had to be separated by a nun. We were made to spend the rest of the afternoon in the chapel, opposite sides of course, and stayed there till teatime. It was very quite and peaceful. We did not speak, and the nun made us shake hands before she would let us out. Usually after a fight you received a good caning but this time we did not, perhaps it was because my brother was a "guest". I am sad to say I was never close to my brother, a fact I can only put down to a subconscious jealousy of his upbringing, compared to mine.

I don't know if it was my imagination but we seemed to have a fair amount of freedom, as I have vivid memories of going into Gravesend, particularly the market. There was a man who auctioned goods from the back of a large van. He used to have us in stitches. Part of his sales pitch was to insult, in a friendly way, women in the crowd. He used to say things like 'don't pick your nose love, pick me.'

He made a few suggestive remarks which we boys didn't understand. He grew to know a few of us and we often helped him by passing out the goods to the customer. We got paid sixpence.

Some of us liked fishing and managed to go to a place called Blue Lake, an old quarry. I think we heard of a boy drowning there (not one of ours), and we were forbidden to go there again. I am not sure we obeyed.

Occasionally we were taken to the "pictures", to the cinemas called The Regal and Majestic. We mainly saw religious films like "The Robe" and "The Song of Bernadette". Sometimes we saw a western with Roy Rogers, Lash LaRue, Hopalong Cassidy and even a young John Wayne.

Whereas I didn't particularly like St. Mary's I was content to stay there, because I knew nothing else. This was not the case with all the boys. Some decided to run away. One particular boy named Peter Asher, I think he ran way more than once and I am not sure what became of him. It was rumoured he came from a rich family and was later sent to Borstal.

I continued working in the laundry, until the law forbade it, but that didn't mean I became unemployed.

One of the Dormitories. Look at the lovely polished floor.

Saturday mornings were polish the dormitory floor time. The procedure was: move all the beds to one side, sweep up the dust, put down the polish, shine it up with the bumper then put the beds back and do the other side. The polish was contained in large tins and we dished it out onto a cloth using a putty knife. Boys being boys we larked about, throwing the putty knife to see who could make it stick in the wooden floor. One day one of the boys got over enthusiastic. I think his name was Church, but would not swear to it, threw the putty knife and it stuck in my hand. I still have the scar. I had to go to hospital and have it stitched. I told the nun it was an accident caused by me. It gave me a bit of kudos as everyone wanted to see my stitches.

As we boys were getting bigger so the punishments seemed to become harder. There was a thing call the feralah (I apologise if I have spelt it wrong). I believe it was a mixture of rubber and leather. We witnessed one poor boy receive six of the best across the backside from Father Baker. He was held over a billiard table. I have never heard screams like it. I don't know his name but I think he was one of the "big boys". Part of the punishment was for us all to witness it. The rumour was he was caught stealing. Stealing was considered to be the worst thing a boy could do at St. Mary's, hence the harsh punishment. It was probably the only one of the Ten Commandments we could break. Adultery was out and we did not know what coveting thy neighbour's wife meant in those days of innocence. Such punishments were reminiscence of floggings given at sea.

I was enjoying school at St. John's, Denton. I was growing and so was pushed around less. Most of the "big boys" were OK and kept with their own age group; there was very less bullying. It was noticeable that each year their numbers dwindled as they moved to "the farm" which sounded to us youngsters as a most forbidding place.

It was the rule at St. Mary's that all boys wore short trousers until they were fourteen. There were some long bare legs in those days, which were often red-raw with chaps in the winter months.

I really looked forward to my fourteenth birthday; unfortunately I never made it at St. Mary's.

On 21st December 1956, a Friday, Sister Gerard told me that I was going home for good. I was given clean clothes to put on, all my worldly goods which was not much, contained in a small brown suitcase, and my coffee table clutched in my hand. I left St. Mary's forever. I do not think I was even given time to say my goodbyes.

I walked to the bus stop and had my last look at Pocahontas and my ten years as an orphan were over. My record with Southwark Catholic Rescue Society (now Cabrini) states: 21st December 1956 "Discharged home to care of mother".

It sounds as though I was leaving prison.

POSTSCRIPT

I cannot say that living at home was easy; in fact it was very strange. There was my brother, of course, who everybody doted on. I was the new boy, the cuckoo in the nest. In my new "home" lived my grandmother, as bad as my mother portrayed her, an aunty, my mother, my brother and myself, all squeezed into a three-bedroom council house. It was crowded to say the least!

I went to school in Orpington, St. Joseph's on Sevenoaks Road. This, like St. Mary's, was an orphanage run by Christian Brothers. It was joined to St. Anne's, another orphanage for girls and the Holy Innocents Church. I was here as a "day boy" as opposed to a "boarder". It was boys only and there was a definite split between the two sets of boys. I found I was comfortable with the "boarders".

Each evening after school my brother and I were supposed to light the fire and peel the potatoes ready for when the grown-ups came home from work. I had no problem with that; years at St. Mary's had conditioned me. My brother never took his turn, and sad to say, he got away with it.

I stayed at home for eighteen months, then aged fifteen I joined the RAF. After St. Mary's, square bashing was a piece of cake. I signed on for twelve years but halfway through my service I developed a rebellious streak, rejecting a life of discipline and regimentation. I survived but could have made more of my time.

Many questions remain. Was I affected by my experience? The answer must be yes. Was it for the good or ill, the answer must be both. I do not think I was damaged by the experience, though I have read many boys were. I truly believe that my ten years an orphan made me a less emotional person. Compassion does not come easy; I have still retained the attitude of "get on with it, there is always someone worse off".

St. Mary's had a strong bearing on me when I became a parent. From having nothing I believe I over-compensated with my children and perhaps spoilt them. I must not complain too much. They have both grown up into fine adults of which I am extremely proud. I thank God they did not have to endure St. Mary's or its like. I have deliberately left out the names of the nuns who I consider had been bad to me. Most were reasonably kind; others were less so. God has them listed.

In all of my ten years I cannot honestly recall being given a hug or comforted when I hurt myself or was in need of a little show of affection; as a result I had difficulty showing the same to my children. I see that as my legacy from St. Mary's.

ACKNOWLEDGEMENTS

I would like to thank (Delvin) John Flynn for his work in perpetuating the memories of all the boys who were resident at St. Mary's, through his emails and information gathering.

Caroline Whitehead for her work in putting our memories together and allowing us to perhaps gain a better understanding of our early lives through the benefit of the passing years.

To all the boys who went through St. Mary's, during my time as well as before and after, you have contributed to my memories for you are a part of them.

The boys who were shipped out to Australia, at last your story has been told and justice, if that is the correct word, seeming to be done.

To all who have contributed photographs of St. Mary's. Having reached the ripe old age of 71, I have only two pictures that relate to my time there. The picture used as a front cover and the one with my "bodge-up Aunt" which only came into my possession this year (2014).

My wife Lesley, who by now must be sick and tired of hearing about St. Mary's, of reading endless rough drafts and acting as a wise and caring "sounding board".

God bless you all.

DO WE EVER FIND OURSELVES?
SEEK AND YE WILL FIND

BY TERRY S. MCKENNA

In life I have found for everything that happens there is always an opposite effect that takes place. I have spent most of my life looking for the reasons why I look like I do. A lot of people spend loads of money changing their inherited looks! I have spent a lifetime looking for mine! When searching for family it seems most parents are desperately trying to forget the child who didn't ask to be brought into the world. I have spent a lifetime looking for my parents! If you approach the Authorities for help to find blood family, you would think there would be a fair and just system in place to assist the sibling, to find what most ordinary folk take for granted. I have spent a lifetime fighting these very authorities!

Instead it seems that even in these enlightened times the parent holds ALL the aces.

Knowing, learning loving and understanding family is the one thing that separates mankind from all other life forms. Due to the archaic laws that still exist in the UK, this fundamental yet basic human right is still being denied to all siblings if the parent simply says 'NO.' There will of course be many opinions on this sensitive subject, which is absolutely right.

For many years governments of the day abdicated their responsibilities to the unwanted, the abandoned and forgotten children, primarily because of the financial cost, and handed out their welfare mainly to the Church. You would have thought the "House of God" was the perfect place for these unfortunate souls to be saved and be given a start in life. How wrong can we be? To be impartial it has to be said that most of the kids were treated reasonably well but sadly a very large minority were not. They were abused in many different ways, not just physically but mentally and emotionally too. A huge amount of kids at these Homes were told their parents were dead. The plain and very disturbing truth is this was an awful detestable lie, concocted by nearly ALL the various organisations and sanctioned it appears, by someone in a very high place within Government. Not for the public consumption! In my opinion I really believe it was an Ethos of: "If they don't know, then they won't ask!"

I discovered that meticulous records are kept for every child that landed up in care. To get this information needs at times a fortitude beyond recognition and alas sometimes the threat of litigation, which is surely wrong. Nobody has the right to deny anyone the knowledge of who they are, just because it's easier to deny rather than tell the truth.

As with most of the laws of this land, decisions are made by people who have absolutely no idea of what it means to be a "child" needing to find his or herself. This may be the age of the Internet and the cyber world in general, where you can find answers for just about anything. BUT, just try to find your birth details if you are from an orphanage or Children's Home, as they were known, and you enter an entirely different world. I have a saying: 'when one door shuts, another one is slammed;

just like an echo.' This actually refers to what happened whenever I got close to something important and then all authorities appear to close ranks. That's what I mean by doors slamming. I can hear the do-gooder objections from here.

Of course there needs to be proper consultation between a child and an authority, as well as the parent; that is obvious and understandable. I know you can't just knock on a door out of the blue (morally at least) and say, 'Hi, I'm the child who was abandoned, given up, or indeed the children who were taken from you.' As the law currently stands (as I see it) if a parent is approached by an organisation in the proper way and simply says, 'NO, I am not interested', then that's it! This surely cannot be right, can it? Yet a parent's current life needs certain understanding but not protection, to stop the probably unknown child suddenly appearing out of the thin air into a family unit that never knew of its existence. BUT this surely mustn't be forever.

What we are told in life is whatever we do come with responsibilities and consequences. There needs to be some form of mediation in a totally private and safe environment. Like a vast number of drug consellors, I sincerely feel this mediation should be run by people with first-hand knowledge and understanding, from BOTH sides. People who have experienced the pitfalls and difficulties this time can and does produce. It is inevitable the mother will be contacted and may be confronted by the child. In this country it is the mother who is always named, whereas in most cases the father is not. So it goes without saying the mother has to deal with the emotional scars she and her child undoubtedly will have.

A thought occurred to me that maybe it's time the father (if known) is named by law. Logic tells me this would make tracing a parent a lot easier for all concerned, mainly because the father's surname remains a constant; unlike the mother's, that may change whenever she marries (or divorces).

This is just one practical idea from me and I'm sure there are so many others. It would not be the child's fault if its being is unknown, that surely must lay with the parent, or as I now know, with government AND the various societies that were undoubtedly responsible for a lot of cruel misery for decades!

I have discovered that most (though not all) siblings from the same family base are usually delighted to learn of an unknown sister or brother. Almost without exception people that I know who search for family are NOT seeking revenge or retribution – a myth that is often banded round by those who pretend to understand. As ever reality is so often the opposite end of a myth. It really does depend from which end of the rainbow you look. Theirs is a simple but genuine need to know. In my case one reason to find my family was to show them the actions taken years ago (whether for the right OR wrong reason) was probably for the best I could have hoped.

I am not set on a destructive mission to destroy the life of an estranged parent. I'm not out to try and lay blame for my life (in most cases) on a single parent. I'm no mischief maker. I simply want to know why I or any other children are STILL denied this information by laws that are so out of date. All we hear these days is the Politically Correct brigade banging on about all and sundry, with not a thought for people like me and there are many, many others who need what could be described as a form of closure.

There are things called The Family Court System in the UK. Why does that NOT include people like me? Am I not a member of a family? I am more than willing to mediate at any level to gain a positive outcome. I am also here to share what I've learned in over half a century of not knowing who I really am! My thought is that successive Government Law Makers don't have the will or guts to address this quite large minority. Or maybe just enough of these stories are not available here in the UK.

There are plenty of us still around who could tell you stories that would make you cry. I have been stunned at some of the stories I've heard.

I belong to a group of many former residents of the children's home that I was in, who regularly email their recollections of their time in care. Yes, there are some that really did suffer. Some spent years having been institutionalised by the system and then were thrust into the big wide world and told to get on with it. Some emails I've read are full of things than can only be described as black humour. Some just didn't make it at all. Some children carry the notion of guilt all their life. Why do we think this happens? Is it perhaps because the lack of nature or love, or guidance of the real world, and how to deal with life as it comes, was never shown to us kids? Is it because we were robbed of the innocence of childhood? Many children (such as myself) tell me how they feel worthless about themselves and carry this with them for the rest of their lives. I consider myself one of the fortunates of these homes. I was plucked from the scrum of obscurity and placed into a family unit when I was five years old. I was given a 'New" identity; a home, a new Mum and Dad and two brothers, after spending over three and a half years in my Orphanage (because that is what they really were). Unusually, unlike most of these residents I actually remember my mother visiting me and although only eighteen months old initially, I have always known my birth name and both of my parents' names. The lies told to others wasn't going to work with me as the years have since proven.

Many people I know tell me I have a penchant for doing myself down; never allowing myself any self praise, which is actually very true. I always thought I'd made a pretty good recovery from my wretched start to life. Maybe I need to re-think that concept! My family really struggled as much as I did to deal with a frightened and unloved little boy and it is true my introduction into the then family unit caused utter mayhem. Parents (to my mind) brave enough to take on the challenge of a disturbed little soul like myself, with no handbook or guidance, must be applauded for their efforts to make life as normal as they could. I never really told my parents, nor indeed thanked them properly for what they did for me because I simply didn't know how.

Despite what some may say, I learned to respect everybody; no matter their colour or religion. I learned good manners, to say please and thank you. I learned family is the most important (or should be) part of life. I also learned that there are times when you have to stand up for yourself. To tell the truth only upsets those that lie! Many, many years of heartache and soul searching with regards to my birth family have now made me realise just how lucky I have been. Both my adoptive parents have passed and wherever they may be I hope they think their boy done Good.

It wasn't always that way! It has taken many years for my brothers and me to find ourselves and my life is so much better for that. Although distance and finances play a major role as to when we see each other, the Internet with web cams are such wonderful tools to maintain mutual respect and friendship that we should have enjoyed many, many years ago. The joy of seeing my brothers' own children growing up in a loving family unit, albeit from miles away, only cements my original statement. Family is important.

Equally important in my mind is the friendships we have during our lives. True friends are just as important as any family member. Two of my closest and early friends held the key to getting me out of the bubble of uncertainty I was trapped in. They were the catalyst for me to learn trust and understanding. Trevor, my life long friend, in reality was closer to me than my two brothers, right until his passing. Life as his friend was uncomplicated for fifty-seven years. In all that time not once did we ever have cross words; a true friend indeed. Anita was the person who held the most important key. The key to my heart changed me forever. Life in the 1960s was exciting as a teenager. The shackles of Victorian attitudes and morals were being challenged. The young were finally being listened to and boy, were their voices heard! With Anita, love and self-respect found a new home in me, which was the most wonderful experience of my life. In fact, life had gone from black and white into colour, and I loved it! For many years, my early life and subsequent adoption was my excuse for everything that went wrong. And there was plenty that did!

Between them, Anita and Trevor will never know what they did for me BUT I do. Along with my adoption and friendships I think I've had far more than my fair share of luck. I am still making new friends who are proving equally as important in my later years. As I write my initial anger with the Authorities, whatever form they have taken over the years have softened (though you may not think so), as I think of the positives and good things in my life. My search and long time battle to find family has to say the least, been a journey of many ups and downs with some surprising results and become the most important thing in my life. Not least resulting in two books.

An author or avid reader is not how I would describe myself but as Bob Dylan sang: The Times They are Changing. My first book "Welcome to your New Home" is the story of arriving at the Catholic Children's Home St. Mary's Gravesent, Kent. My adoption into the McKenna family and consequent battles to find birth family, and how I went about this. This chapter is mainly to show that attaining the Holy Grail itself throws up many unforeseen problems that need to be resolved. As ever, no handbook to refer for guidance. The reaction of the missing family that you may find if you are as determined and at times as lucky as I was, can be very strange indeed.

When after almost sixty years my birth mother was found, her initial reactions it seemed were just great. The first contact from an organisation (in my case Cabrini) must throw up all kinds of emotions for the parent. I can't imagine how I would feel in those circumstances, but then isn't this the price to pay for earlier possible indiscretions! I am amazed sometimes at the total disregard afforded to a child when this is brought to the attention of a parent. Maybe a self-defence mechanism sort of kicks in after living a "lie" or worse, a deception for many, many years. The stigma that went along with the mothers who bore children through their own lack of responsibilities, or the unfortunate women who were left to bring the child up by one absent father must have been very traumatic. As stated earlier, I'm not an unfeeling person and truly realise that there should be a system in force that gives both sides an equal chance to come to terms with possible future outcomes.

Even so, in my mind the balance is so very unfair for the child and needs to be brought to a level playing field, with every effort made for a positive result. My dealings with the authorities lead me to believe they think a child is always out for some form of revenge. Without exception I have found this to be completely unfounded. Inevitably when families are reunited or discovered there will be times of discord, and maybe latent feelings will surface that perhaps were thought not to be there from both sides! Without doubt the questions of why and how will begin to take over from the natural desires.

I have found in my case that my thoughts changed dramatically from the original need to know, the need to understand, and is difficult to keep in check. The support of your adoptive family to me is an absolute must if this stage of your life is to make sense

My advice to anyone on similar journey to mine, is to involve the family that have made you into what you are today, because it will be as fascinating to them as yourself. Their backing and understanding and support is important and may keep things manageable, particularly when the search hits any minor or major setbacks. And this will happen! Many of the TV programmes that feature similar journeys only show the initial joy of discovery but not many of the ups and downs of learning about your new family and of course yourself. The initial response from my mother led me to believe that everything was going to be rosy in the garden. And for a brief while that was what it seemed. Then came the changes. Within a few short weeks of discovering my birth mother was still alive at eighty-three, I was told that I had TWIN half brother and sister, eight years younger than myself and brought up by our mother. Told to me: not by my mother but the adoption society. This should have rung some alarm bells within me. Why did mother not mention this instead of them? We still had to meet but had shared plenty of what I might term as informative phone calls, or so I thought! You would have thought mentioning a further three half siblings almost obligatory but apparently not. My first reaction was one of sheer delight to discover further siblings; a sister and brother came as a welcome surprise nearly sixty years down the line. Then I discovered they had no knowledge of me either or indeed another half brother that I did know of, who was three years younger than myself and whom I had also be searching for. Sadly he died in his mid-twenties. He too had been adopted (which I had discovered) and I informed my mother as I said I would. She said she didn't know he'd been adopted! I resisted pointing out to her that she would have had to give her permission for this to happen. Just as she had already done for me. He was in fact adopted by my mother's sister and her Polish husband. My mother obviously didn't share my openness and honesty and this is when the cracks started to appear.

I had told her about my first book "Welcome to Your New Home", although at this time it was in manuscript form and I had read and given it to her. When told of having some other siblings I didn't know what to say to Mother. Things like: 'why didn't you tell me?'

And 'why did it have to be the Children's Society that told me?'

I suppose I was so involved with my joy of finding family that I missed (or just ignored) the signals from my mother. The secrecy of years gone by were apparently alive and well. To further complicate matters my sister who lives in Italy and her daughter were told by my mother within a few weeks of my finding her. YET my brother, her TWIN, who lives just a few streets from where Mother does, still doesn't know and neither does his son. I have to time my visits to Mother when she knows he won't be around or is unlikely to drop in unannounced. This is something that really frustrates me immensely because I hate living a lie. To me it's astonishing that Mother is happy enough to deceive yet again, almost as a second nature, which I find a little disturbing.

To try and keep together the section of the family that know of me I reluctantly agreed not to reveal myself to my new brother until after Mother passes on. This does not sit at all well with me and has now created a widening gap of silence and denial from my Mother. Something has to give sooner rather than later, which is not what I had anticipated at all. I am a man of my word but am finding it increasingly hard not to reveal myself.

On one hand Mother, my sister and her daughter (who I have met and is a delight) have threatened to have nothing to do with me IF I should tell him. On the other hand, I feel he should know of me. My thought is why should he be denied as I was and if he decides he wishes to have nothing to do with me then at least it would be his choice! The emotional blackmail being used by my mother and sister is so tasteless to me that I have a major struggle not to break my word. As I said earlier this is the less than rosy side of finding family. Instinct pushes me to tell him but I was brought up by my adoptive parents to be honest and faithful. One of these concepts will become a casualty in the not too distant future. That truly disturbs me.

Another reason for a balanced non-partial system that needs to be in place to help families overcome just this kind of impasse. One of my biggest complaints is simply; there appears to be an attitude, a lack of feeling and understanding for those seeking family. Is it because it's not a vote catcher? It's not the News Headlines on a daily basis, is it?

I genuinely think that this attitude still exists: "If we do nothing these people will just give up and go away."

When I was trying to get my book published, I hawked it around to several publishers and the various media sources and not one of them even replied to an initial contact or enquiry. Does that tell you a story of the closed shop that operates within these organisations, OR do the people who run these companies have no concept of life as it really is? Through a very helpful friend, an ex-Pat who now lives in Canada, I was able to get my book published from there in what seemed like no time at all.

I say again mine is NOT an unusual story. There's a large minority of siblings as well as parents that sincerely need help. I would urge anyone who reads my stories and many others that are available, to just sit back and think about what they have read, then go to their local MP and see what reaction you will get from him or her. Then you may get an idea of the battle that lays ahead for all of us! I should have realised from day one just what a journey I had in front of me when I tried to get my original birth certificate. Living in England, the scenario that you would NOT wish to encounter was simply: Born in Scotland AND adopted through the Catholic Church. There is a sort of expression we have in the UK: A Double Whammy! Basically the two worst things that could happen to anyone under such circumstances. Scotland and The Catholic Church were my double whammies, when I set out on this intrepid journey (it sounds like Scott and that epic trek to the Antartic in 1912). And it feels as though the laws of this land are still in a time long before that amazing event.

Remember that in the nineteen-sixties there was no Internet and Freedom of Information was very restricted, especially if seeking knowledge of yourself let alone family. Although I knew my birth name in full, where I was born and when, my mother's maiden name and even my father's, this simple request took me three (YES, 3) years. With just a telephone (landline) and writing letters as my only choice of weapons it was easy to be pushed from pillar to post. Despite obvious changes since the sixties it still feels like nothing has changed.

Over thirty-years ago I was sent six letters that had been written by my mother to the Catholic Rescue Society as it was then called, and were her basic thoughts to the local Parish Priest as to how and why she had made this momentous decision. They were a revealing read. It was obvious she was not able to cope with a child and wanted me to have the best chance of a decent and most importantly happy life, that she realised she couldn't give me at that time.

On each of these letters her various addresses were obliterated by the Catholic Authorities. Sadly some years ago my home was burgled and amongst the items stolen were these six letters. Lost forever; or so I thought! When I told this to one of the St. Mary's Old Boys (my group of emailing friends), he said that The Catholic Rescue Society (now called Cabrini) would still have the records of these letters. And he was right. So I contacted Cabrini to ask for copies of the said letters, carefully explaining that they were for my own files and not for publishing and guess what? I was informed because I'd made contact with my birth mother they couldn't resend me copies without her consent.

Let's recap for a second. Letters sent and admitted in writing by Cabrini to me some thirty-years ago now couldn't be sent. The reason for this: The letters may belong to Cabrini BUT the contents belong to my mother. I remind you this is 2012, NOT 1912, or indeed 1812! And to confuse matters even further, apparently what they (Cabrini) decide relates to me IS however allowed to be sent but not the rest! I really haven't made that up!

After several emails and telephone calls THEY have decided they can send me extracts from these letters! Well that was a month ago and all the letters were much less than 100 words each and guess what? NO letters YET! Maybe they are literally cutting, sticking and pasting by hand the individual letters onto another small letter. This of course could take years! I have to be seen as fair and even handed so I will try! Cabrini says it's the LAW of protection and privacy and the data safety protection act that doesn't allow them to be sent as they were written. This is the same data act that permits unsolicited telephone calls and junk emails in volume to me on a daily, if not hourly basis. I did suggest that their original letters sent must have been an illegal act on their behalf.

Although that comment was meant as a sarcastic aside, it was greeted in total silence. Perhaps at last an admission of guilt. What do you think?

If I was still at school and had written what I just have for an essay, I would probably had electrodes attached to my head, because I would have been deemed as mad. I'm not targeting Cabrini: it's just that this organisation (especially from several years ago) is the group that I have mostly dealt with. From what I hear other societies are much more forthcoming. In the spirit of fairness, I have to applaud the wonderful and compassionate help the lady social worker, Irene Coppock from Cabrini, who eventually found my birth mother and other details, was just brilliant. A real shining light from within a dark background and perhaps the much maligned Catholic Church organisation. My thanks to her are very geniune.

After a great deal of soul searching I have come to what for me is a stressful decision. Remember I earlier said there was going to be a casualty with one of my values in life. Honesty and being Faithful. I have decided to send my half brother my book "Welcome to your New Home", with an accompanying letter, explaining who I am and why I've gone down this route. My mother and to a lesser degree my sister have left me no choice. Nearly four years of no effort on their behalf to inform him of me. The emotional blackmail laid at my door to keep the secret going has finally proved too much. I am fully aware that this action alone will be the perfect ammunition for those from this family of mine to abandon me again. In an ironic twist until recently, the thought of being abandoned had never been mentioned by me. I have for years stoically defended my mother and the actions she took regarding my future life and strangely enough do actually agree what she did was the best thing that could have happened for me at that time.

Where is the mechanism of reason and debate and resolution that I need? I have broken my moral ethos of NOT knocking on the door out of the blue and saying: 'Hi, guess who I am?'

The results of my actions will no doubt feature later in this book. Already I had a reaction from my older adoptive brother after telling him what I have just done! I must admit that he, his wife and my younger brother and his wife all did suggest a couple of years ago to make the best of and accept what I had already achieved. Finding my birth mother, discovering two half siblings and sadly learning of the death of the half brother I knew of. As I touched on earlier I have kept my family, my brothers up to speed with all events as they unfold and I value their input and advice. So why break that, I hear you ask?

The urge to meet and discover an extended version of another family that I was once part of, albeit very briefly, is an instinct that seems to take over. My older brother wrote to say he thought I was wrong to just suddenly land the information at my brother's door without any warning or caveat. And in a way I have to agree with him; to a point. My mother and sister have had nearly four years to have made steps to ready him for the knowledge of a brother he (and my sister) never knew of. Though I have never seen my sister I have had the pleasure of meeting her daughter, my niece, and she is an absolute delight. A credit to her mum and dad, and I have to say we got on really well. I had hoped her modern outlook on life might help to breakdown a few of the barriers. It is with some regret that my niece has been dragged into this very messy situation and I have repeatedly apologised to her for doing so. And now it is plain to see why there is a need for a system of arbitration and reconciliation for ALL parties. My older brother does not agree with what I've done BUT he is entitled to his opinion and I did ask him. We will not fall out over his thoughts. Why should we; we are family.

As a diversion and a chance to recharge my thoughts and memories, I have just bought on-line and now read a fascinating book written by Margaret Humphreys. This was originally called "Empty Cradles" and is now call "Orange and Sunshine", to coincide with the release of the film of the same name. Without revealing anything of the contents of a book that left me as angry as I was delighted to see confirmation of what I always knew in print and had been telling people ALL my life and incurring a lot of disbelief from an extraordinary yet ordinary person from Nottingham, has vindicated some of my apparent rants against the authorities earlier. Maybe I should have done it years ago. BUT like most of us kids from this background, people just didn't want to know. Even my adoptive parents used to say, 'That can't be true; it's a figment of your imagination.' Not any more, it isn't!

I have recently discovered several books that deal with the trauma so many people went through in their early years and nearly all of them are quite harrowing accounts. None appear to have a happy ending. Unless you actually experienced what these people (myself included to a lesser degree) went through, it is difficult to comprehend. Everyone knows what you become and how you deal with the vagaries that life throws at you, is usually predetermined by the way you were brought up. NOT just a simple case of learning the meaning of wrong and right; but love, understanding and compassion. These are the tools that you need to live your life with proper meaning. A void of just one of these attributes can cause mayhem for the rest of your life. It's a bit like having a missing gene in your personal make up.

My earlier reference to the letter from my birth mother has taken another turn! After about three months of waiting patiently for a reply from Cabrini, with regards to the letters and NO response again, I decided to send a letter to remind them and then after emailing back I actually rang them. At my behest (not theirs) I suggested that I could meet someone from a local branch in Bristol to see what they had decided I could see. Well that meeting has taken place and I met two pleasant and young ladies and introduced myself to them. To break the ice I showed them the folder they (Cabrini) had given me which contained ALL the original and now sepia faded documents of their dealings with my mother and the process along the way up to and including my official adoption by accreditation with the Kent County Adoption Court. I brought this folder with me because the lady I'd made the appointment with was a student learning her trade. She had quite properly asked if I minded another person being present; presumably to oversee the interview. I guessed she's never seen someone's life in that fashion before and from as long ago as it was. And I was right in my assumption. She was very grateful that I had thought about her situation.

There was as ever a method in my madness! It was to show them I was the thoughtful person I'd always told Cabrini I am and wanted to show them as such. I also said that I am a very determined soul and wasn't going to be easily put off in my current quest. An hour or so passed very pleasantly as she read the snippets that they had deemed was for my eyes and about me. They also gave me a copy of what she'd read out and I dutifully thanked them both. I also reminded them of my determination to get the six letters one way or another, even if that means taking some form of legal action to do so. One of them asked why I felt the need to do that. I politely pointed out it had taken me almost sixty years to trace my birth family and that this was due to many reasons but mainly my fight with the Catholic Authorities and their cloak of secrecy. Although it is so much better today because of the change in certain Laws of the land and not so much the change in the Catholic church.

After the publication of my own story, "Welcome to Your New Home" and the positive feedback, I have now read many books from other authors and the extent of the abuse most of them suffered at their various homes, I was very, very lucky and don't recall such problems for myself and the huge veil of secrecy is mind-blowing! Then of course there is the matter of the thousands of British kids and their mass transportation to Australia and other Commonwealth countries and the vile part governments played with their web of lies and deception.

Little did I know that hundreds (not just a handful) of British children were still being sent to the Antipodes even in the late-sixties! Not only that there was the practice of not telling the parents of those children had been sent without their consent, knowledge and most certainly no authority to do so for most of them (though not all). These kids were often put through severe hard labour and were transported from as young as five years old. How can you send a five-year-old to the other side of the world alone and completely lost? A simple apology is just not enough; it never will be!

It took the brave efforts of Margaret Humphreys to expose these terrible wrong doings and most importantly re-unite some of those kids with their blood family. By the time Mrs. Humphreys got the facts it was too late for so many: children and parents alike. "Sunshine and Oranges" is a book and film that will live with me forever and has made me realise just how lucky I was with my own adoption. My own birth mother was one of the few mothers who were asked about me being sent to a "lovely" new life in Australia and she readily agreed to this, thinking that she was giving me the sort of opportunity and life that she could never provide in the UK. It seems my adoptive parents unknowingly, saved me from God knows what!

It has now been a couple of months since my meeting with Cabrini and there has been no further response. No phone calls or emails regarding my visit, which does not fill me with confidence or indeed bring me to believe that the Catholic Church has really had a serious change in its ethics, morals or understanding of us children! I did suggest that they might try and contact my mother either by phone or a letter and wished them well. Needless to say there has been no response from them OR indeed my mother. My half brother who I know has now received my book and the letter that I placed with it, has not responded either. Maybe I shouldn't feel surprised: why when you receive something as important as a book and a letter from a very close and unknown member of your own family there is no reaction at all. Perhaps it runs in the family? This is supposed to be the age when nothing surprises us anymore, isn't it? When I found out about the twins my immediate reaction was: fantastic, tell me more!

Not a single negative thought from me despite missing nearly sixty years of knowing them and searching for birth family, not one!

In my mind the Catholic Church has not changed one bit in several hundred years. It is the law that has changed, slightly! In fact the Catholic Church is so far behind the times I'm surprised they don't speak in Latin. Every new Pope trots out the same old dogma and they wonder why they are losing followers they will never get back. When are they going to learn? When are they going to be honest? When are they going to move forward? When are they going to apologise to us kids? When are they going to be held to account? I often wonder what God will say to these people, past and present, when they meet? Surely it would have to be at a halfway house and probably never in heaven!

THE BAKEHOUSE
BY THE PRISON WALL

BY MICHAEL MCKENNA

CHAPTER ONE

Mt. Thom is a fairly insignificant mountain by most standards; it separates Cape Breton Island and Pictou County from the remainder of Nova Scotia. It is however high enough to create a microclimate, and as my car crested its final rise the grey rain I had been wrapped in during my drive down from Halifax began to break and the patchwork fields of Pictou County bathed in late summer sunlight stretched out in front of the windshield.

Nova Scotia was now my home. Settled first by immigrants of Anglo-Scottish descent it later became a haven of black townships, created at the end of the underground railroad by those fleeing the harsh bonds of slavery. More recently still as the social structure of Canada changed it had become culturally diverse, cosmopolitan but without many of the negatives associated with wealthier and larger Provinces.

My cell phone buzzed. 'Michael – it's Shaun – Mum's in hospital, but don't worry it's not serious, I'll keep you posted.'

Shaun was the younger of my two brothers, I being the oldest. Our father had passed a few years previously and our aging mother lived at this time quite comfortably in a nursing home in England.

Shaun was eleven years my junior; we maintained fairly close contact emailing each other with regularity. He was articulate, educated and amusing, and had created a successful career as a playwright after a brief stint on stage. Both younger brothers lived in England still, but there was little real contact between them, totally different in outlook and attitude, the three of us managed a closeness of sorts. The casual observer would have been hard pressed to recognize we were raised in the same household, influenced differently and loved unequally. Shaun had no children of his own, although he had two older stepdaughters from his marriage, who he adored. Luckily they were of an age that they never intruded on his completely self-centred existence, one which in fairness he lived honestly and without excuse.

The brunt of looking after our Mother in her later years, emotionally at least, fell to him. I had provided financial support for a number of years and until she became too frail to travel entertained her royally for a month each year in Canada. Shaun accepted this responsibility grudgingly but handled it with humour and equanimity. As the favoured child he felt he could pillage her bank account as needed and his visits were often prompted by financial need rather than filial responsibility. Shaun was clever and artistic. I had always believed he may well be gay, however he married a charming lady, albeit one fifteen years his senior, enabling me to state that he had "married his mother." A small minded position I chose to adopt because of my jealousy of Shaun always being favoured. Years later when the three of us reconnected I discovered how unfair this perception was; the burden of expectation placed on Shaun's shoulders was immense. I had run away. The only expectation of Terry was that he would be troublesome, leaving the entire responsibility for meeting parental expectations, and keeping family peace on Shaun's young shoulders.

Shaun was adored by both parents. He was the child that matched or exceeded all of their expectations.

His birthright was a little cloudy as a few months prior to his birth Mother had run off with a man forever identified as "The Swiss Guy". The question of parentage was never discussed, at least during our Father's lifetime. In post-war working class England secrets were seldom alluded to, kept close to home, and never discussed. A sharp slap upside the head, the accepted consequences of loose lips.

The more spiteful of the street's matrons might be overheard gossiping over a gin and tonic in the snug bar of the local pub. 'Heard she had a fling with a furrin fella then,' but it would have been a brave soul indeed who let Dad overhear any such talk.

My perception was unfair as I had witnessed my Father's breakdown at the time. His was a world in which men didn't cry, but on this occasion I came across him sitting on an upturned beer crate in the back yard, holding a telegram with tears streaming down his face. He poured out the whole sorry story of our Mother's defection in hurt and angry desperation. I was eleven years old, too young to handle such a burden and yet proud to be considered man enough to share his pain.

I wrote to my Mother that day, a cruel, childish letter that was a direct result of my father's pain and my own lost innocence. That letter effectively tainted, and ultimately destroyed whatever fragile love we shared; it ripped the security away from my young world, its effects rippling into the infinity of our existence. She did eventually return home, and on one memorable afternoon some weeks later the "Swiss Guy" made the mistake of showing up unannounced on our doorstep. If it hadn't been for the intervention of old Mr. Dobbin who ran the greengrocers across the street from our shop, a good kicking may well have turned into grievous bodily harm. He saved Dad from himself, and in the process allowed us to maintain both the deceit and our diginity.

Terry was my second brother, always in trouble; poor bastard never met Mother's expectations. I must confess that throughout most of our childhood I ignored him, seeing in him the interloper who took away my status as only and therefore favoured child. He never found much in common with Shaun, who was always more cerebral in his hobbies and pursuits. The fact that Terry who was four years my junior always bore the label "the adopted one", was never perceived as odd or exclusionary. What chance did he ever really have? Like the sandwich boards outside cheap cafes advertising home cooking the intent of the phrase masked the paucity of the execution. By today's standards he was abused, even in the storm of our childhood both Shaun and I recognized he had a harder time than either of us.

His life was tough from the beginning, having been born to a member of the servant classes who, not being allowed to have children and keep her job, hid him in a closet for the earliest months of his life before being forced to put him in an orphanage. A likeable and thoroughly irrepressible soul, he could never quite provide the adulation Mom thought she deserved for being such a good woman (she had, after all, taken the poor waif into her home) but once the initial wash of adulation over her good deed had passed she was stuck with the reality of a troubled small boy who was hers to cherish forever. The intentions were no doubt good in the early years, but the practice of bringing a child, even your own into an unhappy marriage, has never proven to work. As boys we never developed a closeness, and age differences meant we only spent a few years of our childhood together. As adults I saw Terry once or twice every decade, and we exchanged phone calls and letters with no greater regularity. He was likeable and gregarious and had I not left my life by the prison wall so decisively behind, we may well have been friends. Time, distance and circumstances left us comfortable with the relationship as it evolved; we were comfortable as familiar strangers.

Terry once enjoyed a brief flirtation with fame and success. A talented soccer player he was picked for one of the first division's farm teams but a blown knee wrecked his chances early in the process. In the intervening years his life had been a series of mundane jobs interspersed with two unlucky marriages. He had no children, no significant other, and coordinated the serving of meat pies and sandwiches in a job at Bristol City football club. He was fifty-four the day the phone rang

I was now in my late-fifties. I had run away from home at age sixteen, returning as infrequently as possible. My career choices took me far away from the bakery, my family and my home. I landed in Canada while still in my twenties, expecting to stay for the two-year term of my contract, and had remained ever since. I was the only one of the three boys to father children and had been married to a woman who had been my salvation for nearly thirty years. Whatever scars I bore when we met she healed; however poorly I had learned to parent she guided me through the morass of trial and error involved in successfully raising children, and most importantly she loved me. Susan brought peace to my psyche, allowed me to be myself, and liked who I turned out to be. Early in our marriage she pushed me to bring my relationship with my family to an understanding of sorts, and my world was better for it.

I was headed to meet her at our small summer cottage on the ocean in Pictou County. We spent much of the season there, and I would commute as necessary the eighty-five mile trip to Halifax. Our kids were grown and away at University, so it was just the two of us when I arrived.

'My Mom is in hospital,' I told her.

'Then you had better get over and see her,' was her reply.

It had been two years since I had last seen my Mother; the somewhat difficult decision to move her into assisted living being made coincidentally with my taking a couple of trips to England as a result of her failing health. The earliest of which marked the first time I had returned to England in twenty-seven years. The bakery was long since closed. My Mother remarried and lived with her second husband prior to his death in a pleasant home just outside the town in which I had been raised.

As we age the habits that society and good manners cause us to adopt to mask the less desirable parts of our personalities, diminish. Mother had become somewhat spiteful and vindictive in her latter years, in ways that reminded me of my childhood. As a result I discovered in myself a return of childish feelings towards her that I didn't care for; I recognized myself in her actions and I didn't like it. After all she had been allowed back into my life only upon the insistence of my wife and then on my terms, she had in conscience acted well and made a real effort to change. I recognized that it was my feelings causing the widening rift. I had been struggling with them for some time, trying while doing so to avoid upsetting Mom, who was after all unchanged, just older and more vulnerable.

I sat on the couch and made selfish excuses, not wanting the intrusion of a last minute trip to England.

"Well they say it's not serious, I'll wait awhile.'

'Wake up, Michael. She's eighty-five and in the hospital. You'd better go!'

Susan wasn't going to allow me to let myself off this hook. Our conversation was interrupted by the ringing of the telephone.

It was Terry's voice. "All right then, Mick? Look, mate, Mom died.'

At that moment I realized that the opportunity I had been trying to justify not taking was lost forever! It was too late. I was disappointed in how I acted and who I had become. It is on moments such as these that life turns.

Terry was completely broken up. I spent a few minutes consoling him, angry at myself for not sharing his grief. Of the three of us he was by far the most visibly upset by her passing; a woman who had at best been a poor mother to him was his last tenuous hold on family. Even at the end when she figuratively slapped his face one last time by purposefully excluding him from her meagre will, he still grieved her loss. As is human nature at times of moment in life, my thoughts turned backwards.

It was fifty-one years earlier when I first set eyes on the Bakehouse by the prison wall. The wall was the ugliest thing I had ever laid eyes on, stretching as far as my seven-year-old eyes could see. The bakery sat kitty corner from the wall in a solid working class part of town surrounded by rows of terraced houses each perched on a postage stamp sized lot. In areas like this the Queen's photograph was probably up on the living room wall, usually adjacent to a trio of plastic ducks caught in endless flight to nowhere. Of course, I didn't know it was considered working class; the constant reminders of our station in the world would come often enough in the ensuing years. I once read somewhere that there are men who become who they are as a result of whence they came, while others rise to greatness despite humble beginnings. There are also men who attempt to leave their beginnings behind, never able to silence the whispers of insecurity echoing from their past. I am afraid I am such a man.

CHAPTER TWO

The first time I saw the bakehouse there was no smoke coming out of the chimney. The massive ovens had been out for months, ever since the dreams of the previous tenant had foundered in the years after the war when sugar, butter and sweets required for baking were unavailable. In fact, it would take a solid week of stoking the fireboxes to build up enough heat in the century old brick to even think of making a batch of bread. That was the only time I would ever see the bakehouse ovens with a puff of smoke lazily climbing skyward.

The bakehouse was built from rough Kentish stone quarried from the South Downs at the turn of the century. It was a two-storey saltbox building, which at one time had an open yard in front; this long since covered with a cheap corrugated iron roof. At the rear of the yard was a stable built of the same quarried grey stone, a necessity of the time when all deliveries would have been made by horse and dray.

Inside the bakery was lined with huge old fashioned bread bins, conical open tubs, once designed for hand-mixing now topped with sturdy board. The centre of the space was dominated by a production bench the size of two dining tables. The rough-hewn wood polished to that rich patina found only in well-aged wood that has been carefully used, and worked on for decades.

The end wall was entirely taken up with two ovens, one large, one smaller, each with an arched steel door braced with brass cross plates and handles. The interior of each oven was about the size of a small bedroom. For over a hundred years huge fires had been built up and kept burning without ever being allowed to go out. You could trace the Industrial Revolution here, first wood, later coal and now, in the post war years coke kept them fed. If the ovens lost too much heat the bricks they were made of would eventually shrink and the roofs come tumbling down. At one point during the time we lived there, this happened, and even after six weeks the brickies could only work twenty minute shifts before they had to concede to the built-up heat.

I stood there with my Father and looked around the space which would mark so much of his life.

'We'll get a fresh load of coal tomorrow but there's enough here to get the ovens fired up, son, then you can help me get this place cleaned up.'

I was seven years old. A young Queen Elizabeth had just taken the throne and we had our own business. What optimism must have surged through my Father's chest as he looked round his bakehouse. He had been a baker all his young life, working in, or running them for others. In post-war England for the average man in the street, owning your own place was an ambition not often realized. It never crossed my mind the years that lay ahead would prove almost overwhelming in the amount of work and heartache they would throw at us. I was a man among men, ready to get to work alongside my old man. I would have been horrified if his expectations of me were any less. The premise of entitlement, one of my generation of baby boomers would learn to embrace, had not yet been conceived. You expected to eat, you were expected to contribute – simple as that and we felt pride in our ability to do so.

'I'll get started down here and you can sort out the loft, son.'

'Where's the loft?' I asked looking round for something, anything that resembled a loft.

In one corner of the bakehouse a square hole about a yard each side had been cut in the roof. A rough ladder of 2 x 4's bolted to the wall with cross beams of the same dimension screwed in place for rungs disappeared into the darkness above. The rungs of the ladder were worn from use in the centres, polished again to a dense patina as a result of decades of use. A year or two prior I had visited the Tower of London and marveled at how the steps leading down to the kitchens and dungeons had worn over the passage of time into smoothly concentric circles. The same pattern of wear was evidenced on the bakehouse ladder. The wood smooth to the point of slickness as we climbed up rung by rung. I was a little scared; only the reassuring presence of my father's bulk below kept me climbing.

'OK, son, pull yourself through and wait for me,' like there was a chance of my going anywhere!

The loft was a gloomy cavern lit only by sunlight filtering through chinks in the slate roof. Mysterious scuffling and rustling in the deeper shadows of the side of the room suggested we had entered a world inhabited by others; who knew what manner of creature lived in a loft?

The space flooded with light as Dad threw a switch for the single bare bulb suspended from a beam over the centre of the room. The scurrying increased as barely glimpsed movements suggested that nothing more threatening than the odd mouse made the loft home. No bears or other dangers lurked in the gloom. The space was huge, covering both the entire lower floor and stable area. Windowless and musty with a pile of canvas in one corner, the floor consisted simply of boards roughly nailed to cross beams which over time had warped and twisted allowing glimpses of the bakehouse beneath.

'This is where we store flour. Watch out for the chute and the ladder,' I was told. 'And don't go running around here too much until I check for loose or rotten boards.'

Each cautious step produced tufts of fine powdery dust, the motes dancing in the air like fog on the English Channel. Every surface was covered with the finest film of flour dust and huge spider webs draped the corners and the exposed beams.

'We tip our flour down the chute into the mixer each night to make the dough,' explained Dad.

The pile of canvas in the corner proving to be a canvas chute resembling a gigantic toeless sock suspended over the bread-making machine a floor below.

'Well, let's start cleaning this place up.'

There was no hot water available; once the fire was stoked and burning we stowed five-gallon jerricans of water in the proof boxes built under the ovens. There may not have been a surfeit of technology in Victorian England but they were inventive. The fire that heated the oven also ensured the horse slept snug and warm as the stable shared a common wall with the firebox. Any heat escaping through five feet of tightly stacked brick kept the loft warm and dry, a perfect environment for storing flour. While next to the firebox below the oven were proofing chambers which held enough heat to warm water overnight.

I filled jerricans at a single iron tap over an earthenware sink the size of a steamer trunk. My father stacked them away one by one as I struggled mightily to help him, the weight of the can and its contents way too much for me to overcome. And there we stood, side by side, man to man in the centre of it all, our new universe.

'Let's get *her* fired up then, son,' said my Father.

I guess it's the male thing that what we love are gender specific: our cars, boats, inanimate things that we hold dear to us are always she. Perhaps because we know they are going to be trouble, out of our control. On that first day he truly loved her, only later, like his marriage would she sour on him.

We started the fires and, once they caught, we shoveled on coal until Hades itself burned no hotter. The dampers (the system controlling the amount of air fed to the fire) were wide open. The flames roared mightily and the ovens stirred slowly to life, bricks creaking geriatricly as they were roused from dormancy.

Eventually we closed the dampers, built up the fire with coal dust to keep it sullenly brooding overnight and pulled the yard gates shut behind us. The ovens would never again go out during the years we lived there. At night they were banked up with coal dustings, and each morning around 4 a.m. they were stirred reluctantly to life. The wisps of smoke rising from the chimneys visible from my bedroom window defined the scope of my life as clearly and abruptly as the omnipresent prison wall defined the limits of the world of those trapped within it.

CHAPTER THREE

The shop sat on one corner of four intersecting streets adjoining the shop; part of the same building was our house, the bedrooms of which were built over the shop. Tacked onto the back of the house were a scullery and an outside toilet both of which sat in a yard, where we stored empty beer crates; the whole surrounded by a ten-foot brick wall.

The bakehouse itself stood immediately adjacent to the yard my bedroom overlooked and from where I could see the chimneys of the bake ovens and two very large signs, one proclaiming to anyone who cared: "Don't Say Brown, Say Hovis", an early and very successful effort at what would later be known as brand marketing.

I attended school in a small village five miles away, a three grade school ruled by Misses Charlton, Peak and Wyse. It was an idyllic country school, high standards expected of both behaviour and academics. We looked out of our classroom windows onto pastureland complete with grazing Jersey cows and a meandering shallow brook. To get to school I had to take a bus. My Mother would walk me to the bus station each morning from where the bus stopped right outside my school. Each of the stops the bus made was clearly identified by the conductor along the route, and once out of town it was not uncommon for the bus to wait for the occasional tardy rider. At one small village en route to school a young girl about my age was always accompanied at the stop by her mother and pet lamb. During the years I rode that bus I watched the lamb grow into a sheep; in later years it apparently walked to and from the stop with no need of human guidance! On my way home each afternoon I caught a local bus from the bus station to the prison stop from which my mother could watch me make my way across the street from the shop window.

One day, shortly after we moved in, I arrived home from school and there, outside our shop, was a team of four dapple grey shire horses, each the size of an elephant. They pawed and snorted in a most alarming fashion, striking sparks from the pavement with their front hooves. I was in complete awe, but everybody else seemed to take this momentous happening in stride. We lived in a market town, built on a bend in the river Medway about 30 miles southeast of London en route to the channel ports. The local brewery was a major employer and took great pride, not only in their beer, but in the teams of horses that delivered it. Kegs, cases and crates of bottles were stacked on flat trays and men of giant stature, at least in my young mind, toured the pubs and off licenses throughout town delivering their bounty.

'Alright then, son?' one of the draymen asked after he learnt that I was the new governor's boy.

'Coming for a ride then?'

I was king of the castle as I rode between the draymen. The horses strained to gain momentum before effortlessly hauling the dray to its next destination. All eyes were upon me – why, the emperor with no clothes could have attracted no less attention. At the end of the street I was dropped off to scamper home bursting with my newfound knowledge of horses, and horse handling.

I came to know each horse over the next two or three years and developed favourites. I always scrounged a piece of apple or carrot from old Mr. Dobbin, the greengrocer. I discovered that shire horses loved old day doughnuts. It was a lesson never forgotten as the draymen, like their charges, were gentle giants, not to be aroused by such foolishness as feeding horses food guaranteed to rot their teeth.

Around our back yard was a three-foot wide strip of dirt, euphemistically referred to as the garden. The English have always had a great love of gardens; no one approaches gardening with greater optimism and enthusiasm than an Englishman faced with a patch of dirt. In miniscule backyards all around our neighbourhood, gardens abounded. Rationing had only just ended and the frugality of the war years remained a virtuous necessity. Runner beans, tomatoes, lettuces, cabbages were all coaxed into life, nurtured, protected from pests and carefully tended before being harvested. A vital ingredient in this process was horse manure. What fell in steaming piles outside our shop was sacrosanct. That was ours, and it fell to me to collect it, if we were lucky enough for the horses to move their bowels during the delivery process. I would scoop it up rather gingerly (as I was never sure how accepting these dappled monsters were of a small boy waving a large shovel in close proximity to their nether regions) and then I would carefully deposit it on our little strip of dirt to be saved for greater things! The value of any commodity is always defined by demand, the demand was such that the progression of the dray, if interrupted by "a natural recycling event" was marked by housewives rushing out of their front door armed with dust pans and brushes ready to pounce on whatever lay in the roadway.

Delivery by horse lasted only for a year or two, falling victim to cost effectiveness and overcrowded roads. The horses lived out their years in splendid retirement interrupted only by special events for which they were curried to gleaming perfection and adorned with brightly polished horse brasses. I swear they knew they were the centre of attention all along.

Young Norman was one of the draymen and blacksmith to the horses. He lived with his widow mother just up the street. There were a lot of widows in the post war years and living at home was then seen as a caring and loving thing, in no way diminishing. Young Norman (never spoken of without the diminutive) was none too bright. His life was his horses and evenings spent over a pint or two and a game of darts at the Greyhound. He was the custodian of the magnificent dapple greys and sometimes he would take me down to the stable where the last of the breed marked the passage of a less restless time. When the last of them died he took retirement, his loss so overwhelming he could find nothing to replace it. Years after I had left home I would see Young Norman, now an old man, stepping out of the door of the little terraced house in which he had been born and would die alone, a man seemingly content with his world containing a garden, a pub and a radius of not more than thirty miles.

The reason we had beer in a bakery was that part of the shop consisted of an off license – licensed premises where you could purchase alcohol for home consumption. In the early days the bakery was separated from the off license by a frosted glass partition etched with the words, "jug and bottle department". Once inside you were faced with a giant mahogany bar, two pull taps for beer, one brown, one mild. Bitter was yet to become a workingman's brew; it was the reserve of county folk in hacking jackets and tattersall checks. To one side was a keg of scrumpy cider, a noxious brew guaranteed to reduce the hardest drinking man to a gibbering idiot after one or two glasses. Behind the counter a couple of makeshift shelves held the odd bottle of spirits; gin was the overwhelming favourite and an assortment of cheap Cyprus sherries and sickly French Sauterne. In crates on the floor quarts of stout, brown ale and pale ale were stacked high. The bakery closed at six but from six to ten p.m. a steady parade of neighbours, most armed with jugs covered with clean tea cloths, yet others with assorted empty pop, beer and milk bottles brought them in to be filled. To ensure fairness we had two pewter and brass pitchers, one holding a pint, the other a quart. Each of these had a line an inch from the top and woe betide you if you poured too much foam or worse yet perceived to be pouring to the line and not over it.

'You'd sell more beer if you filled the jug, son,' or 'if I wanted a half pint I'd bloody well order one,' were likely to be heard.

We all worked in the shop watching TV in the room behind it, alerted to the presence of a customer by the ringing of a bell attached to the top of the door.

Our street was lined with Plane trees; in spring and summer their leafy shades gave the illusion of a much grander locale. The terraced houses, immediately around the bake shop fronted directly onto the street. Further along towards the monied end of the street where homes increased in value, small patches of front yard gave way to spacious walled gardens. That end of the street was the one furthest away from the prison wall.

When first constructed in the era between the wars the small front yards were genteel reminders of the social elevation ascribed in living in a semi-detached rather than a terraced home. At one time each yard had been enclosed behind a decorative wrought iron fence. These had all been cut off and melted down to make tanks and bombs to support the war effort. Winston Churchill stirred the country to make the contribution of their scrap iron but the post war government never provided funds to replace the fences.

Few families had the disposable income to undertake the task themselves, and as a result the low brick walls surrounding these modest grounds were punctuated at four-inch intervals with rusting lengths of protruding iron.

The majority of the neighbourhood was solidly working class, mill and factory workers and other occupations comprising the blue collar class. The class system still defined British society, the nuances subtle but always clearly understood.

The prison wall loomed over us all. Crews of prisoners on work release programmes, under the watchful eye of prison guards, were a common sight in the neighbourhood as they marched or jogged to whatever tasks had been allotted to them for the day.

It was common, in those days, for open spaces of land to be allocated to neighbourhood allotments. The prisoners were responsible for supporting the prison budget by tending plots devoted to the growth of basic vegetable crops. They also did clean up work around the neighbourhood, keeping drains unplugged and on occasion undertaking household maintenance work for homes that has lost their man in the war. It was a close knit community in which one always felt safe.

CHAPTER FOUR

Each street corner in the area by the wall housed some type of business, although part of the larger community of a bustling market town, our patch was like a walled medieval village. The English are renowned for building walls and fences to separate and enclose their space. Within the area bounded by the prison wall and the main road at the end of the street were many small fiefdoms, the confines of each clearly understood and accepted by the residents.

On the opposite corners from our shop stood Mr. Dobbins Greengrocers and Mrs. Coveney's general store. On the next block over you would find the Greyhound, the local pub which anchored the community, while a hairdressers, builders' yard and a second off license completed the block. A short distance up the road a butchers and a corner grocery store could be found. If we had a candlestick maker to boast of we would have completed the trinity popularized in the old nursery rhyme.

It was a happy and uneventful time, my parents were working as a team with a common goal, and my world orbited theirs. After coming home from school I would generally drop off my satchel of books and run up to the bakery to see Dad. Baking followed a very orderly regime. Each morning at 4 a.m. Dad would go off to work. Doughs were mixed, ovens fired up and pans and trays greased for the day ahead. Once mixed the dough was scooped out onto the huge production table where it was hacked into the required size, scaled and molded to its finished form.

While the bread was proofing, the production of morning goods began. Doughnuts, Swiss buns, buns of all sorts were lined up ready for the oven in serried ranks a general would have envied. My Father could gauge the temperature of the oven simply by laying a hand on the oven door. Once he decided it was ready the flash goods were loaded. These cooked quickly at high heat and soon the smells of cinnamon and spice would pervade the air. After the first goods from the oven were loaded back into racks to cool it was time to ready the oven for serious business. The fire was raked down to a bed of glowing embers giving off a solid almost baleful heat – next the warm brick of the oven floor was "scuffled". This process involved an old bread sack lashed to the end of a twelve-foot pole, this then dumped into a pail of water kept oven side and scuffed vigorously over the oven floor removing any ash or soot, as much of the bread was baked directly on the brick floor of the oven. Finally the oven was loaded. Gently and deliberately, because by now the loaves had risen into the full form, any rough handling would cause them to collapse, wasting not only the ingredients but several hours work. The bread had to be hot and fresh in the shop by 10 a.m. each morning.

The loaves were loaded deep into the oven using a peel, a device which resembled an egg lifter, but one about 12 feet long. Placing eight two-pound loaves at a time with a very long and heavy stick in the deepest recesses of a hole in the wall hotter than Hades was hard physical work. On occasion as Dad backed up in the effort to delicately place a load in just the right spot, he would encounter behind him a rack full of hot trays of buns recently removed from the oven. I have learned many colourful phrases over the years, in a number of languages, none matching in scope and inventiveness the colour, mostly blue, my Father brought to the English language on such occasions.

By the time I returned home from school around 4 o'clock each day this process was long completed. Afternoons were devoted to fancy goods. There were eclairs that had to be dipped in chocolate, Victoria sponges waiting to be sprinkled with icing sugar, cream puffs to be piped full of whipped cream and countless small and repetitive tasks that, while mundane, delighted my eight-year-old soul.

I would spend an hour balanced precariously on a 28 lb jam tin "helping" my Dad with his routine, surreptitiously licking chocolate covered fingers and sneaking the odd squeeze of cream from the piping bag. Next it was off to help in the shop for an hour. The ornate brass cash register, marked in pounds, shilling and pence, made a very satisfying ringing sound when the correct combination of keys were pressed. In the back, behind the shop, was the cake room where trays of finished goods were held in readiness to restock the shelves. My job was to sort and organize the cake room.

It was in the shop where I met most of our neighbours popping in on their way home from work for breads and cakes for that most glorious of mealtimes – tea! Dinner was a meal served at noon, a time not easily missed as the air raid sirens now pressed into peacetime service announced lunch break not the threat of German bombers. Tea usually consisted of slabs of fresh bread, sometimes slathered with butter and jam, other times toasted and topped with baked beans, a staple of blue collar British life. Usually one could expect a sweet treat as well, perhaps a jam tart or slice of Battenberg cake. There was no time that was designated as "quality time" so popularized by the Spock generation. I did of course get to spend time with my Mom and Dad, although we were usually working. I developed social skills by interacting with customers in the shop, and learned math by deducing how much change one gave from a shilling after deducting the cost of the cottage loaf and two lemon curd tarts.

In those early years we spent time after tea, generally around six, "improving" the shop. The jug and bottle department was manned by Auntie Vie, who always had a healthy ruddy complexion. I think she used to get into the scrumpy. No blood relative, Aunti Vie, she or any other adult acquaintance of one's parents received the honorary title of auntie or uncle. We would labour mightily to rip out magnificent mahogany counters to replace them with tawdry but thoroughly modern chipboard. Light fixtures were updated, new glass shelves installed in the front window and bright white paint slapped over richly veneered and panelled wood walls. I learned the hard way that the colourful expressions I had picked up from my Father's odd accident in the bakery were not at all suited for general expression.

Saturday was my favourite day. I got to work in the bakery learning the skills necessary to identify by eye how much dough weighed two pounds. Dad could always do it in two cuts; I was generally happy to take three or four stabs at it before hitting the right weight on the scale. Frying doughnuts was another early accomplishment of mine. A huge cast iron vat of oil bubbled over an open gas ring. Today we wouldn't let a child within twenty feet of such a thing, but I quickly learned how to scoop a freshly proofed doughnut off its tray with my left hand and drop it into the boiling fat. The trick was to avoid splashing the hot oil on oneself or worse yet, underestimating the degree of skill one had acquired and dipping your fingers into boiling oil.

On Fridays we had a night baker to get ahead of the inevitable demand for fresh baked goods on Saturday, the busiest of the week. Once I arrived, the last of the bread was in the oven and all the finished bread and baked goods needed to be carried down to the shop. This was done using large flat trays, which were balanced on our heads. At age nine I had to be content with a half size tray, my ever thoughtful Father having made one especially for me, my load was still six or eight loaves of bread weighing a total of twelve pounds. I didn't care, I was working alongside the two people I loved the most.

Sundays were a great day. We followed the biblical habit of resting, one I maintain to this day. There was no deep rooted religious basis for labouring six days, just the sheer necessity of rest after working a seventy-five hour week. Mom and Dad had a lie in. I made tea and raided the cookie bins in the shop before we all had tea in bed. Mom and I went to Church; she was Catholic Irish (my Father was a profound agnostic but had to agree to raise me as a Catholic in those days before the church would allow them to marry). It was a race of time between overcoming his lack of belief and my Mother's rapidly swelling mid-section. After church it was home. Mom made dinner and Dad went to the pub. Back in the day pubs closed at 2 p.m. on Sundays, and without exception Mother would have dinner on the table promptly at 1.45 p.m.

Giving the timing Dad was always late, and we would then spend a thoroughly miserable hour over our meal as Mom pointed out in great detail how thoughtless and selfish my Father was to want to spend time with his friends. In those early days none of her ill will extended to me. In later years I apparently became "more and more like your bloody father". A self-fulfilling prohecy for sure and one that seemed unfair as Dad was always particularly agreeable after coming home from the pub.

One day after the dishes were done Mom said, 'Michael, we have a surprise for you.'

I was excited at the prospect of a surprise. Surely a trip to the seaside or the zoo was in order, especially as Dad had borrowed a car from Uncle Cyril – again no relation, just an honorary title.

We drove out of town my face pressed eagerly against the rear glass seeking a clue as to what the great surprise might be.

'Where are we going, Mom?' I asked.

'Wait and see, it's a big surprise,' came the reply.

My excitement grew. A big surprise. Perhaps a pony. We had a stable empty and ready after all. At the very least I was sure something truly momentous was about to occur in my young life.

After what seemed like hours, the car turned into a driveway with large stone gateposts on either side.

A huge castle-like house squatted at the end of the drive with an imposing flight of broad stone steps leading up to the doors.

'Here we are then,' said Mom.

Upon entering the building we were greeted by a Nun in a flowing black habit. She held a whispered conversation with Mom and Dad at the far end of the room while I was sent off to play with three or four freshly-scrubbed boys. They were all wearing well polished and worn lace-up boots, a fact that sticks in my memory as it was an oddity even then.

I recall quite clearly the absence of any real toys, and the presence of both a strong smell of disinfectant and a sense of desperation. Each of the boys in turn was paraded in front of my Mom and Dad and then we loaded back in the car and drove off. The Nun stood on the steps and waved until we were out of sight. The small boys nestled under the bat-like wings of her habit.

'Did you like the boys?' I was asked. It was a matter of complete indifference to me.

'They were all right,' I replied.

'I really liked Terry,' said my Mom. 'Perhaps he can come to tea next Sunday.'

The whole thing washed over me like water off a duck's back. Obviously there was to be no pony. In fact, if they thought this was a surprise my parents were obviously not very bright but I found it in my heart to accept their flaws. That night after we returned home I fell asleep, watching the smoke slowly rising from the bakehouse chimney.

The next week passed uneventfully enough, but come Sunday at 5 p.m. the table was laid for tea. It was a tea so splendid as to be momentous. Not only sandwiches, but bread and dripping, a salad dressed up with egg and beetroot, plates of cakes and cookies and wonder of wonders, a bowl of trifle; heady stuff indeed!

Add to this the fact that I had been dressed up in my best and even my Father, who was normally asleep snoring in his chair at this time of day, was sporting a dress shirt and tie. Shortly after five there was a knock at the door which opened to reveal not only Terry and the Nun, but with them a rather grey man wearing a priest's collar. Tea was an illuminating affair. Mon had developed a "posh" accent overnight, Dad seemed to be going out of his way to pay attention to Terry, while everyone except me was beaming with pleasure at things I just couldn't catch on to. After tea I was sent to show Terry my room, shortly after that they all left for the evening and I thought things were back to normal.

'Michael, your Dad and I have a surprise and we want to talk to you about it.'

I knew with all the wisdom of my eight-and-a-half years there wasn't going to be a pony involved.

'Terry is going to come to live with us. We don't want you to be an only child and grow up spoiled and I can't have any more children. Won't it be nice to have a brother to play with? It will be so much fun.'

At that point I had no concept of what being spoiled might mean. The passage of time subsequently helped me realize quickly that I stood in absolutely no danger at all. Having a brother seemed rather a pleasant idea given the absence of either a puppy or a pony but one I had given no thought to. Terry seemed harmless enough and I only gave a passing thought as to why my Mother could have no more children. I was pretty familiar with the process, knowing it involved both birds and bees with a stork playing a role of some sort, and so Terry, forever after identified as the adopted brother, moved into the bakery by the prison wall and our lives.

CHAPTER FIVE

Maidstone was a pretty little market town in the late '50s; the Medway River weaving its way through town crossed by a single bridge carrying the main highway to London some forty miles west. The riverbank was a popular spot for fishermen, and with a short walk along the towpath we were deep in the countryside. Every few miles there were locks, which had over time, become social centres where country pubs served real ale and freshly made sandwiches.

High Street ran through the centre of town, and the history of the British Empire was all around for those who cared to look. A large cannon, a relic from the Boer War, and a magnificent monument to Queen Victoria stood in the middle of High Street breaking traffic into two distinct streams. Much of the architecture of the buildings lining the streets dated back to Dickensian and Tudor times. The busy commercial street, Week Street, crossed High Street at the top of town. The original buildings lining Week Street had been demolished over the years to make way for concrete box stores, mass market retailers. Boots the chemist, Woolworths, Marks & Spencer's, British traditions all – lined Week Street. There were no supermarkets in Maidstone at this time and the streets running across both commercial routes were lined with upscale stores located in magnificent 14th Century buildings on streets leading down to the river, which prior to the widespread use of the motor car was the major link for market towns.

Barges were a common sight in those years, many had been motorized but the odd one could still be seen being pulled by a large horse ambling along the towpath. The Bargees, river people, were like the Romanys, a nomadic, insular group, interacting with the townspeople only as required. The gypsies as Romanys were known to travel the countryside in brightly-painted horse-drawn carts. The women sold sprigs of herbs, dried flowers and clothespins door to door. The men were tinsmiths, repairing and selling teapots, kettles and pans. They would also go from door to door collecting rags and old clothes, the best of which they wore themselves.

Kent was a farming county, fruit orchards, vegetable gardens but most prominently of all hops, fields of which stretched for miles in the countryside. Picking season brought the Romany to town each summer, gypsy camps springing up overnight at crossroads and in fields in the outskirts of town. The gypsies themselves were viewed with suspicion. They had a reputation for being sharp and light fingered. Every so often the local bobby would roust the camp, and they would pack up and disappear into the night only to reappear at a village a few miles down the road the next day. Gypsies and tramps who shared their nomadic lifestyle developed a system for marking curbs and gateposts of houses in the towns and villages they passed. Coded symbols indicating work available, hot meal, guard dogs, and other such invaluable information was scratched with chalk for the next traveller who passed that way.

The roads travelled by the gypsies had been trod by man since 54 B.C. The old Roman Road still in parts showing the original cobblestone construction wound its way across the South Downs passing the immediate outskirts of town. The pilgrim's way, which was the chosen path of the faithful on route to the walled city of Canterbury and its famous Cathedral, followed much of the old Roman way. Churches, castles and palaces built by the faithful to glorify God and deify the rich mark its route to this day.

At the bakery life was proceeding uneventfully, although signs of strain were becoming visible in our parents' relationship. Some of this resulted from trying to work together, some the result of bringing Terry into the house. Terry was proving to be a bit of a handful, his childish pranks drove Mother into fits of rage completely out of proportion to the offence, whether real or imagined. We learned to keep our distance on Monday. That was wash day, and one of the few days Mom's mood could be accurately predicted. On wash day the gas fired "copper" – essentially a large cauldron located in the scullery – would be fired up. Each piece of dirty clothing, and household linens, had to be boiled clean, wrung by hand through a large wooden mangle before being dried on clothesline strung over the backyard. To simplify the process the clothes were stirred around then removed from the copper with a large stout stick, euphemistically known as a copper stick. Mom would stand red-faced and perspiring with a scarf holding her hair back, ready to explode at the slightest opportunity. Terry came home from the local school for lunch and invariably would do something to set her off. He had more coppersticks broken across his shoulders than I could count. On rare occasions Mom would pursue him up the street waving her copperstick like an Archangel's sword of retribution promising dire consequences if she ever caught up with him.

Terry and I were close as we would ever be during these years. We played and joked together and explored the woods and riverbanks when allowed. We had a dog, Sandy, rescued from the pound and like the rest of us, doomed to become a constant source of annoyance to Mother as he did all the usual doggy things, most reprehensibly chew, shed and defecate. The animus between Mother and child had its genesis in this period. I once ran away from home with Sandy on one of the many occasions when she threatened to put him down. I lived in the woods by my school for two days existing on food brought to me by my school mates only to be eventually turned in by one of their parents. I remember the ride home with Dad; we spoke man-to-man of the problems. He explained Mom was difficult to live with and promised my dog would be safe. I in turn promised to try harder. It was like playing Russian roulette.

On Tuesday nights Terry and I were sent to catechism classes to learn by rote the Creed of the Catholic Church. Father Moore taught our class, and always enjoyed playing with the young students. His favourite game was wrestling! I remember being pinned across a table during one such game aware even then that his closeness and the pressure of his limbs on mine were best avoided. I was not popular with the priests. I asked once why we put money in the collection plate on Sundays and then delivered a case of liquor to the refectory on Mondays. It was an honest if naïve question; the vehemence of the response my only clue that it was not welcome.

Strict class distinction prevailed in those years, even after the social renaissance and liberalization created by two great wars. It had not yet become an issue we were aware of and we stuck pretty much with our own. I had begun to notice that some of my friends at school took inside toilets, and even central heating as commonplace. In our house a mad dash to the one fire kept burning and freshly stoked in the living room before getting dressed each morning was considered normal, a rudimentary lick and a promise over the kitchen sink served as morning ablutions, our only relief coming with the installation of a two-gallon Ascot boiler delivering a slow and reluctant stream of hot water, luxury indeed!

My parents took up the sport of tennis during this time in our lives. By today's standards not an earth-shattering decision but in the immediate post-war years sports such as golf, tennis and squash were played mainly by the well to do. Rugby, for example, perfectly acceptable to the Upper Classes. Football very much the sport of the masses.

I can only guess that this was an effort to elevate our social standing. We had recently acquired our first car, a Ford van of dubious ancestry which had been sprayed a particularly virulent shade of blue. My Father would have been forty, and this was the first car he ever owned, the rear seat was out of an old bus and was stuck in the back of the van as required. On rare occasions when the tired old engine could muster a peppy start, any unwary occupants of the rear would tumble backwards, legs in the air.

The neighbourhood kids would gather in awe to see "Mac the Baker" resplendent in crisp white flannels and shirt as we set off to play tennis on Sunday mornings. Within a year he had moved on to white tennis shorts and a short-sleeved athletic shirt. As the sight of a grown man in short pants was very rare, even at the seaside where the concession to casual ended at rolling your pants up to the knee, the shorts caused much merriment to the local urchins.

The business seemed to be going along OK and looking back it was a period of relative calm and normalcy. We were "moving on up" having hired Uncle Cyril to help in the bakery with the increased workload as in addition to our shop we supplied not only one of the big chain stores with baked goods but had a route of neighbourhood corner stores and pubs taking bread rolls, pasties and pies on a daily basis.

Life has a way of gob smacking the complacent; we should have been warned by experience. At age eleven the English education system (at least at that time) separated the children into three aptitude streams. Grammar – academically bright; technical – still more bright but more likely to become engineers than lawyers or accountants, and secondary modern – a morass from which only the brightest would break free of the blue collar stigma.

I passed the 11-plus exams with flying colours, and was bound for glory at the local grammar school. Mom had started taking vacations alone around this time as Dad couldn't or wouldn't tear himself away from the bakehouse for more than a few days. She returned from a package tour of Switzerland full of stories of the bridges of Lucerne, the bears of Berne, and the romantic tale of Mount Pilatus.

As I look back this was the first widening of the cracks that would eventually bring our parents' marriage crashing down. Unwittingly I was to play a role, as reward for my achievement in passing the 11-plus.

Mom announced, 'Michael, next year you will be in the grammar school. To celebrate I am taking you to Switzerland.'

CHAPTER SIX

The Grammar School was a red brick institution, sitting on the outskirts of town on the road leading to Canterbury. Approximately 850 boys were enrolled from Grades 3–6, the equivalent to Junior High and High School. There was both a boys and girls grammar school; only in the secondary modern were boys and girls unceremoniously lumped together. We wore uniforms, the idea of which was to eliminate any difference in class, status, or religion. The harsher reality being that the very uniform designed to eliminate any social inequality served only to accent it, isolating the hoi polloi in the process. Of course I knew nothing of this when we went shopping at one of the two approved haberdashers to purchase everything on the list we had been provided. Blue Blazer

(1), Grey Slacks (2), White Shirts with collar (3) School Tie (1), and the ultimate in status symbols – a school cap! I was one of only three boys from my three-room school to have successfully passed the eleven-plus, so I was alone in this vast new school, the other two electing to attend a school in Tonbridge, a nearby town.

Things had been really bad at home during the summer break. Mom's moods had worsened since her return form Switzerland and constant bickering became a way of life. That was the year when the wheels fell off. We lost the British Home Store account and with it much of our business. Mom and Dad's relationship was deteriorating daily and I never knew if she would be there when I got home from school. She left with frequency to stay with one or other of her seven sisters. Divorce was not an option for Catholics, apparently living in hell on earth was considered an acceptable price to pay to assure one's place in heaven. The high point of the summer was the two weeks Terry and I spent on a farm in Hampshire. We thought it was camp, only years later, learning that it was a refuge for troubled boys, our trouble was simple – we pissed our Mother off! The farm was great, our main tasks being to collect eggs, take the goats out to pasture, and milk them at the end of the day. It was run with ease and compassion by a Swiss couple known (of course) as Auntie and Uncle. It was a time of great personal freedom. Although we had the responsibility of helping out around the farm, we had all sorts of time to fish, hunt for wood pigeon with homemade catapults and laze by the stream with Uncle's fifteen-year-old niece, Priscilla. The first girl I kissed and the first I loved! She dumped me after a week for a sixteen-year old East end reprobate who constantly bragged about feeling her tits.

At summer end we returned home, I gathered my school uniform together with pride, polished my best shoes and readied myself for the adventure that lay ahead. My generation was the first year of what would become known as baby boomers. The year I showed up at school there were 150 new boys – all bright – all eager – all with high expectations of and for themselves. I was in 3A, the top stream reserved as our tutors and professors informed us for the "cream of the country's intelligence". Having spent the last seven years in a 3-grade schoolhouse, answering only to Mrs. Peak, Charlton and Wise, I was overwhelmed. I didn't know how to act, was thoroughly intimidated and unused to the cold arm's length discipline expected and maintained. For the first time I had different tutors for different subjects. Our form Master, Mr. Caley, was an arrogant, cold, pretentious man who took an instant dislike to me

'You, McKenna, are one of the inevitable clots amongst the cream,' he invariably reminded me.

I despised him and then set out to make his life hell. Not for me the simple tack on the chair, I glued pages of his textbooks together, pinned dead frogs from the biology lab on the underside of his desk which were often not discovered for weeks, the odd smells being attributed to vague drainage problems.

I also invented the nickname Wanker Caley, by writing it on our home-room blackboard, a name, which I'm happy to say stuck throughout my time at school.

I made no friends that first year, no one from my neighbourhood had made it to the grammar school, and so not knowing how to behave, I acted up, becoming the boy who elicited the cheap laugh at the teacher's expense. I switched chemicals in labs, causing interesting and sometimes alarming reactions, mocked the effete English lit professor and generally made their lives as miserable as I perceived mine to be.

Of course looking back I simply didn't fit in. I didn't know the difference between cheap grey flannels and smooth wool worsted but for the first time I knew I was poor. Still, we did get to shower after gym classes, a treat because bath time at our house involved hauling an old tin tub in from its home on a nail in the backyard. After being dragged into the scullery this was filled with the two gallons of hot water the Ascot heater grudgingly provided, and the family bathed in order of perceived grubbiness. My first year at the grammar school was indeed an eye opener.

The feud between Wanker and myself reached its zenith the end of the term. I had hidden myself in a closet in his classroom, armed with a water pistol, my weapon of choice. At opportune moments when his back was towards me, I would squirt the unsuspecting Wanker. Sooner rather than later the titters of the class and outright betrayal by one "Woodthorp

Junior" caused Wanker (who was quite amazingly scarlet around the gills) to discover me and drag me off by the ear to the Headmaster's study for retribution.

School was divided into four houses. School, College, Corpus Christi and a fourth whose name escapes me. Each morning we all assembled in the Great Hall for the day's announcements.

'Schoolhouse won the inter-house rugger tournament. Jefferson 6A accepted into Oxford. Butcher Jr. placed in the top ten of 100 yard dash.'

Today was different.

'Boys, we have not had a boy in our school publicly caned in twenty years.'

'For the utter insolence displayed by a member of Corpus Christi House we have decided this is the only suitable punishment. McKenna 3A, step forward.'

My walk towards the raised stage was, I flatter myself, quite insouciant, I was a rebel and for once the eyes of all 850 boys were on me. After six of the best administered to my flannel clad ass the shamefaced scuttle back to my seat struggling to hold back tears was less auspicious. Of course I was suspended, nearly expelled, I shamed my family in the process. This series of events did nothing to help smooth the troubled waters at home. I was duly punished and nearly lost my trip to Switzerland. Had I only been so lucky!

Mom and I spent a week at a pensione situated on Lake Lucerne. The journey involved a channel ferry and a lengthy train ride but at last we were met at Lucerne station by a very nice taxi driver, or so I assumed. This pleasant and thoughtful man accompanied us on our trips up the Engadine, drove us to the Rhone glacier, and seemed to expect nothing in return. Years later, after Mother died, Shaun discovered and sent on to me some old snapshots taken that day, each of us balanced precariously on skis, looking very chic and sportif. My Mother was smiling, carefree and beautiful. She would have been around thirty-nine. She should have stayed with the Swiss guy – at least five people would have been happy.

After dinner the taxi would pick Mom up and take her out. I was allowed to watch TV, then bed at ten in our shared room. She was always there when I woke in the morning. That vacation was in August. By

September she was gone and the events I described earlier unfolded. It was during this time period when I came across my Dad seated in the backyard clutching the letter from Mom. She eventually returned home after a few weeks and although we didn't know it, our lives would never be the same.

One day shortly after her return I was working in the bakehouse with Dad; it is clear in my mind, we were decorating Yule logs in readiness for the Christmas season. I had taken to hanging out with Dad at each available opportunity as Mom had by now received my letter, and was not a forgiving soul!

The door to the bakery opened and Mom came in dressed in street clothes. She was red in the face and had obviously been crying.

'I got the results,' she said nodding meaningfully towards my Dad. 'What will we do?'

There was silence – then 'We'll make the best of it, luv,' he replied.

I knew all was not well. Once Mom left I badgered Dad for more information.

'Mom's pregnant, son, you're going to have a baby brother or sister.'

Oh shit – all I really wanted was a damn pony!

*Antony Hayman,
aged 9.*

*Antony Hayman and
wife, circa 1954 or '55.*

St. Mary's School.

Demolition – end of the road.

Catholic clergy.

Charity nuns with priest and young boy.

Group of St. Anne's and St. Joseph's boys and girls, Orpington, 1930s.

Unbeaten St. Mary's Football team 1937–38. "Sadly several of the boys were killed in the last War."

Circa 1937-38, part of a religious procession through Gravesend, carrying a statue of the Virgin Mary. "I can only assume the Irish connection was because most of the Sisters were Irish as were quite a lot of the boys. My brother Bernard is directly under the L in the Ireland banner."— Antony Hayman

The refectory at St. Mary's – "No sign of flowers in my day."

*Priest
serving Mass.*

William Marshall, top, with friends at Bletchingly Farm, Surrey 1940.

John Flynn in Victoria, BC, Canada, 1994.

PROTECTION OF **OUR** PERSONAL FILES

Editor's Note: A letter dated December 4/2014 from the Diagrama Foundation to Cabrini of 49 Russell Hill Road, Purley, Surrey, England was the first indication of a takeover. The personal records of all Catholic children put in care dating back to the 1900s and held for many years in the Purley Archives, were to be handed over to the Diagrama Foundation.

A copy of this letter was sent to (Delvin) John Flynn of the London "network" of old St. Mary's boys who in turn sent copies to group members, including myself as honorary member. This triggered off sparks of concern (a) why these records of a personal nature were being transferred in the first place (b) the environmental condition in which they would be kept for future generations and (c) why was this information of a takeover not forthcoming to advise those concerned, worldwide, of an already done-deal, without being given the opportunity of expressing an opinion.

Quote:

> *"I am delighted to be able to write to you with the exciting news that Cabrini Children's Society has transferred the Adoption, Fostering and Residential Services to the Diagrama Foundation.*
>
> *For some time now Cabrini has had ongoing concerns around how best to continue the very valuable work that Cabrini has been renowned for.*
>
> *In April this year we saw the transfer of all our community projects, except the nursery at Vauxhall and the Fountain centre which sadly closed. This left us with the core service*

of Adoption (including Access to Records Services), Fostering and our residential unit at Orpington. Over the past year it has become apparent, in order to move forward and for our services to continue, that the best option is for all remaining services to transfer to the Diagrama Foundation. Cabrini is due to close officially in the Spring of 2015.

Diagrama has an ethos and very similar values to those that have been provided by Cabrini over the years. The Diagrama Foundation is a charity for children and young people who are experiencing social difficulties, at risk of exclusion or who are similarly disadvantaged. The work of the Diagrama Foundation is based on quality of care, openness and transparency, the involvement of children in the design and delivery of services, the participation of children in decisions which affect them individually and collectively, collaboration and benchmarking best practices and raising public awareness, research and international cooperation.

This is an exciting time for both Cabrini and Diagrama, and we are all looking forward to seeing the continuation and expansion of the wonderful work of these two organisations under a new remit.

Please let me reassure you that these organisations changes will not affect the level of service that you have received from Cabrini Children's Society. Cabrini, as part of the Diagrama Foundation, will still continue to offer all our children and their families a lifelong line of suppport.

If you do have any questions or concerns, please do not hesitate to contact Ian Forbes, Head of Services on 0208 668 2181.

Yours sincerely,
Hilary Brooks,
Interim Chief Executive

From Cabrini Children's Society – Important December 6/2014

Caroline Whitehead

I am currently out of the office. If your enquiry is urgent, please contact a member of the Purley Administration Team on 020 8668 2181.

Sharon DaSilva, Cabrini

December 7/2014

Sharon DaSilva; (Delvin) John Flynn, London Group; Irena Lyczkowska, Cabrini

Dear Sharon,

It is with concern to learn Cabrini will be handing over all children's records who were placed through the auspices of the Southwark Catholic Children's Society from the early 1920s, to the Diagrama Foundation located at Dunstable, Bedfordshire.

It is my understanding this international organisation was founded 2009 and has no connection I believe to the Catholic Church, and is registered as a charity.

My question: where are these social historical records to be kept and under what environmental conditions?

Hilary Brooks, Interim Chief Executive, in her announcement specifies transparency, openness and accessibility to records. If these are moved to another country what chance does the inquirer have to establish family history?

Due to the importance of these records, did not Cabrini consider first approaching the Archives in London of Family History before making the decision to leave children's records in the hands of an unknown Foundation?

Perhaps you would be kind enough to give me your answers?

Thank you.

Caroline

Member of London KOKO group

December 7/2014

To: (Delvin) John Flynn Mavis and Pat Heffernan, Australia

Hi John,

Did a quick search on the net regarding this Foundation. It appears this is an international organization, located at Dunstable, Bedforshire, founded 2009. Not sure if it is connected in any way with the Catholic Church or its organizations.

There are groups in Germany and Spain. I'll continue to search for other details as I feel within this international organization there must be more countries.

To convey our concerns where the children's records from Cabrini are to be kept and stored prompts me to question their survival. Moving them out of the country, perhaps for economical reasons, was one point we mentioned.

Will keep you posted so all members are aware of what's happening to their records beyond April 2015.

KOKO

Caroline

Hi Caroline,

Like you I am very suspicious of the name Diagrama Foundation! Certainly something I've never heard of. They claim to be certified by Bureau Veritas Certification. I looked BRV up on line and it seems the only "qualification" they have is a self-proclaimed one! The certification is NOT recognised as a quality of repute ONLY as a registered charity. So why Cabrinin have gone to a Belgium company first known as an insurance company in 1996 and in 2007 proclaim to be world leaders in child care is beyond me. I noticed Cabrini have closed the Orpington wing of their company (where I believe we went to last year (2013), and my thoughts are that the "Rats are leaving a sinking ship!"

The Catholic Church is not adverse at doing this; hence the name change to Cabrini from the Catholic Rescue Society to avoid "complicated investigations" in 2008/9. As I wrote in my comments in my WTYNH follow up: someone is abdicating its duty and responsibilities. I haven't sent this to John F. because I have no wish to upset him OR the others of our group such as John O'Donnell. Maybe I am being unfair! I just harbour a sneaking feeling that sadly I'm right. This "new" company will of course NOT be responsible for past misdemeanours of the Catholic Church! It wouldn't surprise me that the Catholic Church are the "money" behind this "unknown" company. We'll see!

Am off to meet two former school friends from the Boys Tech I went to in Maidstone. One of them is on a visit to the UK from Australia visiting his family and with another friend Paul (who lives just over the Severn Bridge) met 2 years ago so we are meeting up again in a place called Aust, which is almost underneath the old Severn Crossing Bridge. I'll let you know how that goes.

Terry McK.

Terry,

Good to hear from you. I've been meaning to ring the past week or so but have much going on; to cough would be time-consuming. Firstly, why are Cabrini disregarding the responsibilities of maintaining our records and handing them over to Diagrama Foundation, who is an international organization and located at Dunstable, Bedfordshire, where it is assumed our history will end up?

How much have these people offered to Cabrini to offload them? Or is it the other way round?

As you commented, I cannot see any other motive other than a transfer of money. That being the case I am even more outraged this would happen! What are the ramifications of the responsibilities of Cabrini to ensure children's records are not only kept safe but in an environment where they survive?

Another matter of concern is not only to do with social history but these records relate to sensitive issues regarding the reason why we were put in care through the Catholic Church.

What connection is there with Diagrama Foundation who was founded 2009 or have Cabrini pulled a trick out of the hat regardless of religion or concern in what happens to our records. What gives them this right to turn over our personal documents to an unheard of organization where they can be transported to Germany, Spain, Italy or heavens knows where, beyond the reach of those who are anxious to determine family records.

Surely, with something as important as this happening, are not government Archives the mainstay for such historical records. I don't think we can allow Cabrini to blindly undertake this course of action without making it known our distaste of this proposed transport of our personal history.

It horrifies me to learn Diagrama is a Belgium company and registered as a charity. It would then appear there is no connection with the Catholic Church.

Once we have been able to tie up all the loose ends with questions to answers from Cabrini and the Diagrama Foundation, the finality of our childhood history records will be the last chapter in the "The Boy's of St. Mary's" KOKO book.

Will keep you and John F. posted on forthcoming events.

Caroline

December 8/2014

Hi Caroline,

As with the earlier email, I am forwarding this one to Ian Forbes, who will be able to address your concerns.

Kind regards,

Irena, Cabrini

Senior Social Worker.

To: Irena Lyczkowska, Cabrini Sharon DaSilva, (Delvin) John Flynn, Ian Forbes

'morning, Irena,

Thank you for your response regarding our London group's concern why our records are being handed over to Diagrama Foundation.

I would appreciate knowing to whom you refer as Ian Forbes and what his connection is to this serious decision of Cabrini's to put the Catholic children's records into the hands of an unknown, foreign, Foundation, who incorporated in 2009.

On behalf of KOKO

Caroline, BC, Canada

Hello Caroline,

I totally understand your fears and worries, but just to reassure you, the records we hold will not be taken/sent abroad – by law they have to remain in England.

Ian Forbes is the Head of Service, Adoption, Fostering and Family support here at Cabrini and he will be able to address all your concerns.

Irena Lyczkowska, Cabrini.

Irena,

I sincerely appreciate your time in assuring me our records will not be sent abroad by virtue of English law, they remain in the country.

We do need to have more information regarding Diagrama Foundation's history and Cabrini's reason for transferring children's records. If financial stress is the cause there is no question in my mind you would have the support needed to continue the safe-keeping of all children's records who were under the auspices of the Catholic Church.

I am sure I speak for others who have spent years looking for family. We would be more than willing to pay a fee towards the upkeep of storing our social history.

With sincere thanks.

Caroline

To: Irena Lyczkowska, Caroline Whitehead, Sharon DaSilva, (Delvin) John Flynn.

Dear Caroline,

Thank you for emailing us regarding your concerns. I hope the following answers your questions.

The Diagrama Foundation throughout negotiations and transfer has always shown a commitment to maintaining the archive records in a safe and proper manner (this was a big part of the decision on to which company to transfer).

The management of the archive is sitting with the same staff members in place as there was when Cabrini Children's Society was managing itself.

Keeping the records alongside our experienced staff would seem to be the best way to maintaining the records and to continue to provide good access, etc.

The Diagrama Foundation is a professional organisation with a strong moral ethos and will continue to offer a high level of professional service.

Diagrama is discussing currently about how to upgrade the archive facilities to improve access and safe-keeping.

Regards,

Ian Forbes, Cabrini.

Ian,

Thank you for your response to my concerns on behalf of the KOKO London Group of "old" boys and girls.

The details outlined regarding the Diagrama Foundation and its capabilities of maintaining our family records, you failed to indicate the location of where our records are to be held. This is a prime factor.

It is appreciated in knowing, by virtue of English law, our records will remain in the country and not shipped abroad. That we are assured your negotiations with the Foundation are based on a commitment not only to maintain these in a safe place but they will not be subjected to environmental damage.

As you are aware, these records are our social family history and we need assurance they will be respected as such, and accessible to those who wish to inspect them.

It would be appreciated if you would give me the Charitable Registration number of the Diagrama Foundation.

Sincere thanks,

Caroline, BC

December 9/2014

'morning, John (Michael Murray)

Not sure if you sent a reply to my previous email asking for help with the address of the Minister Responsible for Children. Somehow, one I just posted was returned. Clitch, somewhere.

If you did send another email to me I did not get the message.

Many thanks.

Caroline

Hello Caroline,

There is no longer a Children's Minister but I located Edward Timpson MP who has children's matters as part of his responsibilities. I have passed the details to Terry Mc. If this fails then there is Adam Holloway MP for Gravesham which includes Gravesend. We must get to the bottom of this.

KOKO

John M Murray

To: John M. Murray, (Delvin) John Flynn, Terry McKenna, Mavis & Pat, Australia, Anny Phyall, Irena Lyczkowska, Antony Hayman

'morning John M,

Your support in helping us determine the legality of Cabrini transferring our personal file records over to the Diagrama Foundation in the April 2015 is much appreciated.

I did manage to find Edward Timpson MP Responsible for Children, House of Commons, London on the net and mailed a letter to him yesterday (Tuesday) asking for his advice on this matter. We can but wait and see what transpires with this inquiry but on behalf of our group of "old" boys and girls it is important for us to know our family records will not be used for financial gain by this organisation and that their intent to maintain these in a friendly environment with accessibility to them will be honoured in accordance with negotiations made with Cabrini.

Irena kindly advised by virtue of English law our files remain in England and not sent abroad to another country.

Ian Forbes Cabrini kindly responded to my inquiry regarding the transfer of records but unfortunately failed to acknowledge where these will be located and under what conditions are they to be stored.

I hope this helps our group. Should Member of Parliament Edward Timpson respond I will forward the details.

Hope everyone is well. We must remain together if we are to satisfy ourselves our records are kept in safe-keeping by a responsible organisation, of which little history is known.

KOKO

Caroline

Hi Caroline,

I saw the email from and to John M. Murray regarding Diagrama Foundation. They are actually a registered company within the Charities Commission (Reg. number is 1128532) fold although this is only for 2013 accounts (delivered 76 days late!) in 2014.

As I was writing this John Murray (Laundry Boy) rang me. Like you he is very concerned about this; Cabrini giving ALL their documentation (shouldn't it be ours?) that is supposedly going to Diagrama Foundation. He like me has found nothing to say this company even has a place in the UK although one assumes there must be a UK address to be able to apply for this status and therefore all the benefits this can produce.

I will be contacting the M.P. who has the responsibilities for children/adoptions/and general welfare. His name is Edward Timpson with a private office Telephone number 03700002288 and has an address at: Sanctuary Building, 20 Great Smith Street, London, SW1P 3BT. I will be

contacting Mr. Timpson hopefully tomorrow or at least with his secretary
to see what he has to say. John M. also gave me the MP for Gravesham
area that includes Gravesend. (Ann Phyall often mentions this area.)
Name: Adam Holloway and I will contact him too. Basically I have agreed
with John that I will email him and yourself whatever I find.

Terry McKenna

Terry hi,

Whether we will be able to resolve this concern or not I don't know but it
is worth a try to determine the validity of Cabrini to casually turn over our
records to the Diagrama Foundation who as you know have nothing to do
with children put in care or connected in any way to the church.

John M. Murray suggests contacting the Minister Responsible for
Children. I have asked him for his address but have yet to obtain these
details.

My request to Ian Forbes Cabrini for the location of where the records are
to be kept has fallen on deaf ears. He has gone pristine quiet! Does that
tell you something?

Have asked John M. Murray for the address of the Minister Responsible
for children in the hope he may advise on the legality of Cabrini
transferring children's records to the Diagrama Foundation.

I wonder if we should make The Kentish Times aware of what is
happening to Cabrini's decision to rid themselves of the records of
all children who were under the care of the Catholic Church covering
London and the Counties?

Caroline

December 9/2014

To: Edward Timpson, MP. CC: Caroline Whitehead, John M Murray.

Dear Mr Timpson,

It is with some concern that Cabrini, based in Purley, will be giving ALL
the very personal information they hold with regards to children who have
been in their care since the late 19th century, originally known as The

Catholic Children's Rescue Society based in Southwark in London until a dramatic change of name to Cabrini around 2008/9.

All of my group of what we call "former inmates" of St. Mary's in Gravesend and some from St.Anne's and St.Joseph's in Orpington, regularly email and help each other with our many questions and advice we can give to anyone who wishes.

As you will no doubt know already the "Right" of a sibling to his/her birth family bears no reality to modern times. By this I mean if you wish to find almost anything about anything (if that makes sense) you just go on line and eh voila there it is! It took me sixty years to find out about my family due in the main to the antiquated laws of today and the total lack of consideration, respect or understanding to someone looking for their heritage, from the various organisations involved and in particular successive governments for many, many years. AND worse of all, if a parent simply says NO then officially that's it! To say that this is a totally unsatisfactory situation is indeed to be polite.

At times with my own story I have had to use the threat of litigation to get any response right across the board: AND if that isn't bad enough we are now being told of the latest piece of skulduggery involving the Catholic Church; to completely block any contact from people looking for their birthright. AND yes it is a right, not a whim of a government or religious group to deny access and possibly a form of closure in our lives. There are still many people who will need these details and will be so for years to come.

The company being "entrusted" with this is: Diagrama Foundation. Originally from Belgium dealing in the main with Insurance! They are registered with the Charities Commission for 2012/2013. Ref. number 1128532. Their own site says they deal with children from troubled families and poor social skills. Absolutely NO official Government decree to do so. I do believe they may have premises in Bedford BUT no telephone or address can be found. In short I would be most interested to hear your views on this matter. Can personal and sensitive records be removed to who knows where without some form of discussion involving ALL parties to a company nobody has ever heard of?

You may contact me by phone on 01179535594. Please bear with me if I don't actually answer when you ring. There is an answer record machine and you can leave a message and I will get back asap OR be in at an arranged time if you wish not to send your telephone number for obvious reasons.

My home address will be made available on request. It hardly needs to be said BUT I really am looking forward to your response regarding this matter. A lot of people will be waiting to hear from me and they will!

Yours most sincerely,

Terry McKenna

December 9/2014

To: Mr Edward Timpson,

House of Commons,

London, England SW1A OAA

Dear Minister, Re: Transfer of Children's Records

It has come to my attention Cabrini of Purley, Surrey are to transfer all records of children put in care from the early 1900s to an unknown charitable organisation call The Diagrama Foundation, in the Spring of 2015. They are not connected to a church or any children's Government programme.

A "network" of old boys and girls worldwide are concerned of the legality of Cabrini, previously known as the Southwark Catholic Children's Society whose headquarters were at 59 Westminster Bridge Road, London, if this transfer of our social family records are within the laws of England.

It is my understanding the records by virtue of English law must remain in the country and not be sent abroad. In discussing these concerns with Cabrini we are notified our records are to be maintained in the Diagrama Foundation archives. At which location of the country and under what environmental condition is unknown.

Because of the nature of these valuable family records our network is concerned for the safe-keeping of these documents for future generations.

Any help or advice you can give regarding the legality of our family records being transferred to an unknown source would be appreciated.

Yours truly,

Caroline Whitehead,

Honorary Member of the London Group

December 10/2014

'morning Terry,

As always, you are on the "ball" when it comes to something as serious as our files being transported to charitable organisation, whose location we have still to determine. No doubt, my earlier message has been received, copy went to Mavis & Pat Heffernan, Australia, who also raised their concern about their personal records.

With the support of the group I feel sure we can find the information we are looking for as to the reason of the transfer (said with tongue in cheek).

Correspondence to Edward Timpson or better still the MP for Gravesend and Orpington asking for the feedback in this matter will at least give us I hope piece of mind our records will not be used for commercial gain or dumped in a pile left to rot! If the group in general contact these M.P.s it is hoped they will confirm the legality of the apparently done-deal by Cabrini to the Diagrama Foundation.

In all correspondence I believe we should keep (Delvin) John F. informed as he is also concerned for the safety of our family files.

Would appreciate the address of the Kentish Times, Orpington and if there is a newspaper in Gravesend.

Upon reflection Terry I am convinced with your thoughts this whole done-deal with Cabrini to Diagrama Foundation smacks of financial benefit.

As a group concerned with our personal files that appear useless as a bag of garbage to Cabrini, we need to go through with this until we are satisfied with their answers and the advice given from MPs with a view to contacting the appropriate newspapers in Orpington and Gravesend, Kent.

Please do hold on to all emails on the subject as it is important we detail its contents

Many thanks for getting the Charity Reg. number of Diagrama Foundation who we are aware are not connected to any children's organisation.

KOKO

Caroline

December 11/2014

Hi Terry,

Have just got off the phone speaking with my "old Navy Commander" friend and relayed to him some of the details regarding the situation with Cabrini and Diagrama Foundation.

His comments:

'There appears to be a financial proposition made between the two parties involved.

'Keep in contact with all Members of Parliament, outlining the group's concerns regarding personal family files. There is also a question of the Confidentiality and Privacy Act in the UK.

'Contact Sue Stafford, Tuart Place, Fremantle, W. Australia and see if you can advise those old boys who emigrated to Australia from St. Mary's through their magazine of the plan to hand over their records.

'You must protect your personal files at all cost.'

As this done-deal with Cabrini and Diagrama Foundation smacks of financial gain until we are convinced our personal files are not used for this purpose, we continue to search for answers to our questions.

KOKO.

Caroline.

Hi Caroline,

Just received your latest email regarding The Diagrama Foundation/ Cabrini situation. It does seem your "old Navy Commander" friend has come to the same conclusion regarding the unseemly actions of the wonderful Catholic Church! Every person I have spoken/emailed to have ALL arrived at similar conclusions. The most obvious as pointed out by yourself is: What/Where/When AND are the legal implications for you and everyone else who have had OR will have dealings with this secretive society, and a number of groups that masquerade as the church purporting to represent the "House of God"!

As in my case alone it took pretty much sixty years of threats of litigation, countless phone calls and several emails and thankfully for me my memory from so long ago and ALL thanks to the devious and diversity of years of denial of the church (and others too). Can you imagine what will happen in the future? It doesn't bear thinking about, does it? Yes I'm STILL annoyed at the total lack or comprehension of our feelings! But then I shouldn't be, should I? Still in fairness I must wait a reasonable time for people such as Edward Timpson to respond to my first letter bringing this matter to his attention. After all he works for a Government of today in the UK who are as interested in our welfare as The Catholic Church, China and Russia are to their dissidents around the world.

Will you send an email/letter to Sue Stafford OR would you like me to do so? Can't take ALL the credit for details of contacts. John M. Murray gave me some great leads (thanks John). Again I must stress that I am NOT laying any blame with the Cabrini of today most of us know; that would be very unfair.

It's their bosses in Rome who should be facing those that have been sadly dealt with for centuries BUT of course they are experts in that department, aren't they?

KOKO as I surely will!

Terry McKenna

Terry,

Many thanks for continuing to establish the reasons for the transfer of our personal files from Cabrini to Diagrama Foundation.

A big question put to me today: Will Diagrama Foundation put these records on microfilm then have reason to destroy them? I did not of course have the answer.

Or is the intent of their acceptance to use them and catalogue these records with other children who were adopted then in the late 1900s? Again I did not have the answer. I could not see the connection.

Another query: why did not Cabrini hand these personal family files into the care of the Latter Day Saints if they no longer wished to be the guardians?

Having put out feelers today the response has been identical. "These records of old boys and girls and other children whose files Cabrini hold and were under the auspices of the Catholic Church must at all cost be PROTECTED."

Due to the fact Ian Forbes, Service Manager, Cabrini has failed to answer all questions relating to his Foundation leaves us no choice but to continue our search in establishing the location of where our personal family files are to be kept, and confirm to our group members worldwide the telephone number of the Diagrama Foundation for future reference, which cannot be found in any UK telephone directory.

There is a responsibility of all parties to ensure our privacy is not at risk and in accordance with the laws of England and confidentiality is preserved.

We will await the advice from MP Edward Timpson, Minister for Responsibilities of Children, House of Commons, also contact Adam Holloway MP for Gravesend with a view to his advice.

Perhaps, Terry, you would be kind enough to contact Sue Stafford at Tuart Place. Many thanks.

As mentioned, the blame is not being left on the doorstep of Cabrini who in the past been supportive in dealing with family records to those requesting personal information.

With sincere thanks to everyone for the input to ensure the group arrives at an amicable solution to this matter. We certainly need closure to the satisfaction of all.

KOKO

Caroline

December 12/2014

To: Sue Stafford, W. Australia. CC: Caroline Whitehead, (Delvin) John Flynn, John Michael Murray, Mavis & Paddy Heffernan, Australia

Hi Sue,

My name is Terry McKenna and I am a former "inmate" at St. Mary's Catholic Children's Rescue based at Gravesend in Kent here in the UK. I am writing to yourself and to ALL people worldwide to advise you of some vital information that has just landed on our doorstep.

Despite the vast majority of my friends such as Caroline Whitehead an author of some distinction, an ex-Pat from England and herself a former resident of St.Anne's/St.Joseph's based in Orpington and run by the same Catholic organisation as my own Children's Home. There is a group of mainly email friends from my St. Mary's Home (and some very welcome and honoured "guests") who for several years have emailed each other with their various stories AND help to each other. This group has been well informed by OUR collective good friend (Delvin) John Flynn. He has over many years built up a rapport with Cabrini which has benefited many of us myself included. WE have been informed by Cabrini that OUR personal records (and we think ALL such records though we are not entirely sure), are being handed over to a company calling themselves The Diagrama Foundation.

This particular company originated from Belgium and mainly deal/dealt with Insurance. They have a site under their name D.F. pronouncing they deal with "Problem" children, i.e. from dysfunctional families where may be drug abuse and violence in the home and the like has taken place. There is NO obvious evidence of child adoption and provision of homing. We have been told they "might" have a place in Bedford in the UK although attempts by me and others has thus far failed to find either premises OR telephone/email contact. Their home page quotes Certification that as far as I can see holds no significance to ANY recognised authority. They are however registered under the Charities Commission since 2009 and their registration number is 1128532 and there is one entry of accounts on line, which shows a loss and was 76 days late of the deadline to produce these accounts.

Needless to say everyone who has their personal files "lodged" with Cabrini, including the thousands ALL over the world should be worried as to their future whereabouts. Will they be safe? Will they be available? Is it in fact legal to actually do this? Who and Where are these people for us to contact and so on?

I have sent an email to M.P. Mr Edward Timpson based with The Department of Education here in the UK, expressing our concerns over this very sensitive matter and will be updating and advising my contacts as and when I get some response from Mr Timpson. His address is: the Sanctuary Building, 20 Great Smith Street, London, SW1P 3BT. Telephone No: 03700002288.

At this point I must stress that Cabrini of today is a much better place than it used to be and ANY critique aimed at The Catholic Church and whoever else is NOT meant as a personal attack on those based in Purley, Surrey (Cabrini H.Q.).

There is a good rapport between them and our group which we hope to maintain. The Catholic Church has a history of "Deception" that should worry ALL of us and why I have alerted you to their latest "escapade". We are deeply concerned at possible implications regarding our rights, personal or otherwise and with good reason. If you wish me to convey to you what we find by email then do please email me back and of course I will do so.

Many thanks to yourself and the good work and publications that you produce in Aussie Land (we all love to read what's going on over there).

Terry McKenna

PS: I received an email from Irena, Cabrini giving me a telephone number, which I am about to call. It is 01582 471854. The address of Diagrama Foundation: Morton House, 52 High Street South, Dunstable, Bedford. LU6 3HD.

Email not UK based. The gentleman, although polite and called Raphael, was a little difficult to understand and I gave him my details Irena provided us.

'morning Terry,

Your message to Sue Stafford, Tuart Place, Fremantle, W. Australia sums up the group's concerns with regard to our personal files. This is not a whim but simply stating categorically our wish to secure all the answers from Cabrini under whose guardianship our records they currently hold.

We have no wish to harbour grievances with their staff who have been supportive in dealing with requests for family history. What we don't want is for our records to be left in the hands of an organisation of which little is known. The little history of them at this time is not favourable in light of their dealings in producing their accounts beyond the deadline, lack of details of location and connections where they can be contacted.

There are old St. Mary's boys living in DownUnder and for this reason we are compelled to advise them where their family records are to be kept April 2015 on.

Also "old" St. Anne's girls living in different parts of the world should be made aware of this current concern.

To all, sincere thanks for your support and in the hope we can soon put this grievance to rest.

KOKO.

Caroline

Caroline Whithead, (Delvin) John Flynn, John Michael Murray

Thought you might like to see this email.

Terry McKenna.

Nathan James Ward. Diagrama Foundation

Hi Nathan,

Just received your email, and thank you for that. If you ring me on 01179535594 I may not answer BUT don't be put off by this. There is an answer machine in place and if you leave a contact telephone number I WILL get back to you.

Terry McKenna.

Dear Terry,

Many thanks for contacting Diagrama regarding the historic records of Cabrini. I have tried calling you a couple of times; however you are engaged. I shall try again later today but in the meantime can I reassure you that fundamentally nothing has changed in regards to the archives and Diagrama are committed to keeping both the personal and social history archives from Cabrini. It would be good to talk on the phone later and maybe to meet in person with a vested interest in the archives.

All the best,

Nathan Ward,

Head of Care and Justice,

Diagrama, U.K.

Terry, (Delvin)John Flynn, John Michael Murray.

Your message through Nathan James Ward, Diagrama Foundation and his response is much appreciated.

As I understand from him our records are to be maintained in the archives. The big question" whose archives – Cabrini's where they are now held – or Diagrama Foundation archives at Dunstable? We need clarification to this confusion of the whereabouts our family records are to be kept and under what conditions.

It has yet to be determined the reason why Cabrini chose to discontinue the responsibility of guardianship of our personal files. I believe it is our right to know the answer? Neither has Mr Ward or Cabrini been explicit to this question. There are no deals made without reason, regardless of them being of compassionate or of monetary value.

KOKO

Caroline

Dear Caroline,

Many thanks for contacting Ian Forbes regarding the archives at Cabrini. It would be good to touch base with you on the phone regarding this and I wondered if you could let me know the best time and number to call you on.

All the best,

Nathan Ward,

Head of Care and Justice,

Diagrama, UK.

Dear Mr Ward,

Thank you for your message. If you wish to telephone me, my number is: 250-655-1510. I am available to speak with you any Saturday at Canadian time from 9 am any day of the week with the exception of Thursday.

It is with deep concern I am supporting our group of "old" girls and boys worldwide to fully comprehend (a) the reason of Cabrini to transfer our personal family records to your organisation, of which we have little knowledge (b) the little history of the Diagrama Foundation that we know, is incomplete and therefore our trust in them to protect our most valuable documents is questionable.

Caroline Whitehead

BC, Canada

December 12/2014

Dear Caroline,

Many thanks for the phone conversation earlier today and I am deeply sorry for the pain and distress the SALE of Cabrini has caused to you and other members of the group.

The sales of Cabrini took place on 27th NOVEMBER 2014 to Diagrama from Croydon Borough Council and I can confirm that there was a financial transaction at the point of SALE. Diagrama are now responsible for the archives which include the "social history" of Cabrini and are keeping the archive in its present location. The staff that have looked after the archives now work for Diagrama and therefore there should be continuity for people who are currently accessing their personal records.

As I said on the phone Caroline, please do not hesitate to contact me if I can be of any further assistance and it would be good to meet with you next year when you travel to England. I have just ordered a copy of your book from Amazon and shall read it when it arrives.

Take good care and please do keep in touch.

All the best,

Nathan Ward

Head of Care and Justice

Diagrama UK

Dear Nathan,

Firstly, thank you for your promised response. Secondly, I fully appreciate your understanding of our group who are worldwide and deeply concerned Cabrini did not have the courage to be upfront with our members whose personal family history was in their care from 2008/2009, having taken this responsibility over from the defunct Southwark Catholic Children's Society in London.

Had Cabrini been honest from the beginning before the group were forced to jump on the merry-go-round it would have save time, energy and frustration. To lie to us our records were to be transferred to Diagrama Foundation next Spring (2015) indicates their lack of transparency.

It was unnecessary and neither were we interested, but assumed, there was a financial gain somewhere with these negotiations to remove their responsibility of maintaining the children's files to another organisation, of whose history we know little.

Before closure to our concerns it would be appreciated if and when you become aware of where our family files are to be kept at Rochester Kent, and under what environmental condition, to please advise us. Since Cabrini advised our leader (Delvin) John Flynn of the KOKO group in London all correspondence to the appropriate parties, a copy goes to him.

We will continue to follow-up events and sincerely hope closure of our concerns addressed to the Minister for children in London UK, will prevail.

Thank you for your telephone call and consideration to support my book.

Caroline

Caroline (Delvin) John Flynn, John Michael Murray, Paddy and Mavis Heffernan, Australia. Sue Stafford, Tuart Place, Fremantle, W. Australia.

Hi Caroline AND everyone else,

I had quite a revealing conversation with a Nathan James Ward purporting to represent D.F. in his position of Head of Care and Justice UK. After the basic introductions we began to talk!

I had earlier spoken to I think a Spanish or maybe Portuguese guy called Raphael who was a little difficult to understand at first: AND not just his accent!

Nathan Ward revealed to me what I assumed was on his prepared "crib" sheet! I don't think I've spoken to a less convincing person in my life. I pride myself, wrongly or rightly at being pretty good at picking up vibes and I didn't like the manner of this guy. He sounded very young (maybe I'm just jealous) and went on about the founder of this wonderful company that he works for. After he went on about the founder of this company apparently strolling around the back woods in Portugal he saw young people not in a great place. So he took pity on them and determined he was going to help them.

All very admirable and of course, commendable. It was at this point I told him I'd looked at his company's very short history and carefully pointed out the only thing I'd found was: Formed at some date in the 1990s. Running 2/3 homes for these unfortunate youngsters. All very good at this point BUT no mention of adoption, housing and long term aftercare OR what was going to happen to OUR (Not Cabrini: Not D.F.) personal details and this was on their own site. I also told him that the certification they proudly "boasted" of from Bureau Veritas is a company formed in 1982 in North America: Their site is http://www.us.bureauveritas.com.

A direct quote from their own site: IS a global leader in Testing and Certification (TIF)! What does that mean? Pay me enough dollars and we will say exactly what you want! Is it just me or do I smell a rat? Even more disturbing was the revelation that: The Catholic Church had approached Diagrama Foundation over two (YES, 2) years ago saying they were looking for a way out and had no money left. No wonder Ian Forbes has not bothered to reply to several requests for information.

For a guy in charge (Head of Care and Justice) he was very loose with his comments and it didn't take much on my behalf to drag this out of him and it makes me wonder what his underlings are like?

I asked him about the strong possibility of his company going out of business. Just look at The Charities Commission on Line (Ref.no. 1128532) and their submission of accounts was over 140 days AFTER the due date AND they made a loss!

He then blandly said that if that happened then the local council would probably – take over. I took this moment to remind that there are thousands IF not millions of people ALL around the world who rely/want/need these personal records and NOT an unheard of "Foreign" company or indeed a local authority in this country. When I asked him about contacts (Telephone and Address) he calmly said: 'Oh well nothing changes there; Cabrini in Purley will remain the same and ALL the staff too!'

All of this now explains some of the "sudden" departures of long established and known to us staff at Cabrini. Although Irena at Cabrini was the person who sent me (and others) the telephone number in the UK of D.F. EVENTUALLY, and I have thanked her for that, it leaves me with a sinking feeling regarding our rights yet again so easily dismissed and abandoned by in our case The Catholic Church. Until I hear back from Edward Timpson, M.P. I wonder other news may filter out?

Watch this space and as our motto under John Flynn says: I will keep on keeping on: you can be assured of that. If anyone else wants a question asked OR indeed answered send it to me and I will do what I can.

KOKO

Terry McKenna

Ann,

I don't see any downside in your contacting Cabrini. They are very nice people but they like us may only be pawns in the game of life. Things may only get better with your intervention.

Love.

Josie & John.

December 13/2014

Good morning John,

I was pleased to read Terry's email to you regarding your personal files etc. and I have to say I am very worried on your behalf. Terry says he smells a rat – I can smell a whole colony of them! I wouldn't mind betting young Caroline is hopping up and down too.

You are right, John, in suggesting folks apply for their records now without delay. It sounds as though your records/YOU are being "sold on".

I noted too, that Cabrini are based in Purley – as are the NCH's (National Children's Homes and Orphanages). I have been based for my work in Social Services for 40 + years and cannot imagine the mayhem if just one case file were to "disappear". It would be tools down until it was found.

John, on Monday I happen to be free. Would you mind if I ring NCH Purley to see if they know anything about Diagrama Foundation? I'll get back to you with anything I may be able to find out and may even try the old "pulling rank" card. On the other hand, I don't want to interfere in any way.

Ann

Terry McK. (Delvin) John Flynn, John Michael Murray, Mavis and Pat Heffernan, Australia, Sue Stafford, W. Australia.

Hi Terry and All,

My recent telephone conversation with Nathan James Ward did not convince me of what he conveyed regarding our family files, NOW in their care. Initially through John F. we were advised it would be Spring 2015 when these would be transferred from Cabrini to Diagrama Foundation.

This was conveyed to John F. by Irena, Cabrini, but the done-deal took place last week. Where was the integrity of Cabrini who failed to give us these details and the factual decisions made when telling us only a few days ago what was happening to our personal records.

It is my understanding from Nathan Ward that Cabrini was experiencing financial difficulties and sold the "business" to Diagrama. This negotiation was done through the Croydon Council who employed an outside company to complete the transaction of the sale. There was most definitely a monetary gain, with legality, according to Nathan Ward. I am also given to understand that when the tender was put out by this unknown company hired by Croydon Council, with the exception of D.F, there were no other bids.

Our records are to remain in the archives at Purley and will be transferred to an unknown source somewhere in Rochester, Kent, as Diagrama will vacate the Purley premises some time next year (2015). Again our concern is where will they be stored and under what conditions?

It is ironic to think of past history when all of us were eager to research our family records in the hope of extracting the smallest of information. It saddens me that Cabrini, once again are we deceived, did not have the courage to give us the full details of the reason why they could not through financial difficulties have come forward and been totally honest with our group.

It appears Cabrini have been supported with funds by the Croydon Council but at which level I have no knowledge. How this was effective to keep them from going into bankruptcy leaves me to believe this cost must have been budgeted by council. Legally, it could not happen otherwise; unless there was a surplus of taxable funds?

Throughout my conversation with Nathan James Ward I clearly emphasized I was not prepared to listen to more lies and wanted nothing more than the simple truth to relay actual facts to our members worldwide.

Will continue to keep you posted.

KOKO

Caroline

December 18/2014

Response to Questions

Dear Ann,

I believe you had the following questions –

Is Diagrama government funded?

No. The Diagrama Foundation is a non-for profit organisation and charity. Diagrama may apply for government grants in the future or take on government contracts. Some of its income comes from offering services to Local Authorities/Councils. In Spain and other countries Diagrama has taken over statutory functions so may have some government funding in those countries.

Are they inspected and approved by government –

The organisation is currently registered with OFSTED under the name of Cabrini Children's Society. An application has been submitted to OFSTED to register all the services under the parent company.

The Diagrama Foundation OFSTED will be visiting the Purley Office in January to start the registration process and this will be followed by a full inspection.

Is there a possibility of a meeting?

(Skype?) with members of the group. John Flynn seems to lead it.

If we were still a Catholic Children's Society?

No, the organisation is not associated with any religion but does acknowledge the Catholic roots of Cabrini.

Please let me know if you have any further questions.

Regards,

Ian Forbes,

Head of Adoption and Fostering

December 19/2014

(Delvin) John Flynn, Caroline Whitehead

Hello John,

I appreciate this is a rather late message, but I have been awaiting a reply from Ian Forbes to the questions I raised AFTER my telephone conversation. You will see that he has replied to those questions left with Wendy – Admin.Dept.

Yesterday (Wednesday) Ian Forbes telephoned me in response to my brief message left on Cabrini's site. That followed a request from him via email for my phone number. He subsequently rang me to discuss my concerns, on your behalf, the reason for personal files of children from Care Organisations such as St. Mary's and other Catholic Children's Homes residents, being transferred to Diagrama Foundation.

Firstly, I had to establish my connection in all this, to which I replied that I am part of a writers group known as KOKO, and that we have all grown up "in care" as residents of Catholic Children's Homes and in my case, the National Children's Homes and Orphanages. That I write specifically to John Flynn and that emails are passed to and from members of this group who are scattered worldwide. I added too, that I am a retired Social Worker and Home Teacher for the Blind for 40+ years and I am familiar with the security of personal files transit and storage of those files.

Ian Forbes explained that Cabrini will not exist after this week and that the Diagrama Foundation had been part of Cabrini for some considerable time. I didn't feel that five years was a "considerable time" and that I couldn't see anything on their site which referred to an after care service or reference to past residents of the Children's Homes being able to retrieve their records.

I have expressed the Members' obvious distress at their records being handed over to any Organisation without their knowledge or consent, least of all to one which no-one has heard of.

Ian Forbes has assured me that Diagrama Foundation was chosen after other Organisations were approached, because they were able to offer the most secure storage of the files in a suitable storage room on site, among adoption and fostering files, and that no-one is allowed to access the room or its files unless they have been appointed to do so, such as a senior social from a specific department.

Ian Forbes is a Senior Social Worker on the Adoption Team and is allowed access, but at all times the room is locked and is secure in every way.

Diagrama is soon to transfer its Head Office to the Old Court Buildings in Rochester, Kent. Personal records and files will be transferred to the Old Court Buildings where security will be as tight. AT NO time will personal files of any nature be transferred out of this country.

I did ask if Ian Forbes would be willing to meet with members of the group and he agreed but suggested it might be via Skype! I didn't think that was very appropriate, nor did I think it was the right way to conduct a meeting about such a serious matter I'm afraid. Though I see in his email tonight, that suggestion still stands.

From my personal observations about Diagrama Foundation site, the children they are working with appear to be those who until recently, were known as "maljusted"; social "misfits", those who are unable to settle in conventional schools or in their own residential homes. Aside from my own work, we, my husband and I lived at a termly boarding school for "maljusted" senior school children for many, many years, so I did recognise the description. Diagrama have two children's homes accommodating these children.

I have to say that, following this fairly lengthy talk with Ian Forbes I do feel reassured that your personal files will be safe and secure and will be accessible by individuals who may wish to apply for details or viewing in the normal way.

I have also had contact with Liverpool University (Ref.D.541) re the storage of files, to clarify their interest and why they store records. The position is firstly, they do not store any records from any Catholic Organisation, only because they have never been asked. NCH and Barnado's do use the facility at Liverpool for personal files of children and staff; children who are 100+ years old and staff records after 75 year. If a relative of any of those files wanted to see those records, they would have to apply in the first instance to the Organisation involved in their care. That is the only way a file can be extracted from the University.

This is a lengthy email I know, and I hope I have covered most of your questions with suitable answers, but do please come back to me, or indeed, Ian Forbes, for more clarification. I have acted merely as your friend and not as your spokesperson.

Tomorrow evening I have to be away until Sunday evening, but you have something to reflect on for the time being.

Much love to you both.

Ann

Ann,

Yours was a lengthy email but very informative. So that files are to be stored under strict security but what is it all about? Storage is expensive. Why does this organisation take on this expense? What is in it for them? What use will they make of the files? I doubt that the files will be as freely available as we have been used to with Cabrini.

Let's hope that we don't learn at some time in the future that there has been a fire and all files have been destroyed.

I have, like others, an uneasy feeling about all of this.

John.

December 22/2014

Hello John & Josie,

I think the best thing to do is to have a meeting with Ian Forbes on the Group's behalf and not via Skype. Like that, you can express your feeling and those of the other members. His email to me suggested that it was I who asked for a Skype meeting. Not so! For I don't believe for one moment this is in any way the correct way to hold a meeting of such importance!

When NCH became Action for Children, we were told officially at the London reunion what was happening to our records, among other things. A survey was done by NCH via a letter for us to complete and return. At the next reunion we were told how those questions and queries were resolved and the changeover was very smooth and satisfactory. I feel Cabrini should have consulted you and the Group before suddenly dumping it in your laps. Just a personal view.

Kind regards,

Ann.

December 23/2014

Re: Response to Questions

So Ann, how was it left? Is Mr. Forbes going to extend an invitation to us all to meet?

We hope you and your family have a really Happy Christmas.

Love.

John

Hello John,

I would imagine he'll want you to contact him and say what it is you want.

I do wonder though, if your files are there, why you can't have them to keep yourself? Those of us from NCH get to keep them once we've seen them (with Social Worker) at the office.

Have a very Happy Christmas, John, Josie too, and let's hope 2015 will be a brighter year.

Much love,

Ann

Ann,

I have a copy of my file contents. I was told years ago that the files are only kept for seventy years.

My file would be placed in the skip but the time limit has, I believe, been revised. This is probably because we are all living longer. I advised our members to make a request for copies of their files. In my case all the documents in my file were photocopies but mindful that Cabrini is a charity I made a donation to offset the costs involved.

Perhaps if we can arrange a meeting in the New Year, the Charity holding the files and so a "This is your Life" and hand each of our members their personal file.

Let's see what the New Year brings.

Love

John & Josie

December 27/2014

(Delvin)John Flynn, Ann Phyall.

Hi John,

Well, if your file is placed in the skip, imagine where mine has ended up. I can't begin to imagine, after a seventy year lifespan. If we could but obtain our personal files from Diagrama/Cabrini I believe this would settle a lot of the hurt we are currently going through – myself in particular as I know for a fact my records at St. Anne's and those of William's at St. Mary's would pull at the heartstrings of anyone reading its contents. But we are a tough crew who with thorough early training are capable of taking on any mammoth task without the blink of an eyelash.

It would be my firm belief in order for each of us to secure our file we would be more than happy to cover any costs involved. I say this with tongue in cheek as the answer stares me in the face.

Keep well.

KOKO with love

Caroline

December 28/2014

John,

With clarity of mind, yes indeed, if we could but take our files from Cabrini/Diagrama it would allow us to rest in the knowing they can never be destroyed. I use this term loosely as we have been advised otherwise. What affects me personally the most, John, is the "silent rule" and if those responsible for the protection of our records realise the devastating effect it has on our group members; myself in particular as I still have no answer why my elder sister's name was changed from Brandon to Marshall. A mystery! No date or reason given. I fully understand the time-frame for holding records. Is it now time for them to be let go?

Hope you and Josie are keeping well.

Caroline

January 5/2015

(Delvin) John Flynn. Caroline Whitehead, John M Murray, Ann Phyall.

Hello,

Just to update everyone with regards to Ian Forbes of Cabrini. I spoke to him on the phone just now explaining our "worries" as a group and individuals with The Diagrama Foundation. Our rights. Our records and contacts, etc. and I have insisted that we have a meeting asap with myself, John Flynn, Cabrini read Ian Forbes and of course Diagrama to clarify once and for all how we ALL stand!

As you can see from Mr Forbes' email the meeting will be in Orpington where Cabrini still retain small premises that Caroline, John F. and myself visited in May 2013. When I get the dates from Ian Forbes I will let you know and take it from there.

I told Mr Forbes of our considerable concerns and distrust as far as the previous years of distrust goes with the Catholic Church let alone this non-British Company being entrusted with OUR personal details. I did make a point of not attaching any blame to those in the Cabrini set up that we have had dealings with for the last decade or so. Our reason for distrust in reality is the past and present record of the Catholic Church and in particular their "Habit" of accidental fires and floods (though not 40 days these days!), magically happening and then hundreds and thousands of records being "lost" forever.

You know me by now when I tell you that I pointed this out to Mr Forbes in no uncertain manner.

I also informed him that I had written to the M.P. Edward Timpson who has the overall responsibility for Children's Welfare as part of his Government remit to ask for clarification as far as the law stands to ALL our rights.

I emailed MP Timpson on the 9th December 2014 and am still waiting for a response. SO I rang them today to be told they are not always the quickest at responding to situations: Well, blow me down what a surprise! I was told by a very helpful "Scouser" called Helen to ring her in two weeks if I had NOT heard from Mr Timpson; which of course I will do, you can be sure of.

KOKO

Terry.

Dear Terry,

Thank you for your time discussing with me your concerns regarding the Cabrini archives. You have requested a meeting as soon as practical in Orpington.

I have agreed to arrange a meeting so a range of issues can be discussed including the background of Diagrama Foundation and its future intentions with regards to the archives.

I will contact you with some dates.

Regards,

Ian.

Terry McKenna, (Delvin) John Flynn, John M. Murray, Ann Phyall

Terry and All,

Many thanks for your update re meeting and concerns with Ian Forbes which I sincerely hope will be sooner than later.

I am reminded of Ann's message to John F. on December 22/2014 when she clearly stated:

"When National Children's Homes (NCH) became Action for Children, we were told officially at the London reunion what was happening to our records, among other things. A survey was done by NCH, via a letter for us to complete and return. At the next reunion we were told how those questions and queries were resolved and the changeover was very smooth and satisfactory. I feel Cabrini should have consulted you and the group before suddenly dumping it in your laps. Just a personal view."

This of course is the way it should have happened between Cabrini and the Group with the changeover of personal records, bearing also in mind there could have been some discussion on the proposition when John, yourself and I visited Cabrini in May 2013 at Orpington. It was a missed opportunity for us and I feel did expose us to this current situation over which we had no control.

Our main concern is not to be critical of Cabrini due to their past record of good work, in particular helping some of our members to achieve their family history, but the way in which this transfer took place without our knowledge of an already done-deal, with no input, and had been in negotiations the past two years. It is a long time to be kept in the dark about something as important as our files.

I trust your meeting with Ian Forbes will prove positive.

Question: due to the importance of all contents within member's thoughts with him on the concerns of our personal files, is it my understanding that none of his emails can be used (verbatim) in KOKO book? Many thanks!

Can someone in the group, please advise?

KOKO

Caroline

January 7/2015

Caroline Whitehead, (Delvin) John Flynn, John M. Murray, Ann Phyall

Re: Edward Timpson MP and The Information Commissioner's Offices.

Having sent you the copy of the email from Edward Timpson's minion one Geoffrey Haynes, I immediately went on line to the Information Commissioner's Office and spoke to an operator by telephone: 0303 123 1113 as shown on the bottom left side of their home site. After explaining who and where I was from, I asked him for details of OUR specific rights regarding information/files held; in our case by Cabrini.

This is the gist of replies to my questions:

ANY such organisation CAN withhold any information they feel is NOT for you to see! I kid you not!

ANY company can take over OUR personal records and keep them wherever they wish AND NOT necessarily in this country (UK). He seems to think that OUR personal records CAN be destroyed after the death of whoever they hold information on, although the seventy year rule (which was never authenticated) would probably extend to about 100-125 years. How will that affect family genealogists searching for ancestors etc. in the years to come I ask?

You can however apply in writing to an organisation requesting YOUR personal details either in writing and/or email and upon payment of any fee that may be incurred that company has to respond in writing/email within forty days (YES, 40 days, maybe of floods to ruin OUR records) setting out whatever THEY feel you need to know!

Keeping email dates is easy: Save what you send in a computer file. The day sent will never be able to be changed if using mail; letters should be sent by recorded delivery. You can only ask for your details (and family) and not on behalf of anyone else. After all of this IF you still have the will and either an unsatisfactory response (OR none at all) you can then take them to court.

To briefly give you an idea of what that means I quoted my own case of trying to get copies of six letters my mother wrote to Cabrini; then known as the Catholic Children's Rescue Society based in Southwark and the fact I was told "Despite" I was sent the original letters thirty-years ago, which Cabrini freely admitted to me by email! He said this was an illegal thing to do with regards to the Data Protection Act (Remember that?) and I would have to take them to court. I kindly reminded this person I spoke to, who in fairness was honest with his replies to me, that there is a thing in this country known as the "Family Court" and did I not deserve the same as anyone else? Am I not a former child from no matter from whatever part of a "Family" in the UK. So as I told him, thank you for nothing and once again it has been hammered home to me that we "Unfortunate siblings, children, waifs and strays" have absolutely no rights whatsoever despite living in these "enlightened Times" of the 21st Century.

If you feel you may wish to comment then please either email me OR ring me OR even Skype c/w web-cam on terry, sean.mckenna. AND of course any questions that ALL our group may have for John F. and I to take to our meeting with Ian Forbes Cabrini, Nathan James Ward

(Diagrama) and I think Irena also from Cabrini, we will take AND ask when that happens.

To sum up, not very good news, is it? Let me know what you think please. I am taking over this problem ONLY to give John F. as much time for him and Josie whilst she is not too well at the moment.

Hopefully she will soon be better and "Normal Service" will soon be resumed with John.

KOKO

Terry

Terry McKenna (Delvin)John Flynn, John M.Murray, Ann Phyall

'morning Terry,

I am too speechless for words to begin to describe the utter feeling of hopelessness with regard to your conversation with the operator from The Information Commissioner's Office. Was there anyone else you could have spoken with to verify his comments?

The major concern here is that your comments re future genealogists searching for past records of family history they will no longer be able to achieve this goal if personal files can be shunted to and from any country at the whim of the current holders. I cannot imagine the cost to a researcher to be searching the records to find there are non available, either through leaving the country and unobtainable or worse still, destroyed. No history from time memorial should be annihilated for whatever reason.

I did not receive a copy of the email from Edward Timpson's minion one G Haynes, so I am curious to know what he had to say,

In my view the meeting between John F. Irena, Ian Forbes/Cabrini, Nathan Ward Diagrama and yourself should still take place.

In point of fact Edward Timpson still has not written to either you or to me so is there the remotest chance we may get a response from him?

KOKO

Caroline

January 8/2015

Terry,

I am "shocked and stunned". Could it now be about time to write to the newspapers regarding this matter? A good campaigning newspaper like the Guardian Daily Mail, The Times might be interested in what we have to say.

A belated "Happy New Year".

Laundry Boy,

John Michael Murray

Hi John and All,

Like you I was initially "shocked" at just what I was told although in reality NOT REALLY. This past sixty years in my case I have learned that it was not only our parents that "abandoned" us. It is the state and successive governments that are still doing the same!

I would be more than happy to bring this "problem" to the masses but sadly I fear unless we manage to get a substantially well-known, well-connected personality on board we may be fighting the establishment for the rest of our lives and beyond. Personally I would be up for that challenge after I receive any other comments to my emails from yesterday. Again I would be happy to meet up and draw a plan of action and go from there.

KOKO

Terry.

January 9/2015

Caroline Whitehead. (Delvin) John Flynn, John M. Murray, Ann Phyall.

Hi Caroline and everyone else.

I have downloaded to my Laptop ALL 138 pages that are supposed to show what Data Protection actually means in the Government eyes at least. If you wish me to send you a PDF file of this I would be happy to do so OR you can look at it; then download if you wish yourselves. I warn you it is 138 pages long! To look at this key in your search engine.

Once I have heard back from Ann and John F. Caroline and John M. have replied already, then I will look into what I can do. To my mind The Data Protection Act is worth absolutely nothing hence the daily bombardment of "nuisance" calls and emails or good old fashioned "junk" mail that we ALL receive.

I'm afraid, Caroline, the offhand and jerky response email from D.O.E. government department is typical of our modern day society. They remind me so much of the almost illiterate persons of years gone by that produced and kept records over the centuries. Just take a look at any birth/marriage/death records and your own personal records you may have been lucky enough to have got already. Some may say that is a little harsh BUT this is my life AND yours we are talking about here.

KOKO as always.

Terry.

Terry Mckenna, (Delvin) John Flynn, John M. Murray, Ann Phyall

Hi Terry and All,

Reading between the lines of your email I don't even need to hazard a guess the ambiguity between the contents of the Data Protection Act and The Information Commissioner's Office when speaking with one of their operators. As we know, the done-deal with Cabrini/Diagrama began with a negative and remains so as far as we are concerned without getting any positive satisfaction or input from either organisation.

The plan of National Children's Homes (NCH) to pass over their records was done in a professional manner, giving each person involved the opportunity to speak out.

John M's suggestion to approach the media might just help. But, Terry, you most certainly touched a nerve when commenting about future family research in that if there are no records to be searched how then will anyone even within the head office of The Genealogy Society in London, world famous, find the remotest detail of past history. This should not be so!

Record-keeping in the past was never the forte of the powers that be controlling orphanages, institutions and homes for children. It wasn't part of their curriculum and obviously did not interest them in the fact records of all children were not as vital as saving their souls.

Let us wait until either Mr Timpson MP responds to my letter – failing that – see what transpires from the meeting between you, John F, Irena, Ian Forbs/Cabrini and Nathan Ward at Orpington. Perhaps, Terry, it may be prudent not to put it off much longer as there may not be a trail on which to hold.

I realise it depends on John F's time and if he is able to get away.

On behalf of the group, sincere thanks for your efforts to bring our concerns to closure.

KOKO

Caroline

(Delvin) John Flynn. Terry McKenna, Caroline Whitehead.

Dear Friends,

Thank you for forwarding your various emails referring to your accessing records etc. All of which I am trying to follow with interest.

However, as some of you will know, my brother Roger has died in Australia on Boxing Day and my focus right now is on my family there. Another family member died yesterday and I am quite beside myself right now – especially with phone calls to and from Australia and the time differences, which mean sleepless nights etc. here.

During last night, I went online looking for "Legislation" to back up your enquiries. I came back to the same page every time!

This morning I rang my own organisation and the lady there knows of Irena and of Cabrini – but not of Diagrama Foundation. I was advised that you need to contact the Care Leavers' Association who have been quite active and I'm sure that this is perhaps your next step for the help and advice you need.

Just go to Google and type in Care Leavers' Association.

You will see that there is to be a gathering in the House of Lords re

Records and this just may be the place to air your feelings and sort your Rights!

My love to you all.

I shall watch with interest any developments!!

Ann

Dear Ann,

During this time of grief that you are able to concentrate on the groups' efforts to put the concerns of the safe-keeping of our personal records where there is not only accessibility to them but also they are kept in a friendly environment and most definitely remain in the UK, is sincerely appreciated.

In the past you have delved into many subjects on our behalf – all of which is much appreciated – and your advice to contact Care Leavers' Association, I am sure Terry would be more than agreeable to assist and dig up any information possible that may be of value to our group and pass his findings on.

Your advice regarding the House of Lords and discussion of Records we hope to follow up and trust our inquiries will not fall on deaf ears.

Sincere condolences on behalf of the group.

KOKO

Caroline

January 12/2015

Caroline Whitehead, (Delvin) John Flynn, John M.Murray, Ann Phyall

Hi Caroline and everyone,

Not an unusual thing to happen regarding what Irena thinks (no doubt through lack of proper communication from Diagrama AND her overall boss Ian Forbes) Cabrini admit to and Diagrama who what little we have seen and heard already does NOT bode well for the future does it? This is so typical of ALL the churches, isn't it? Just last week in of all places Gravesend, a Church of England run premises is being accused of yet more heinous crimes against children in their care and trust! And so it goes on and on and on!

Be assured everyone I will not be afraid to ask BLUNT questions of Diagrama and Cabrini that may embarrass themselves. That would be their fault, not mine. To "upset" Cabrini and/or Diagrama does not bother me. They have been doing that to you and me for years, haven't they?

Just to remind you, do please send me ANY questions you feel should be asked AND they will be asked.

KOKO

Terry McKenna

Letter dated December 26/2014

to the Office of Jo Johnson, Member of Parliament, (Orpington), House of Commons, London, UK, SW1A OAA.

Dear Mr. Johnson,

I belong to a group of "old" girls and boys worldwide from Orpington and Gravesend, Kent, and we are concerned our personal records dating back to 1900s relating to children put in care, are now transferred from Cabrini, Purley, Surrey to Diagrama Foundation whose location next Spring is at Rochester, Kent. I would like to know if this transfer is within the jurisdiction of English laws.

The group is concerned for the protection of our files and the environmental conditions under which they will be stored.

Thank you for your advice and help. Your reply is appreciated.

Caroline Whitehead,

BC, Canada.

January 13/2015

Response from Spencer Chilton,

Office of Jo. Johnson, Member of Parliament for Orpington, Kent.

Dear Ms Whitehead,

Thank you for writing to Jo Johnson MP about the transfer of your personal files. Joe has read your comments with great interest; however strict parliamentary protocol prevents MPs from contacting non-constituents.

Nevertheless, I recommend contacting the Diagrama Foundation directly via the below link, in order to raise your concerns.

Kind regards,

Spencer Chilton

Dear Mr Chilton,

Thank you for responding to my email to Jo Johnson MP of December 2014, in which I raised the concern of my personal records being transferred from Cabrini to Diagrama November, 2014.

As you have kindly pointed out MP Johnson has read my letter with great interest; however due to the fact I am not a constituent in his riding he is unable through protocol to assist me. This of course is very disappointing in view of the fact if I cannot find help from him or the UK government, where can I go?

While I appreciate where this all comes from, it does not of course satisfy my London group of "old" boys with a negative reply.

Sincerely,

Caroline Whitehead, BC.

Terry McKenna, (Delvin) John Flynn, John M.Murray, Ann Phyall.

I have just forwarded a message to you back from Jo Johnson, MP for Orpington with regard to his response concerning our personal files and my reply.

It leaves one with the feeling that bureaucracy continually has one banging a head against a wall. Having tried and failed within this circle, the door is well and truly closed.

With Diagrama Foundation the die is already cast, and despite their assurance of accessibility, transparency I foresee difficult times ahead for researchers trying to extract the files from them. With their background of constant moves from one location to the next and insufficient accruement, the future of careful management of our records leaves it in question.

Ann's suggestion to contact Care Leavers' Association may provide some guidance, also inquiring through the House of Lords. Again, instinct tells me this will be a negative response.

John M's idea of contacting a London newspaper might just give us the lift we need to jolt Diagrama and Cabrini into realising we still need answers, honest ones at that!

Terry, the meeting with yourself, John F. and other parties involved, is it possible to establish a date when you can get together, albeit we already have the answer to what will transpire at this meeting.

The history of child abuse within any religious organisation will never stop until exposed. Heinous crimes to children will continue in history, sadly!

If someone could forward me the email of Sunday Express, would appreciate it. Thanks!

KOKO

Caroline

January 14/2015

Hi Caroline,

Regarding John F's last email comments! I'm fairly certain that both Labour and The Conservatives already have their "Chimpanzees" in place. Just look at Cameron: Buffoon Boris Johnson: Clegg and Milliband: Need I say more?

I have just spoken to Ian Forbes re: future meeting and he says he's waiting to hear from Nathan at Diagrama! I suggested he took a leaf out of my book and instead of just emailing, phone him just like I have done with you.

He then started to say that meeting at Orpington is most unlikely because: that complex is a home for the elderly! YES he really said that! I politely told him of our meeting in May 2013 with yourself, J.F. and Josie, Teresa Downey, Irena and myself and that wasn't a very good delaying tactic. He didn't like that but that's his problem, NOT mine. Speaking to

John after on Skype he said we could meet at his home for any meeting with tea and biscuits available.

Might I suggest not to holdback with regards to Bruce and the printing preparation. I have a feeling it may be some time before we get what I might term as a responsible and constructive reply (IF at all) to our questions AND in writing. Obviously as soon as we might get that I would let you know at once. I don't think it is worth holding up our book though of course if we get any sort of response in time it could still make the book OR maybe the next one!

Over the next couple of days I am going to read ALL 138 pages of the Data Protection Act that will be of use to us so we (John and I) know not only what questions to throw at them BUT what their answers should be. Wish me well with the reading!

KOKO

Terry McK.

Caroline.

Dare I say it, but officialdom have a low regard for emails and perhaps you and Terry should send "hard copies" when writing to MP's with particular attention to copying the prime minister. The trouble is some MP's have safe seats and don't have to work or acknowledge letters.

Conservative and Labour are in the happy position of having safe seats and in each case you could put a chimpanzee for election and it would be elected.

(Delvin) John

John,

The old adage: nothing ventured, nothing gained, spurs me on with your email to David Cameron which I will most certainly use, today.

I smiled at your postscript: so typical of political rhetoric!

Well, we are shooting arrows in the dark but could there possibly be light somewhere within the darkness?

What great mind used the phrase: Hope Springs Eternal!

Take care.

Caroline

'morning John,

Just on 6.15 am – thought I'd update you on The Boys of St. Mary's manuscript.

Our final chapter relates to Protection of OUR Files and it depends on your meeting with Terry, Cabrini and Diagrama how the chapter ends. I am not feeling good about the end result as I'm sure we both have the answer already.

We have had no positive feedback from lobbying Edward Timpson MP, who directed Terry's email to the Information Commissioner's Office. The MP still has not replied to my letter of December 2014. Failing a response by next Monday I will contact his office.

Antony Hayman sent excellent photographs of St. Mary's – the refectory, chapel, dormitories and the building. Good for reprinting. None of the photocopies of photos are suitable when reprinted by the publisher.

The photograph taken of you and me taken at the Gorge in Victoria, when you visited moons ago, I would like to use. If you agree!

Hope you and Josie are all right.

Caroline

January 15/2015

Terry hi,

Many thanks for your comprehensive message regarding your colourful description of certain Labour and Conservative members of the British Parliament.

In your telephone discussion with Ian Forbes regarding setting up a date and place of meeting between you, John F. Cabrini/Diagrama it seems to me that Ian Forbes is using delay tactics in the hope you will give up on the idea. Am I to assume Nathan Ward is superior to him in his position at Diagrama; therefore, it does not allow Forbes to approach him on the matter. There is definitely something amiss here. For Forbes to make the excuse the complex at Orpington is for the elderly does not mean it is inappropriate to hold meetings there. A poor excuse to get out of a meeting with a one on one, face to face. This tells me a great deal of his attitude towards the whole messy business and I can now fully understand why the transfer of our records was done in this unbusinesslike manner.

It is kind of (Delvin) John F. to even suggest holding the meeting at his house when he is already carrying a heavy load.

I will wait till the end of January before closing off the manuscript as I feel the final chapter: Protection of OUR Files is crucial in its closure.

Do keep us updated on further correspondence from Cabrini/Diagrama.

KOKO

Caroline

Caroline,

Once again I see you are an "early" bird. I told Ian Forbes almost exactly what you thought about his feeble effort to "delay" said meeting! And again I believe he is the monkey NOT the Organ Grinder. A sort of workplace! In limbo, doing Purgatory time.

John F. sounded and looked in good form yesterday when I saw him.

KOKO

Terry

Ian,

When I spoke to (Delvin) John Flynn yesterday after our call I told him you thought meeting at Orpington may be a problem so he suggested that he would be perfectly happy to meet at his home. He lives in a place called Lee, which is fairly close to Bromley in Kent.

As you can see I have also emailed Nathan Ward this message.

I hope this eases the awkwardness of any meeting place?

Many thanks.

Terry McK.

Terry,

Thank you for your message re: a proposed meeting with (Delvin) John F., Ian Forbes, Nathan Ward Cabrini/Diagrama and yourself, which it is hoped will be sooner than later.

Our group member worldwide need closure on this matter concerning the environmental condition and accessibility of our personal files once they are moved from Purley Surrey to Rochester Kent, Spring 2015. This assurance is needed in writing from Diagrama Foundation.

For future generations our records must be protected at all cost.

KOKO

Caroline

Terry,

Ian Forbes and the others have to realise we won't give up until this meeting has taken place and we have it in writing their assurance our personal records are maintained under the conditions of their done deal negotiations between Cabrini and Diagrama Foundation, to our satisfaction. This written document is all we have to rely on for the protection of our files and the accessibility of them to future researchers.

KOKO

Caroline

January 20/2015

(Delvin) John Flynn

Hello,

I was there in 1951 at three years of age with my brother who was then ten; his name was Ted Standen.

I remember the Coronation parades. Father Baker with his Honny TV, Andy Pandy at 2.15p.m. Sisters Vincent, Margaret, Cathrin, Saint Rocs dormitory, and Mrs Galliger, used to bath us all.

I can tell you more especially the names of friends at that time; example, Raffial and Gabrial Ferrari brothers.

Please get in contact asap. I am sixty-seven years old now.

Anthony Standen

(Delvin) John,

Thank you for sharing the news of Anthony Standen, an old St. Mary's boy.

Isn't it amazing the number of old boys that continue to come out of the woodwork. The connection with Anthony is great! I hope he stays in touch with the group.

KOKO

Caroline

January 21/2015

Nathan Ward. (Delvin) John Flynn, Ann Phyall, Irena Lyczkowska, Cabrini

Dear Nathan,

Lack of transparency –

Would you please advise me where is the transparency between Diagrama/Cabrini and our "network" of old boys and girls in North London?

It appears all attempts between Terry McKenna and our leader (Delvin) John Flynn, both of whom are willing to attend any meeting, at any time, between yourself and Ian Forbes are being side-tracked with ongoing excuses why this meeting cannot be held.

First it was the location – previously suggested at Orpington. Second the excuse now is that Ian Forbes has to wait on you for the answer when this meeting can take place. It is with a firm resolution to advise you we cannot wait any longer for this gathering which is essential to our group in the knowing that many of their questions to the long awaited answers to them are needed to be heard now, not later.

If you will do me the courtesy of a response, it would be appreciated.

Caroline, BC. Canada

Caroline, (Delvin) John Flynn, Ann Phyall, Ian Forbes, Cabrini.

Dear Caroline,

Many thanks for your email regarding a meeting and I am sorry that you feel that there is a lack of transparency.

Ian is indeed waiting for me to come back with a date for the meeting and until Friday this week my diary is not "fixed" and therefore I cannot confirm any date. After Friday any date I do confirm will be "confirmed" opposed to now where any date I provide will be tentative.

As expressed in my phone calls before Christmas, I am looking forward to meeting up with members of the group and will confirm a date at the very latest by Monday (26th) next week.

Nathan Ward,

Head of Care and Justice,

Diagrama, U.K.

January 25/2015

To: The Rt.Hon Simon Hughes, MP

102 Petty France, London, England, SW1H 9AJ

Dear Minister, Re: Legality of Transfer of Personal Files

I belong to a "network" of old boys and girls worldwide whose base is in North London, and who regularly email their recollection of their time in care.

Our personal family records dating back to the 1920s of those children put in care at St. Mary's Gravesend and St. Anne's, Orpington, Kent were under the guardianship of the Southwark Catholic Children's Society. The Society changed its name in 2008/2009 to Cabrini, located in Purley, Surrey. Our records remained in the same archives under Cabrini's care.

At the beginning of December last, it became known to our group that Cabrini sold its business to an unknown organisation called The Diagrama Foundation, whose headquarters we understand are in Belguim.

Negotiations for the takeover between the two organisations commenced two (2) years ago but it was not until these negotiations were completed in December 2014, did Cabrini advise our group leader (Delvin) John Flynn that all our personal records were to be handed over to The Diagrama Foundation. There was no dialogue up until the time Diagrama's Interim Chief Executive, Hilary Brooks' letter of December 4/2014 addressed to Cabrini confirming the transfer of services, a copy of which was sent to (Delvin) John Flynn. In turn he advised our group their personal files would be handed over to The Diagrama Foundation Spring of 2015; however, it became known this transaction had already taken place without prior notification or input from our members whose files are involved in this issue.

If there is any advice you can give us regarding the legality of the transfer of our personal records from one establishment to another, it would be appreciated.

Thank you.

Sincerely,

Caroline Whitehead,

British Columbia, Canada.

February 1/2015

Hi Caroline,

I was only joking re keeping the various emails. Indeed I have them ALL safe; still have enough room to store many more so no problems there.

Maybe an addendum was the wrong word to use. Maybe either under the Prefix introduction or acknowledgements section just stating that The Diagrama Foundation were given time and warning to respond to our "fears" regarding ALL our records and their availability and continued safety.

The conclusion from our little group can then be listed. Others who read the book can soon draw their own conclusions, won't they? We really shouldn't delay our book or incur any further costs because of the ignorance of Nathan Ward. If they want a "War" of attrition they have picked the right guy for the job: ME!

KOKO

Terry Mc.

Terry,

Thanks for yours. I will give Nathan Ward just this week to respond to a proposed suitable meeting date with you and John F. and if this is not forthcoming I most definitely will close the last chapter of the manuscript with the obvious conclusion of getting nowhere with the supposedly transparency of The Diagrama Foundation.

From the beginning I had the feeling we were dealing with a micky mouse operation and it is showing its weak signs of business in the way they have not been dealing with simple answers to simple questions. This tells me a great deal about an organisation and leaves in my mind why many of its business deals in the past have not functioned. All I can say is heaven help our records with the attitude of couldn't care less and that they are dealing with individuals past of unwanted children left in orphanage care who to them are not important. It is this latter part that strikes a nerve to the limit.

If your next overseas plan is to visit Australia it would be great if you could fit in a trip to see one or two of our group members. Paddy and Mavis Heffernan, who respond to emails. What about Sue Stafford at Tuart Place? I am not sure if you had a response from her to your inquiry of space in the magazine.

My letter to Simon Hughes, Minister of Justice, he should receive this week. The big question: will his response be any better than those from Jo Johnson MP for Orpington or Edward Timpson Minister Responsible for Children and Families bring us any nearer to closure to the issue of concern regarding our family records? Million dollar question!

KOKO

Caroline

February 2/2015

Caroline and Terry,

I had some spare time today as my daughter met up with Josie for a shopping trip, so taking advantage of the bonus free time. I telephoned Cabrini about our concerns re: the takeover of Cabrini by another charity.

In essence I expressed my concern about the fate of my personal details being passed to another organisation and the possible fate of my file. Naturally they couldn't discuss anyone else's details with me. I was assured that the only change that will come about as far as personal files are concerned "is no change". I laboured my concerns and again, was told that there would be "no change". All the information on my file would still be available and the change of name of the charity would not impact on this whatsoever. Information in the file denied to me in the past may still be denied if the original reason for withholding the information still existed and was reasonable. For instance if sensitive information was on file that could impact on family members still alive and leave the charity open to a possible court case. Again if there was a risk of third party confidential information on file entering the public domain then that could be a reason for redacting names and addresses and sensitive information to avoid litigation against the charity. The new organisation would be run under the same regulations as applicable to any existing care charity and the new organisation would be precluded from exporting our information out of the UK.

Although I was not speaking to the chief executive of the organisation I felt confident that I was given a true picture of how all parties are bound by the Data Protection Act irrespective of any change or mergers or takeovers of any charity involved in the care of erstwhile children irrespective of when they were taken into care. However, if any children's charity does not hold proper records for whatever reason then obviously they can't hand over information that they do not have. Then the question needs to be asked why the information is not available. What further action a person can take if this is the case, in my opinion, to take further advice. It may be that files between difference organisations dealing with a child were not handed over and if Cabrini can show that they kept proper files from when the child came into their care they may be able to demonstrate that they can't be held responsible if they were not give a comprehensive file in the first place so long as they kept proper records from then onwards.

We know that at best our files could have held so much more information but in those far off days charities were run for the most part by well meaning middle class ladies who needed to fill their time with "good works". They were at best gifted amateurs. It's different today.

So let's KOKO

(Delvin) John Flynn

(Delvin) John F.

John hi,

Appreciate the long and interesting message you were able to sit down and write while Josie and daughter went on a shopping spree. Just hope there were a few pennies left for the man of the house.

It is quite obvious after your lengthy telephone discussion with Cabrini it prompted Ian Forbes to act quicker than normal and that he came up with the promised meeting date for February 10th, which may be agreeable to you. I have listed a few questions in a previous email simply to establish the background of The Diagrama Foundation without appearing to be prying into their financial stability.

Rightly so, as mentioned, Cabrini is unable to discuss with you details of any one of the group's personal file, but that was not your intent in the first place so one does not jump to conclusions without reason. Although the assurance was given to you nothing will change due to the takeover while it appears they are trying to allay our fears of the protection of our records, it is the lack of knowledge of The Diagrama Foundation's background that cause these concerns plus they are not connected to any government programmes, no church connection, and their past history is questionable when they open facilities only to close them down through lack of funds.

If they are paying high salaries to people like Interim Chief Executive Hilary Brooks and Elaine Brewster who lives away from the main office and no doubt is paid a hefty salary, it leaves many doubts in my mind the reason in particular why they need to hire a freelance person unless they fear confrontation from an outside source.

The fact Diagrama originated in Belgium and has other interests in European countries we should ask them in writing to confirm our records do remain according to the laws of the UK and they will not be transferred outside of the country or used for financial gain, OR destroyed.

Were you able to get the name of the person you spoke with on the phone?

The records of children kept years ago were not the priority of the care-givers and stated only pertinent details, entry and date of leaving, religious instructions. Sadly, curriculum achievements were not considered important.

What I did find disturbing not only with my records but those of others, is the way addresses of families were obliterated. The reason, obvious! The knowledge, disastrous!

It is the records not necessarily of my generation dating from the 1920s but of those children put in care in the '50s, '60s and on, that concerns me. A particular recent case of one of our members who had a run-in with Cabrini about his file was advised he could only extract family information from them but it was not to be used for publication. Again, addresses were obliterated.

Although I am of the mind Diagrama will have no choice but to comply with The Protection Data Act a dark cloud still lingers doubts of them functioning as a charitable organisation. There is John definitely a vibe of suspicion I cannot shake off about these people. Basically, it is the initial underhanded way this takeover began and the fact the three of us saw members of Cabrini in 2013 but nothing was mentioned of the negotiations between them and Diagrama. It leaves a bitter taste in the mouth.

Let us see what transpires from your meeting on February 10th, which I hope will provide questions to our answers, truthfully.

KOKO

Caroline

Terry McKenna, (Delvin) John Flynn, Nathan Ward, Ian Forbes, John M. Murray, Ann Phyall, Elaine Brewster.

Terry,

Thank you for the update from Ian Forbes, Cabrini/Diagrama and the suggested date to meet with you and John F. on Tuesday, 10th February 2015. This is indeed encouraging and I most certainly appreciate Ian making a concerted effort on our part to resolve some of our concerns regarding our personal files. If this matter can be discussed at whatever venue is chosen and we have the assurance of the Diagrama Foundation/Cabrini our personal files will not be compromised in any way we will be able to put this issue to rest. It is hoped John F. can be available for this meeting with all concerned. Today he contacted Cabrini by phone and from his conversation with them, it sounded positive. In the past, Cabrini have always been helpful with our group members who wished to search their family history in their records. This service with Diagrama we hope will continue with the same transparency.

KOKO

Caroline

Terry, (Delvin) John Flynn, John M. Murray, Ann Phyall.

Terry,

I have just read your second email re meeting with Ian Forbes on 10th February. Place of venue, Chatham.

When John F. rang Cabrini with his concerns I believe this resulted in the message from Ian Forbes to act quickly. I can but agree with your assumption why Ian contacted you. Since my rather threatening email to Nathan Ward I did not get a response from him which was no surprise. For him to say he cannot meet with you tells me the kind of people with whom we are dealing. Bit of a sad state of affairs when promises are made and not kept. It doesn't matter about the reason; it is the principle that counts.

No doubt, underlying vibes at the meeting will prevail but I am confident your questions to answers from them will drive home the fact we want the truth and not lies.

My question is exactly where are our personal records to be held once they reach Rochester, Kent and under what environmental condition, transparency and accessibility to our members. How long will they remain at Rochester or will they be like the proverbial Romany gypsies with no fixed abode?

I contacted Care Leavers' Association with our issue and if and when I receive their advice I will pass it on.

KOKO

Caroline

February 3/2015

Caroline, (Delvin) John Flynn, John M. Murray, Ann Phyall

Hi Everyone,

The PDF attachment you should have received with the latest email is what I have discovered on line and more or less covers the doubts we have with this company and I'm afraid a complicit once again Catholic Church. As before I lay virtually no blame with the Cabrini we have come to know this last decade or so, especially John F. They (Cabrini that is) do however have some issues of releasing information for ALL of us and therefore must be included in "discussion" with Diagrama next Tuesday (10th) assuming they agree to the place and time we have offered AND NOT what they are trying to foist upon us!

Ian Forbes emailed me yesterday and tells me that our "original" contact Nathan James Ward suddenly is NOT available seemingly at ANY time!! Ian informed me that he would be accompanied by someone called Elaine Brewster. No mention of Irena whom we all know and was originally coming along too. This lady works as a Freelance Head of Communication. Professional: Available to the highest bidder! How appropriate for the Catholic Church! She also has a great deal to do with Core Assets, a Fostering organisation headquarters in Bromsgrove, Worcester. Just down the road from Birmingham.

She is not listed with either of these companies in any capacity. Her other main business interest is with G4S! This is the former Group 4 Securior Company that features regularly in the National news for losing prisoners and fiddling their actual figures that has cost you and I! So all in all a fine CV then!

Hilary Brooks we were told is the Interim Chief Executive for Cabrini (OR is it Diagrama?) though she is not listed in any capacity on line. Is it me or am I seeing a pattern here? I wonder what would happen if the "Devil" were to cast his famous net? What a catch!!

Anyway I do hope this is not too much of an overload of information. I haven't even started yet. John F., it's a good job you hopefully will be with me because I am now ready to ask some hard questions. Remember this boy DOESN'T ever give up. I will of course behave in a civilised way.

If you have a question for (Delvin) John F. and I to ask, please do so asap.

KOKO

Terry.

Terry, (Delvin) John Flynn, John M Murray, Ann Phyall.

Terry,

I have read your message loud and clear plus the attachment concerning the history of Diagrama and it is my contention the reason we aim to have honest answers to our questions is now obvious to us all in that the protection and safe-keeping of our personal records is paramount.

Noted on their website, and this interested me more than anything, (Private, Limited by Guarantee, No Share Capital).

Under Aim of Charity, No.5 on the list, I ask myself in what capacity are they able to undertake these causes without the support of government programmes – Economic Stability/Fighting Unemployment. Again – who are they trying to help – young ones (what age?) elderly and old people. Those most vulnerable, with no voice and would not appear in this category of help in the first place.

Their financial details – Income versus Expense shows overbudget on two items. Income of 77,312 pounds, expenses 34,105 pounds, and income of 18,731 pounds, expenses 16,327 pounds, neither of these statements appear correct unless they drastically cut expenses, which would greatly surprise me!

But this is not of course our concern. Our intent is to recognize the stability of those who are now the holders of our files. Having said that, there is still the risk of selling valuable material to the highest bidder regardless of whose personal records are involved. Sorry, but my doubts on this item remain on the highest alert.

Three trustees on the Board. Two Spanish, One British. The Director is Elizabeth Jane Davies (b) 1972 UK. It would be interesting to know in what capacity they function at Diagrama Foundation. There appears to be a crack in the system with overseas trustees and the expenses incurred if and when they attend meetings, etc. in the UK. It is unlikely however we would see an entry in the latest financial statement outlining these costs.

For Ian Forbes to advise you Nathan Ward is no longer available at any time does ring the alarm bells and I am apt to agree with your findings which are an added concern to our group in what we feared two months ago despite the conversation between Cabrini and John F. who assured him everything was above board with Diagrama and our files would be maintained in a professional manner. I still have doubts! As I said earlier it is our members who fall within the later age groups, 50s, 60s and 70s whose records are more at risk and need protection.

Hilary Brooks in her letter to Cabrini on December 4/2014 states she is the Interim Chief Executive. Elaine Brewster, freelance, attending the February 10/2015 meeting, we have little knowledge of her background. Can I assume Nathan Ward will be at this meeting? Why does he need the protection of an outsider to attend what I consider a one-on-one meeting, without an agenda? Having said in previous emails he was available at all times, Nathan Ward, even at this early stage of negotiating with him the flaws show clearly in the Diagrama Foundation.

I will drop an email to David McQuire, Diagrama, Dunstable, copies to all.

KOKO.

Caroline

February 11/2015

A meeting held on February 10/2015 at the home of (Delvin) John Flynn, London.

Ian Forbes representing Cabrini.

Elaine Brewster speaking on behalf of Diagrama,

Terry McKenna and John Flynn attending on behalf of our writers group.

A bit of background. It was a very pleasant meeting, robust but friendly, with Terry for the most part putting across our concerns about the changes that are in the process regarding the takeover of CABRINI by DIAGRAMA. These changes have been going on for some time with little bits of information leaking out leading to uncertainty about the organisation that cared for us during our childhood.

Recently, Cabrini has been in financial difficulties losing money in carrying out their day to day services then on top of this Cabrini needed to substantially prop up the staff pension scheme with the staff being asked to contribute more. So it was decided to look around and find an organisation with the experience in all aspects of the work at present being undertaken by Cabrini and thus Diagrama was the chosen vehicle.

Perhaps it would be disingenuous not to mention politics which in recent years has changed the face of Cabrini and how they were obliged to operate within the change in the law regarding adoption. In the past Southwark Catholic Diocese had a very important role in the operation of Cabrini but an important piece of legislation was passed obliging all adoption agencies including Cabrini to cease discriminating against same sex couples seeking to adopt. The church found this completely contrary to their ideals and beliefs. In their view same sex couples were not suitable to adopt children and since the law did not leave any discretion in the matter the church felt there was only one course open to them which was to exit from Cabrini and divest themselves of all future responsibility for the organisation.

Terry had prepared his list of concerns and Ian addressed these on behalf of both organisations, Cabrini and Diagrama. As in the business world true diligence had to be exercised to ensure Diagrama was a fit organisation to undertake the work formerly carried out by Cabrini and in this respect we were given a history of the company whose services embraced 35 different organisations, far too diverse to enumerate here except to say adoption and child care is the biggest part of their operations. It is however important to stress that whilst our personal files are important, especially to us, and will be properly maintained and accessible as before, this is only a small part of Diagrama's business. At

Terry's request Ian has given an undertaking to write and tell us about the improved plans for storage, security and accessibility of the archives and once this is received Terry will pass the information on to our members.

Those members who have examined the Diagrama website will not have felt reassured by the lack of information but Elaine Brewster has taken this in hand and will be working assiduously to represent Diagrama with a more effective and more comprehensive website showing the full range of services provided by the organisation and also the various interest groups like us who will, from time to time, need to log onto the site to learn information.

Terry may feel he wishes to add to this report since it was a long meeting and he may wish to expand on other topics raised and in this respect he may wish to send a separate email.

KOKO

(Delvin) John Flynn

John,

Many thanks for your message re the meeting between yourself, Terry, Ian Forbes and Elaine Brewster, which went well.

If we are to wait on Ian Forbes report before we close this final chapter of our book let us hope it is with transparency, openness and we are provided with the name of the person dealing with the accessibility of our personal records.

KOKO

Caroline

(Delvin) John Flynn, Caroline

Hi John,

Thank you for your prompt sending of what you noted down yesterday, much appreciated. When I first arrived home I sent a message to Caroline confirming the meeting had gone ahead as planned. I did explain that you had been unwell over the weekend so we sort of agreed that you would take notes and I would ask the questions. I think Caroline was expecting an immediate answer in total of our meeting but I explained to her that when I got your comments AND Ian's reply to the set of questions I emailed him yesterday I would report to everyone as we have planned.

I pointed out that if we are to proceed further on at a later date with the feelers we already have out: Ian's promised response in writing is very important! We must if/when necessary produce facts and not just our thoughts; and your comments and Ian's will give us exactly that! So although I sort of hi-jacked the questioning of Ian and Elaine I thought our combined efforts took them rather by surprise: especially Elaine Brewster. A trick I learned years ago is that if you put someone on the wrong foot (in a sensible way of course) they often blurted out answers, without proper thought usually give you answers that are nearer the truth and NOT the prepared responses they would have loved to use.

Did you notice how quiet Elaine was because I genuinely think she did not realise how much this whole scenario means to the likes of ALL of us. And I still think Diagrama is NOT the way forward with any confidence.

I also don't buy the very lame excuse of "Pension" funds being the reason for a "Sale" of Cabrini. They (Cabrini) simply didn't have the numbers of staff to justify that argument. When Ian disassociated the church from Cabrini it struck me as "Towing the Line". After all, he has a job to protect, doesn't he?

I heard nothing to convince or assure me that our futures are safe with this company. What we need is to look at Ian's response in proper time and not rush into a situation without the full facts. So all in all I thought yesterday went down well just like the sandwiches and cake!

Regards to you and Josie.

KOKO

Terry McK.

----
212 February 11/2015

Terry McK., (Delvin) John Flynn

Terry,

Your second message is explicit of the outcome of your meeting with Ian Forbes and Elaine Brewster on February 10/2015

Again I reiterate the strategy used to obtain the answers to our questions must have hit them between the eyes! But we are not here to damage anyone's character but to simply hear the truth not only concerning the safe-keeping of OUR records but how they will be handled in the future. I am concerned that one individual has the power to destroy files as he sees fit! It is not a good scenario, to say the least!

The consensus why Cabrini sold the Diagrama does not hold constructive reasoning in that it relates to "pensions" but to whom, when few were on staff? From my perspective this arrangement in itself does not ring true anymore than what we were told after a done-deal Diagrama is pathos, transparent, accessible. The only way they can portray pathos is to be truthful! We had Hilary Brooks initially on the scene to advise the transfer of records, then Nathan Ward who for no reason given has now disappeared. Do we know or can guess the exact position of Elaine Brewster's involvement with Diagrama?

Unless we can see our concerns resolved, in writing, and I am sure many of our members feel likewise, the character of goodwill and confidence of transparency, accessibility from Diagrama/Cabrini will remain an insolvable question.

The generous time-frame to Ian Forbes to come forward with his answers to our questions, it is hoped he will not delay when he returns from his week's holiday. But I totally agree, not to rush, but rather ensure satisfaction and closure to this longstanding concern of our group members.

KOKO

Caroline

Hi Caroline,

Sorry if I caused a little bit of confusion! We did get answers to our questions though in my eye not necessarily the ones we wanted. I literally just got home when I emailed you and I wanted to let you know that the meeting had gone ahead as planned. We agreed John would take notes and I would press for answers. Rather than misquote a wrong response I will wait for John's version of the answers he wrote down; look at that and THEN when Ian Forbes responds (as he promised John and I he would).

That last bit is important because it will be a reply to my email to him and proof in writing which is exactly what we were after. Ian is going on holiday next week for a week and to be fair to him I have to give him the appropriate time to respond. His reply may after all be the starting point of future discussions with other people. That being the case we must present true facts not just our thoughts to perhaps achieve and resolve our collective worries in effect not only our past but ALL our futures.

The seventy-year thing that we were worried about, the "Destruction" of records will NOT happen. Rather disturbingly he, Ian, did say in good faith that he is one of those "Special" people who not only can look at everything on record (wherever they are held) on anyone he can, if he wished, actually remove said records! As soon as he said that I immediately jumped on him and said: Nobody has the right to destroy my life's details at their behest. He was a little taken aback when I attacked him although he was in fairness just quoting to John and I what the law says he can actually do IF he had a mind to!

The way of the meeting was that I challenged almost everything that was said to at least promote a response. A trick I learned years ago because in the "heat" of the moment responses often reveal the TRUE feelings or answers that are not actually given. Elaine Brewster was very quiet because I got in first telling her what I knew about her before she even spoke and I also knew why she was at the meeting. You know me I actually told her that we were not going to be pushed around so don't even try. Her immediate response was: 'Oh, so you googled me?'

My reply was simply: 'Some of us are prepared and do our homework.'

Instead of being the bully I'm sure she was meant to be she hardly said a word and I think was quite surprised at our knowledge, not only of Cabrini/Diagrama but herself too! It seems her remit is to totally change the home site of Diagrama to which I sarcastically replied the two days a week she does for them will simply NOT be enough!

I hope that my email makes things a little clearer and as I said before when I get Ian's reply I will inform the group pronto. Last but not least John and Josie were as usual excellent hosts.

KOKO

Terry McK.

Hi Terry,

Appreciate you giving details, you did get answers to questions but not the ones you wanted. How come?

Good to hear the meeting went as planned with you and John. I was sorry to hear he had not been well and thank heavens you were at the meeting to take some of the load off him. I appreciated your email when you arrived home, which tells me you drove back to Bristol shortly after the meeting.

Smart move to have Ian Forbes send an email so you can keep on file what he promised you and John in writing, which is what we wanted. I must confess to being disturbed when he said he had the authority to destroy any records within the law. You were right to attack him on this to even say or think of destroying one's records at his behest. The law must be an ass to allow the destruction of files by any organisation as they think fit!

The strategy you used was perfect in catching Elaine Brewster and Ian Forbes off guard with the information the group have extensive knowledge of their rights and concerns of their records, before they could upstage you and undermine any questions pertinent to the reason why the meeting was important to us in the first place. Your analysis of why Elaine Brewster accompanied Ian Forbes speaks for itself. But where was Nathan Ward? What also is the position of Hilary Brooks who classifies her position at Digrama as Interim Chief Executive? We are looking at a "dummy" run here!

The trick you used to prompt fast responses in the heat of the moment was a good psychological move and one I am sure they did not expect as you doggedly pushed forward your questions before they could get a word in! From the start, Terry, your move was in the right direction and forceful. Thank you for that!

With John and Josie – always the excellent hosts.

KOKO

Caroline

Terry.

I am further confused, also of the opinion in your previous email you did not get the answers to our questions from Ian Forbes and Elaine Brewster at this meeting. Are these to be forwarded on later? If so, what was the point of having a meeting in the first place. Please do elaborate so I don't think myself dumb-headed and lacking in comprehending your two emails.

KOKO

Caroline

Hi Caroline,

By now you should have received my email I sent to Ian Forbes as agreed at our meeting on Tuesday. It is the questions that were asked and (Ian) agreed to reply to me ALL the questions. John F. took notes of what was said and he will eventually send that to me and then we can see how close the two lots are!

Of course as soon as John F. does that I will send on the info asap.

Speak soon.

KOKO

Terry McK.

Hi Caroline,

Maybe I didn't quite put it right when I said we didn't get the answers we wanted (which we didn't).

We got answers to all the questions for sure, primarily because I pushed them in that direction which was our remit. John F. has/will be sending you the email he sent me of his thoughts from our meeting. He actually asked if he could send it to the group. I reminded him that this is his group not mine and he could do whatever he wished BUT I won't send my report until I hear from Ian Forbes.

I did mention Hilary Brookes and asked: "How can someone be an Interim CEO of a board and where is she now?

Ian said she only did it for a brief period whilst negotiations were ongoing between Cabrini and Diagrama. Ian also said there were several other companies that were approached. At that point I yet again interrupted him and said that simply wasn't true. He denied that but couldn't produce one single name of another company except Croydon council. Pleasant person though I.F. is I didn't believe a word of what he was telling us and as for Elaine Brewster's contribution Cabrini should claim whatever she charged back.

Nathan James Ward is now apparently doing other things. As I suggested: "Do you mean he has been taken out of the firing line?" This produced a deafening silence.

To be honest, Caroline, I feel the continued skulduggery of the Catholic Church lives on and repeatedly I told them so! Without mentioning names I also said that one of our members was advised by Cabrini her records were in the hands of the Canterbury Guardians and when contacted we were eventually told they had none! I also said that the copy of the court order placing these children into the care of the said Canterbury Guardians was sent (by me) to C.G. and still they denied this. The only thing missing was the crowing of the morning cockerel! Another reason for my total distrust of Cabrini/Diagrama uncle Tom Cobley and all remains as concerned as before if not now, more so.

KOKO

Terry McK.

February 22/2015

Terry hi,

Your dramatic dialogue I fully understand your reason, to which you are entitled. What is more, I totally agree!

What you discovered with Hilary Brooks is nothing short of a red herring as Pimpernel as they come. It does not take a scientist to determine why her letter was sent to Cabrini in the first place but neither did she or Diagrama envisaged the onslaught from our group when their devious ways of takeover was discovered. The more I hear how this organisation operates with little financial background, staff that come and go and the skulduggery they think will work on us, they are badly mistaken.

That you will not advise members until Ian Forbes's report is known to you, I agree. Not much point putting the cart before the horse, is there?

The consensus of how the transfer of our records were negotiated and for Ian Forbes to say other companies had been approached which is entirely untrue, leaves me frustrated for words! My view of the whole situation and the way these people are trying to fob us off with mix'n'match answers is not good enough.

KOKO

Caroline

February 22/2015

Caroline/Terry Mc.K (Delvin) John Flynn, John Michael Murray, Ian Forbes Diagrama/Cabrini, Ann Phyall.

Dear Caroline and Terry,

Thank you for your emails addressed to David McGuire. He has asked me to respond to you as he remains heavily involved in a government bid and will not be available to respond properly until after the bid is submitted on 25th February/2015. This is rather a long email so please bear with me but I felt that it was really important that we address your concerns.

The first thing I would like to clarify is on the point made in Caroline's email relating to "John's supposition of stonewalling" and "this doesn't come within the category of transparency". Nothing could be further from the truth here and I hope that this email will give you some level of reassurance in this regard.

At the meeting between Terry, John, Ian and myself on 10th February, Ian said that it might take a couple of weeks to respond to your questions because:

He was just about to go away on a week's leave.

He may not have all the answers to hand – please bear in mind that at the meeting we had not had sight of the questions.

David was heavily involved in the bid and a delay in response would not be because he didn't care, but simply because he did not have enough hours in the day to do so properly.

Now that we have seen the questions, we realised that we definitely do need David's input; not only because some of the questions relate to how the Foundation is set up but also because David cares passionately about every aspect of Diagrama's business in the UK and wants to be involved in our response to you. I hope you can see that David's personal involvement demonstrates the importance that he places on Cabrini, both in terms of securing its long-term future and safely preserving the archives.

We do absolutely understand the concerns you have with regard to the archives and, in between dealing with bid matters, David has been in touch with Coram to find out how they manage their archives so that we can learn and find the best possible solution for our own records.

I note your comment about minutes. From our side we believed that this first meeting was informal, and had been arranged to begin to give reassurances, particularly around adoption records. John took detailed notes which we assumed he would share with your group. We did not see the need for formal minutes on this occasion; however we take your point and when we have further meetings we should discuss at the start of each meeting whether there is a need for minutes or not.

With regard to the various comments about who has or has not been involved in the dialogue, both at the meeting, in the questionnaire and also in subsequent emails, we appreciate that this has led to some confusion so I thought it would be helpful to provide some clarification, as follows:

David would have preferred to come to the meeting himself but for reason already stated above, he simply couldn't do so.

Nathan Ward is supporting David in the bid submission and his diary didn't have any flexibility prior to the 25th February. Hence, David and Nathan asked me to attend on their behalf.

I have been employed by Diagrama on a contractual basis for two days a week since January 2015 to provide strategic and tactical advice on communications, marketing and stakeholder engagement. If you want any further reassurance on my credentials, please do visit my website or take a look at my LinkedIn profile.

You raised concerns about being able to contact Irena and copy emails being returned. Irena is definitely still working in the business and is passionate about continuing to provide a good service. This does sound like a technical issue so the best way to resolve this, I think, is to ask you to forward the relevant emails to Ian. He can ask Irena to respond and also investigate why they were returned in the first place. Ian is back from leave on Monday 23rd February.

Having said all of the above, we appreciate that you and your group are anxious about how things will work in the future. Please be assured that Diagrama, and David in particular, are committed to providing the best service possible going forward. It is an unfortunate matter of timing which has caused delays up to this point and for which we can only apologise.

As I have already said David will be available to complete the questionnaire after 25th February so we will ensure that we give you the answers you need by latest Friday 27th February.

I have copied in the other group members who were included in Caroline's original email which I hope is helpful.

If you have any further concerns, then David, Ian and I are here to help.

Kind regards,

Elaine.

February 23/2015

Hi Caroline,

Transparency and being upfront is NOT part of the Catholic Church Ethos, is it? It hasn't taken E.B. long to "settle" into deflecting of truth, has it! She said they could not answer our questionnaire because we did not send them before we met. Surely that would make us a bit like Turkeys voting for Christmas OR Thanksgiving. Just how stupid do they think we are!

How was my "tactic" of badgering every answer they gave going to work if I gave them time to have prepared answers? And this woman is supposed to be a high flying and heavy hitter!

Not heard from J.F. for a few days and don't wish to pester him with too much whilst he is coping with other matters.

I will be amazed if we get a response from David McGuire (or his possible successor) by Thursday. Do you think I am being a little sceptical?

KOKO.

Terry.

Terry McK. (Delvin) John Flynn, John M. Murray, Ann Phyall, Irena Lyczkowska/Cabrini, Elaine Brewster/Diagrama

Terry,

The letter from Elaine Brewster while it appears that Diagrama appreciate our concerns, I think we go back to the basics of how this whole scenario of transferring our records played out without our knowledge. I believe had transparency prevailed at the beginning of a done-deal and our group were fully advised as to the course of action Cabrini decided to take it would not have put up the barriers of questions how our personal records would be handled in the future. It was not done in the professional manner I would expect.

Irena has always been instrumental in listening and helping those who wished to search their family record and that she will remain within the Diagrama organisation gives us some confidence in that with future inquiries we will be heard.

I will respond to Elaine Brewster's email and trust thereon we can continue dialogue in a respectable and civil manner.

The fact we are unable to have David McGuire's input to our questions at your meeting with Ian Forbes, Elaine Brewster, John and yourself because of other commitments, does not bode well with this continued delay for answers.

KOKO

Caroline

Elaine Brewster, (Delvin) John Flynn, Terry McKenna, John M. Murray, Ian Forbes/Cabrini

Dear Elaine,

Thank you for your informative email outlining the reason for the delay with answers to our questions to our worldwide group of writers which were discussed at a meeting between yourself, Ian Forbes, John Flynn and Terry McKenna on Tuesday February 10/2015 held at John's home.

It is appreciated David McGuire to whom I was given to understand would collaborate with Ian Forbes in ensuring our concerns of our personal files would be addressed after Ian had returned from his vacation but cannot do so at this time, due to negotiating a government bid.

Reference made re stonewalling forthright information to our group does cause one to question the sincerity of transparency from the Diagrama organisation and appear to continually come up with reasons why this information is not available at this time. However, noting your comment Ian said it might take a couple of weeks to respond to our questions i.e. going away, and not having all the answers to hand is within reason. Again I was surprised you did not have sight of the questions at this specific meeting which all intents and purposes answers to them were requested at the time to enable us closure so we can advise our members across the world how we stand with our personal records.

It is fully understood David McGuire is unable to accommodate us due to being involved in a government bid. Because of this urgency in finalising contracts between both parties I would like also to stress our closure of the answers to our questions concerning transparency, openness, accessibility to our members will be finalised without further delay, beyond February 25/2015.

We do understand your need to negotiate with Government bids. You must also understand our group's needs are as important!

Our interest in the history of the Diagrama Foundation and how it began and what its future involvements will be in securing the safety of our files and indeed accessibility upon request, is to understand the background of the organisation to whom our records are now held in their care. I am unware of Coram and would be interested in learning what their policies are in relation to managing their archives.

I too understand your meeting with two of our members was informal; hence there were no Minutes taken but of course when something important as this subject is discussed between two parties it is necessary to have it in writing.

Your clarification regarding the staff at Diagrama is appreciated. Nathan Ward was supportive in all emails I sent to him, to which I acknowledged.

Your own involvement with Diagrama while it is important to know with whom our group are communicating, it does not come within the category of permanent staff but I understand, as an adviser.

With Irena who has been most supportive of our group and given us confidence in the past with whatever questions we raised they would be answered within a reasonable space of time. Without this communication between the two parties we would be left groping in dark tunnels and that is not how our group wishes to function.

If we have your assurance Diagrama and David McGuire will provide all inquirers with the best possible service, we trust we can have closure of our concerns relating to our family history records. For future generations, these cannot be allowed to be destroyed at will by any one!

On behalf of John whose wife Josie is unwell, Terry and I will continue to communicate with Diagrama/Cabrini and provide information to our group, all copies directed to him and members.

Again many thanks.

Caroline

February 24/2015

'morning Terry,

I hope you were able to digest my response to E.Brewster's email. I tried covering all the points she raised and the questions why we thought we were being stonewalled by them to avoid honest answers.

We now know David McGuire is negotiating a government contract; hence his lack of input at this time. We also know the time-frame with Ian Forbes stands beyond 25 February/2015.

Another name that has come to the fore is Coram and it appears

Diagrama are now through Elaine Brewster, establishing how Coram manages their archives. I will leave you with your thought on this one!

KOKO

Caroline 220

February 26/2015

Hi Caroline,

The reason there are no written responses regarding how our records will be held and maintained is simply because they are still looking at various systems and Ian Forbes said: 'Until they get a solid and 'fool proof" system in place they are going nowhere.'

In their obvious indecent haste to get rid of the responsibilities that the Catholic Church should have and are to be held to account for, this "little" matter seems to have been "missed" but Ian assured John and I this will be resolved! Make of that what you will….

KOKO

Terry McK.

Meeting with Ian Forbes and Elaine Brewster - 10/02/2015.

This meeting being held at (Delvin) John Flynn's home is to ask on behalf of our group of friends from ALL around the world questions to Diagrama and OUR family records.

Those people in attendance: (Delvin) John Flynn, Terry McKenna, Ian Forbes (Cabrini) Elaine Brewster stated as being from Diagrama.

The name of the Chairman of the Board at Diagrama? Francisco Legaz.

(2) The number of member on that board? Three

(3) Exactly where are and will be their Headquarters? Floor 5, Anchorage House, High Street, Chatham, Medway, ME4 4LE

(4) Who are Diagrama's Accountants and Auditors? Francis Clark, Chartered Accountants, Lowin House, Tregolls Road, Truro, Cornwall. TR1 2NA Telephone: 01872 276477 Fax: 01872 222783

(5) Who approves their source of income – Governments home OR

abroad. Listed as a Charitable Organization and Private Donations? Our income comes from a variety of sources. This included Local Authorities who purchase our services and donations from private individuals and corporate entities.

(6) Where do Diagrama hold their Annual General Meetings? England.

(7) The names and Telephone numbers of contacts for file accessibility? For file access: Cabrini part of the Diagrama Foundation, Adoption Team, 49 Russell Hill Road, Purley, Surrey, CR8 2XB Telephone: 020 8668 2181 Email: archives@cabrini.org.uk

(8) The role of the so called "Interim" C.E.O. Hilary Brooks and where does she work from? Hilary Brooks was employed as the Interim CEO from November 2013. She worked full-time from her start date until the 31 December 2014. She was based in the Purley office. As CEO she acted on behalf of the trustees to ensure that the business of Cabrini Children's Society was carried out in accordance with statutory regulations and the society's business plans. Hilary is working a few hours per week now until the registration with OFSTED of the adoption and fostering services is completed. This is expected to take place by the end of February 2015.

(9) When does Diagrama actually close Cabrini offices in Purley and then where are the offices to be relocated? NO REPLY!

(10) Apart from (1) year the accounts for Diagrama have shown considerable losses for such a relatively small outlay over the last seven-years. How long before this MUST have an effect on Shareholders and just who is subsidizing these continued losses?

The losses will be reduced over time as Diagrama grows its portfolio and the services it provides.

(11) Can we please have YOUR version of the truth as to why Cabrini (Re: The Catholic Church) actually did this business in secret two years ago AND why were NO other tenders put out?

The Catholic Church was not involved in any way with regards to the selling of Cabrini Children's Society. A decision was taken by the trustees around October 2013 to sell Cabrini due to its financial position.

Due to the sensitive nature of the work undertaken by Cabrini, tenders were sought with known reputable charities instead of advertising within an open market. Several companies/charities expressed interest and a process of due diligence was undertaken. The Diagrama Foundation was the best option.

February 28/2015

Terry McK. (Delvin) John Flynn

Terry,

Having requested from Diagrama/Cabrini for a written response to our questions the decent thing is not to procrastinate which is what appears to be happening. I am not convinced they are still looking at various systems to determine the safety of our records, after our communication with them of three months since December 2014. I would have thought by now they had a firm plan in place but it does not appear to be the case. Communication going on between Cabrini and Diagrama for the past two years and still no positive plans despite convincing us of transparency, openness and accessibility does not bode well. Although they are trying to appease us in every sense of the word, the run-around is obvious.

Since John F. set up the old boy's network in 1988 our group have always been upfront and unafraid to speak up on any issue. We have learned through these communications there are always good and bad experiences. The business world today is on a different stage compared to when I began my career. The calibre of staff is what makes a company tick when they are on solid ground.

Comments to Answers:

Item (3)

Headquarters of Diagrama: We have no telephone number or person's name whom to contact!

Item (4)

Accountants: Francis Clark in Truro, Cornwall. Why do they deal with accountants living far away from the mainstream?

Item (6)

Headquarters in England? Which part?

(8)

Short time for Hilary Brooks to be employed as Interim CEO, November 2013 to December 2014. A temporary position to negotiate the takeover from Cabrini. Do I understand she will be part of the team from February 2015 on?

Item (10)

I fail to understand the parameters of their financial position which indicates a serious lack of capital funds with which to operate between "fine" lines. Diagrama appear to be running on a "shoe-string".

Item (11)

The fact Cabrini was verified as having been sold, I question its feasibility unless initially it was set up purely to function as a business, therefore yours and my records were part of the deal. This we are fully aware.

In concluding, and I am sure John F. and yourself will feel the same, other than the telephone number and name of the person to connect for accessibility of records, there will be no further dialogue between us and them?

John, I sincerely hope this concern of the group has not added to your already heavy schedule. If so, apologies. But we did need to delve with answers to questions and had we not done so the upper hand would not have been ours or that of future generations.

KOKO

Caroline

March 2/2015

Meeting with Diagrama Thoughts:

(Delvin) John Flynn, Caroline

After meeting with Ian Forbes and Elaine Brewster at John Flynn's home on February 10/2015 to try and get some answers to the many questions, we had to ask the former Cabrini and The Diagrama Foundation, I am even less certain as to what will happen to OUR personal files.

To Questions

1. Chairman of the Board is Francisco Legaz. Fair enough.

2. Members on that Board. Three women are named if you check the Diagrama Foundation on line!

3. The Headquarters at Chatham, Kent. Apparently so new that Elaine did not provide a telephone contact number and I couldn't find one either!

4. Francis Clark, Chartered Accountants, Cornwall. Fair enough!

5. Who approves Diagrama's income? Diagrama's income comes from a variety of sources. Local Authorities do purchase Diagrama services (just as Cabrini do). Donations from private individuals (just as Cabrini do). And Corporate Entities. The first two answers are standard responses that any adoption society would give. Upon checking Diagrama before our meeting (unlike Elaine and Ian, I did my homework). I saw absolutely no evidence or any truth to this statement. In the seven years that Diagrama have been "established" in the UK they have made a loss year upon year with no explanation as to why this has happened. Do I see a pattern of lies here by omission at least! If I were a shareholder in this company I would be very worried indeed.

6. Where do Diagrama hold their AGM's? In England came the reply. An international company that has only just started in the UK apparently hold its AGM's in the UK! Why does that sound like a hollow response to me?

7. The names and contacts for file accessibility remain as before at Cabrini. I find it a little strange that Cabrini in effect, is no more entrusted with OUR personal records. A company that at best will decease "trading" next February 2016.

8. The role of the so-called "Interim" CEO Hilary Brooks! She was only a very temporary appointment for the duration of the "takeover". Not sure how that works but once again a name thrown at us and now no longer! Do I see a pattern developing here?

9. When does Cabrini actually close its Purley offices? After our meeting you may remember I stated that Elaine Brewster went straight to the Cabrini offices in Purley. If I were skeptical I would suggest she went there to "warn" the staff to say nothing to our little group of friends if questioned. Unknown to her and those at our meeting, sorry that includes you too John, I had already discovered the answer to the question (9)

a few days earlier from someone who works at Cabrini whom Caroline, John and I saw in 2013.

10. Has been answered in question (5).

11. Can we please have YOUR version of the truth of why Cabrini (read the Catholic Church) actually did this business in total secrecy two years ago? And why were other tenders not given the chance to "invest". Ian Forbes said that there were several other parties asked! When asked he couldn't name one of them. In fact only The Diagrama Foundation and Croydon Council were approached as I had discovered. As I told Elaine Brewster and Ian, I did my homework. The ill-conceived tale of woe produced by Ian Forbes and blaming "Pensions Funds" just didn't ring true at all. Simply put there are/were not enough staff to affect the finances of Cabrini in this way. This I feel is the Catholic Church at their most devious in my opinion. Nice person that Ian Forbes tried to be I am afraid he left me with a feeling of total distrust and as for Elaine Brewster, the hard-hitting bully produced to block us simple folk, I do believe Diagrama should claim her expense costs back. But then of course they won't because they always run at a loss, don't they? Well, as I said, I haven't pulled any punches BUT once again must stress that these are my thoughts. I look forward to both your responses. Terry McK.

\-

March 3/2015

Hi Caroline and John,

As promised, these are my thoughts regarding our meeting with Ian Forbes and Elaine Brewster on 10th February 2015. These of course are my views as I have stated. See what you make of them and I look forward to your responses as always.

KOKO

Terry McK.

\-

Terry McKenna, (Delvin) John Flynn

Terry,

The details you forwarded are much the same as those sent by Elaine

Brewster in answer to your question with the exception you have outlined your own views and comments.

Can you advise if all our group members have been given a copy of the minutes from Elaine Brewster of the meeting held February 10/2015 with John, Ian Forbes and yourself. Also, what is the next move with this latest report from you?

I did give my comments on Elaine Brewster's answers to your questionnaire, to you and John.

Thanks Terry,

Caroline

Terry McKenna, (Delvin) John Flynn

Hi Terry,

I feel sure John as well as the two of us will be happy to see closure of further communication with Diagrama since we have answers to our questions, albeit, the telephone number of their headquarters at Chatham is unknown to us. This is important. Perhaps one of us can drop David McGuire a line for this detail.

To any group member who wishes to add conclusion to the last chapter of KOKO maybe either you or John can let them have a copy of your views on the questionnaire answered by Elaine Brewster and if and when they respond I can include them in the manuscript before closing it off.

Terry, I am sure if John doesn't have the time he can let you have the list of members for you to forward them a copy of what you sent to me. If John M. Murray and Ann already have Elaine Brewster's original email from the meeting held February 10/2015 they may yet respond.

John, time and energy permitting, can you please press the final button to our members for their final responses, if any, (last opportunity) to this ongoing communication with Diagrama on behalf of our worldwide group so we can have closure.

I am sure we all agree this long-drawn out process is not what we expected to be involved in from December 2014 to March 2015 to determine the security of our personal records.

Hope you are both keeping well.

KOKO

Caroline.

Hi Caroline,

Good to get your latest email regarding my response and what you feel you will now go ahead and do.

Just hope John is in total agreement with you and look forward to seeing the book as soon as possible; which will be great.

Not too sure if you think I/we should send my response to ALL of our friends in the group OR let everyone wait to read it in the book. Let me know OK? Whatever you put in the book I do hope you mention that we are very grateful for the help of certain members of staff of Cabrini, i.e. Irena and Teresa and in my case the social worker before Irena, Irene Coppock who was outstanding in my case.

I feel an important message to send out.

KOKO, as always.

Terry McK.

March 3/2015

Terry McKenna, (Delvin) John Flynn

Hi Terry and John,

Yes, it would be good now for us to sit back with the news of our BEST to secure and protect the rights of our personal files, now in the possession of Diagrama. It is due to our forthrightness to have come this far and unless we did so, perhaps down the road, there would be regrets of not doing anything at all. I believe everyone involved in our group needs to pat themselves on the back with their input throughout these communications with Diagrama. (Honorary members, plus!)

To you John F. and Terry, my grateful thanks!

I will conclude with a final note in KOKO with or without responses from members regarding the February meeting and both your comments, verbatim!

Please do look after yourself.

KOKO

Caroline

Hi John,

I guess you have received Caroline's last message with regards to the email of my thoughts. At her suggestion I would be more than happy to send on the original response from Elaine Brewster to the questionnaire I sent after our meeting; albeit, I was expecting Ian Forbes and David McGuire to have answered, not Ms. Webster!

Anyway, if you wish, John, I will send my result and thoughts that I sent to you and Caroline yesterday to the rest of our group BUT I don't have most of the addresses to allow me to do that. And of course you may wish to do so yourself. As Caroline said we do need to put this part of our ongoing "battle" to bed asap. We must not delay any more with our book. Time is money.

KOKO

Terry McK.

Terry,

I have yet to read John's response to our suggestion to send all members a copy of the minutes relating to the meeting held February 10/2015, also the response from Elaine Brewster to our questionnaire which the three of us followed up with our own comments.

I will of course acknowledge the good work of Irene Coppock who was instrumental in assisting you with your own background history. Also Irena and Teresa have always in the past maintained a good relationship with our group. They were not only trustworthy and upfront with questions put to them by our members but also they were willing in every respect to help us in every way. For their services, we are extremely grateful.

The "Boys of St. Mary's" manuscript is a project so important to social history I would not wish to rush. I am always of the opinion a slower approach is better than a hasty one that often leaves a person in full regret.

Your suggestion to acknowledge past and present Cabrini staff is appreciated.

KOKO

Caroline

Terry and Caroline,

When you come over next time I will let you have the addresses. In the meantime send your thoughts to me and I will forward to the rest of the group. As you say, not to delay. Hopefully all the records will be as safe as formerly by continuing to be held at Russell Hill Road, Purley.

Perhaps Caroline can do a postscript to the book along the lines about outstanding issues to be resolved.

KOKO

(Delvin) John Flynn.

(Delvin) John Flynn, Terry McK.

John,

Although we are fully conscious of the caring of Josie and the fact you find the time to say a few words, it gives everyone the courage to keep on keeping on. It is a philosophy worth preserving and like our personal records, to be treasured.

Your suggestion to Terry to send his comments to you so that you can forward on to the rest of the group will give them time to respond, if so wished.

Your idea to do a postscript to the book I have already begun to draft the outstanding issues yet to be resolved. I was disappointed that the Rt. Hon Simon Hughes, MP, Minister of State for Justice and Civil Liberties, House of Commons, London, England, did not acknowledge my letter asking his advice on the security and rights of our personal records; albeit, he is now in the throes of an upcoming General Election. Also Care

Leavers' Association did not respond to my email with the same request, recommended by Ann Phyall.

Our prayers and heart goes out to you and Josie.

Caroline

(Delvin) John Flynn

John,

Thank you for forwarding the addresses to Terry, to distribute the information to our group members.

It is hoped if anyone would like to comment on the latest communication between Diagrama/Cabrini, yourself and Terry, perhaps they could forward this early as possible. As we have fully outlined our concerns with Diagrama and our group, with tongue in cheek, we hope future contact with this organisation and their staff there will be transparency, openness and accessibility to our personal records.

To you, John and Terry, and I feel sure the entire group agree, it is much appreciated what you have dealt with over the past three months on our behalf.

Caroline

Hi Caroline,

I deliberately sent the response from me in the form of the questionnaire that was set out for IF and EB to show you both my thoughts for each of those said questions; if that makes sense to you and John. I wanted to ensure that I didn't miss any of the points we set them to answer. AND as ever I wanted to reiterate that these are my thoughts and I leave it to you and John to decided if/how our total responses would then be passed on to the rest of the group. I feel that a final nod from you and John is the proper way to inform our group. Of course either you or John may disagree with my thoughts partially or totally.

As I stated, so far with regards to the set questions only you and John have been sent my response.

John M. Murray and Ann Phyall were sent the same original response email from Elaine Brewster from our meeting on the 10th February but I have heard nothing from either of them. Of course Ann has been very busy with her own family and rightly must be dealing with all that entails.

Once you and John have decided what the final form our response as a group should be, then I assume John will distribute an email to ALL as I don't have the emails of everyone.

KOKO

Terry McK.

EPILOGUE

When a group of writers, worldwide, began their dialogue with a "network" of old boys formed in 1988 by (Delvin) John Flynn of North London, England, it was their intent to record the personal memories of childhood during the time they were in care at St. Mary's Home for Boys at Gravesend, Kent.

These remarkable stories, told through the eyes of a child, outline the pattern of their lives and how it dramatically changed, some from birth, others as toddlers who were taken from the arms of their mothers for reasons unknown to this day, and put in Catholic Homes.

The irony of their memories show a familiar sequence how the structured religious upbringing affected them when reaching adulthood and how through this process some of them used an identical pattern of child-rearing, when bringing up their own children. For the simple reason they knew no other way.

The similarities of those memories will strike a chord to the reader, with a visual image of the strict upbringing and dominant rules of the Catholic Church and the effect it had on those children in their care.

Many of the St. Mary's boys turned out honourable men, who gave their lives to King and country during the Second World War. Some rose to the rank of officers. Others were instrumental in taking further education to allow them entry to the professional field of engineers and the business world.

Some went on to become professional football players. The highlight in their education was to give their best on the sportsground both at Gravesend and at other local districts to play to their limit, to win or lose.

Their determination to win for St. Mary's sparked a note of praise from the opposing team and onwatchers alike.

Early December 2014 it became known to the KOKO group that all personal records dating back to the 1900s of children put in care at St. Mary's, Gravesend, Kent, were to be transferred from Cabrini who had taken over this responsibility from the Southwark Catholic Rescue Society, London, England in 2008/2009.

The records were to remain in the archives at Purley, Surrey.

A letter from Hilary Brooks, Interim Chief Executive acting on behalf of The Diagrama Foundation advised Cabrini of a take-over of their business effective November 27/2014. A copy of this notification was sent to (Delvin) John Flynn who in turn advised his group members of the transaction concerning their personal files. Negotiations between Cabrini and Diagrama went on for over a period of two years and when this information was known to our group of writers they became concerned because when they asked for details there appeared to be a lack of communication with Cabrini/ Diagrama. The big question: what will happen to our records?

For three months communications were "strangled" to the point that unless answers were given to our questions the dialogue would remain stunted. It gave cause to our group to become suspicious of the done-deal without being given the opportunity to provide input to this important issue, plus the fact Diagrama staff had taken their time to send emails to our questions simply because their answers were not then available to them. The course of delay, as advised, was due to the fact that The Diagrama Foundation currently were in the process of negotiating a bid to provide services with the UK government. David McGuire was dealing with this bid and therefore unable to either attend the February 10/2015 meeting with (Delvin) John Flynn and Terry McKenna, Ian Forbes and Elaine Brewster or, be involved in providing the information necessary to the group's questionnaire.

Elaine Brewster acted on behalf of Diagrama as a freelance adviser.

The stability of the Foundation who initially started their services in Belgium and in our opinion were insufficiently funded to establish a long-term commitment to ensure the protection and safety of our records, as shown in their financial statements, caused the question to be asked: 'Can they be fully responsible for the security of our personal files? Or, in the long term, sold to another organisation?'

The questionnaire put to Diagrama was responded to by Elaine Brewster who provided most of the answers, with the exception of the name and telephone number of the contact person where their Head Office is to be located in 2016: Anchorage House, Floor 5, High Street, Chatham, Kent.

Assurance given by Ian Forbes and David McGuire there will be transparency, openness and accessibility to our personal records; despite these assurances our group of writers will continue to oversee where and how their files are kept. The tenacity to protect and ensure future generations to have the opportunity to learn more of their family history became a major issue in the dialogue between The Diagrama Foundation and our group members.

At Terry McKenna's request, Ian Forbes has given an undertaking to write and tell us about the improvised plans for security and accessibility of the archives and once this is received, Terry will pass the information on to our members.

At the time of publication there is yet more to be told to this story, but until the answers to those outstanding questions are known to us by The Diagrama Foundation it is only then can we advise our group of KOKO writers by email the results of those final questions, to provide closure.

The final chapter of the story of "The Boys of St. Mary's" whose motto Keep on Keeping On will prevail, as will their history and stories of events during the 1900s.

What we learn today, is the history of our tomorrow!

ABOUT THE EDITOR

CAROLINE WHITEHEAD was born in London, England, and raised in an orphanage in Kent. Knowing the importance of family relationships, she pushed forward for forty years to discover her brothers' and sisters' identities, overcoming many obstacles so the siblings could experience those ties – and their stories could finally be told in a sequence of three books.

Married in 1944, she emigrated to Canada in 1967 and lived in Ontario before moving to British Columbia in 1987. Her husband died in 1999. She has one daughter, three grandchildren, two great-grandchildren, and a wealth of proud memories.

Made in the USA
Charleston, SC
08 June 2015